THE FICTIONAL CHRISTOPHER NOLAN

UNIVERSITY OF TEXAS PRESS, AUSTIN

THE FICTIONAL CHRISTOPHER NOLAN

BY TODD MCGOWAN

Requests for permission to reproduce material from this work
should be sent to:
    Permissions
    University of Texas Press
    P.O. Box 7819
    Austin, TX 78713-7819
    www.utexas.edu/utpress/about/bpermission.html

 ∞ The paper used in this book meets the minimum requirements of
ANSI/NISO Z39.48-1992 (R1997) (Permanence of Paper).

LIBRARY OF CONGRESS CATALOGING-IN-PUBLICATION DATA
McGowan, Todd.
The fictional Christopher Nolan / by Todd McGowan. — 1st ed.
        p.   cm.
Includes bibliographical references and index.
ISBN 978-0-292-73782-2 (cloth : alk. paper)
1. Nolan, Christopher, 1970—Criticism and interpretation.   I. Title.
PN1998.3.N65M35 2012
791.4302'33092—dc23   2011048569

For my mother, Sandi McGowan,
and in memory of my father, Bob McGowan,
who both ensconced me in a fiction from early on

CONTENTS

Thanks to the *International Journal of Žižek Studies* for permission to publish a revised version of the essay that appeared as "The Violence of Creation in *The Prestige*," *International Journal of Žižek Studies* 1, no. 3 (2007): http://zizekstudies.org/index.php/ijzs/article/view/58/120. Thanks also to *Jump Cut* for permission to publish a revised version of the essay that appeared as "The Hero's Form of Appearance: The Necessary Darkness of *The Dark Knight*," *Jump Cut* 51 (2009): http://www.ejumpcut.org/archive/jc51.2009/darkKnightKant/index.html.

I owe a tremendous debt to my students at the University of Vermont, who have constantly advanced my thinking about cinema in general and Christopher Nolan in particular. I'm also thankful for the support and generosity of my colleagues within film studies at the University of Vermont—Dave Jenemann, Sarah Nilsen, Hyon Joo Yoo, Deb Ellis, and Hilary Neroni. Outside of film studies, Joseph Acquisto, John Waldron, Emily Bernard, and Eric Lindstrom have been invaluable.

Thanks to Andrew Barnaby for reading and providing extensive commentary for the chapter on *Memento*. The inspiration for that chapter came from our joint teaching of the film.

I am grateful to Jonathan Mulroney for his catholic perspective, which sees what I tend to overlook.

I appreciate Jean Wyatt and Quentin Martin's careful reading of the chapter on *Inception*. Whatever clarity it now has is due in no small part to their efforts.

Thanks to Slavoj Žižek for his many forms of assistance and generosity, which are always done without concern for recognition or plaudits.

Sarah Nilsen and Michael Ashooh provided challenges to my certitudes and infusions of new thinking.

Danny Cho read several chapters and provided suggestions that sprouted into entire new sections of the book.

I am grateful to Jennifer Friedlander for her invitation to speak on *Inception* at Pomona College and for her penetrating questions. Most of all, I am indebted to her and Henry Krips for being theoretical comrades.

Thanks to Sheila Kunkle, who has provided years of dialogue and incessant construction of new forms of fiction, without which I would be floundering.

ACKNOWLEDGMENTS

I am grateful to Fabio Vighi, whose reading of the entire book helped to make the philosophical arguments evident to me.

Hugh Manon provided so much additional information for the book that, if the book were better, he should be listed as a coauthor. His reading was one of the most detailed I have ever received, and his insights were always clear and to the point.

Walter Davis, Paul Eisenstein, and Hilary Neroni have all traced the logic of my lies to the point of truth, for which my debt remains inexpressible. My relationship with each has become one of true speculative identity.

THE FICTIONAL CHRISTOPHER NOLAN

THE FICTIONAL CHRISTOPHER NOLAN

The lie plays a central role in every Christopher Nolan film. In his first feature, *Following* (1998), the film's protagonist, Bill (Jeremy Theobald), becomes entrapped in a deception that frames him for a woman's murder. Nolan's most popular film, *The Dark Knight* (2008), depicts Batman (Christian Bale) hiding not just beneath a mask but also behind the fiction that he is a murderous criminal. Characters in Nolan's films constantly find themselves deceived by others and often caught up in a vast web of deceit that transcends any individual lies. The predominance that deception has within the content of these films has a clear homology in their form. The typical Nolan film has the formal structure of a lie designed to deceive the spectator concerning the events that occur and the motivations of the characters. Nolan uses the form of deception to constitute an ethical philosophy rooted in the ontological primacy of the lie. Nolan's films do not abandon the idea of truth altogether, but they show us how truth must emerge out of the lie if it is not to lead us entirely astray.

Nolan's lying structure does not consist, as one might expect, in showing events that aren't really happening. Such visual deception would force spectators to conclude that they simply cannot believe what they see—and thus creates a dead-end street in filmmaking.[1] Nolan's films, in contrast, show events that actually transpire in the filmic universe, but the formal structure leads the spectator to misinterpret these events. The structure of the films deceives the spectator about the meaning of the events seen. The deceit exists in the form more than in the content, which suggests that deceit is a structural phenomenon and not simply an empirical one. By exhibiting the structural nature of deceit and its ubiquity, Nolan demands a revaluation of the prevailing ideas of truth and fiction.

This dynamic is most apparent in the openings of Nolan's films. We often see an event but draw incorrect conclusions about its nature. Rather than directly manipulating spectators in the manner of a film like *The Usual Suspects* (Bryan Singer, 1995), Nolan's films tend to begin

INTRODUCTION
THE ETHICS OF THE LIE

in a way that causes spectators to trick themselves simply by adhering to standard cinematic codes. For example, the opening of *Memento* (2000) shows Leonard Shelby (Guy Pearce) shooting Teddy (Joe Pantoliano) for the murder of his wife. Though the film moves backward, it is clear that Leonard shoots and kills Teddy, and Leonard's narration leads the spectator to believe that he has discovered that Teddy is the murderer of his wife. At the conclusion of the film, however, it becomes evident that Teddy did not murder Leonard's wife and that Leonard sets in motion the events that will result in Teddy's death just because Teddy has angered him by telling Leonard what he didn't want to hear. The truth behind the murder of Leonard's wife has nothing to do with the killing that opens the film, though the film deceives the spectator into thinking that this is in fact an act of revenge.

The opening of *Insomnia* (2002) involves a similar though less dramatic deception. Shots of blood staining a white piece of clothing appear throughout the film's opening sequence, and the subsequent depiction of a police investigation leads the spectator to believe that this is the blood of the murder victim. But the end of the film reveals that these bloodstains have nothing at all to do with this murder investigation. Instead, they are the result of a police detective, Will Dormer (Al Pacino), planting evidence to frame a suspect in an earlier investigation. The structure of the film creates a deception in which the spectator misinterprets the opening images, and this initial misinterpretation paves the way for a series of misinterpretations that end only when the film's conclusion enables the spectator to recognize them as such. But in each case, the deception marks the beginning and occurs before any truth. The spectator begins the Nolan film with a mistaken idea of what has happened and what's at stake in the events. The movement of the typical Nolan film is not, as in most films, from ignorance to knowledge. Instead, the spectator moves from mistaken knowledge to a later knowledge that corrects the mistakes. The beginning point is not a blank slate but an initial error.

Other contemporary filmmakers also privilege deceit, though none do so to the extent of Nolan or in quite the same way. M. Night Shyamalan, for instance, is famous for the trick ending that reveals to spectators that their understanding of the filmic reality was entirely wrongheaded. In the most celebrated case, *The Sixth Sense* (1999) reveals that the hero of the film, Dr. Malcolm Crowe (Bruce Willis) has actually been dead throughout most of the film's running time. The difference between Shyamalan and Nolan—or between *The Sixth Sense* and *Memento*—is

2

that the former does not include the deception as part of the truth that the film reveals. A clear line of demarcation exists between the deception and the truth in *The Sixth Sense*, and once one knows the truth, one can watch the film again from this new perspective to examine how it constructs the deception. With *Memento*, such a strategy is not possible because it is only through immersing oneself in the deception that one arrives at the truth. To remove oneself from the deception, which is possible when re-watching a Shyamalan film, would cause one to miss the truth altogether.

The structure of a Nolan film plays on the spectator's investment in the idea of truth, but this investment always results in the spectator being deceived. Insofar as we believe in what we see, Nolan's films lead us into error. The idea of truth as what is immediately visible blinds us to the fictional structure that mediates the visible world and creates meaning in it. In each instance, Nolan's films show how this fictional structure has an ontological priority and shapes what we see, providing the ground against which truth can emerge.

The lie of the Nolan film is not simply the depiction of events on the screen that have not occurred—or are not occurring—in the world outside the theater. What the lie means in Nolan's filmic universe goes far beyond this rudimentary lack of correspondence between representation and flesh-and-blood reality. The lie, as Nolan depicts it, is what misleads both characters and spectators. Lies encourage us to draw incorrect conclusions and to misunderstand actions and events. The victim of a lie fails to recognize what motivates characters to act as they do. But the lie also points to the truth that it hides. Lies are not immediately visible as lies in his films but rather are part of a formal structure that exists only insofar as it covers a truth. We understand the lie as a lie through its relationship to a truth that we finally distinguish from the lie. Nolan's films define the lie as a disjunction between what one believes and what happens, but this disjunction becomes apparent only when one transcends it.

As a result of its attitude toward the lie, the cinema of Christopher Nolan is not a moral cinema in the traditional sense. He does not illustrate the priority of deceit in order to denounce lying and insist on the importance of truthfulness. But it is an ethical cinema all the same, as Nolan redefines the relationship between ethics and truthfulness. The experience of Nolan's films reveals the importance for ethics of understanding the ontological priority of the lie. The failure to recognize the priority of the lie leaves one entirely in its thrall, and one gains freedom from deceit only when one fully submits to it. This is the paradox that Nolan advances and explores throughout his cinema. By accepting and recognizing the priority of the lie relative to truth, one can access the freeing power of the lie and discover its link to the origin of subjectivity.

Memento goes further than any of Nolan's other films in its foregrounding of the lie. The film's hero, Leonard Shelby, spends the running time of the film searching for the murderer of his wife, and the film encourages the spectator to invest in this ritual of detection that aims at discovering the truth of a crime. Despite the atypical disruption of forward-moving chronology that gives the film an exceptional structure, *Memento* appears throughout to share a widely held conception of truth. Truth is what we seek and what we discover when we uncover all the facts of an event. But the film does not conclude in the fashion of the usual detective thriller. Instead of ending with the truth of what happens to Leonard's wife, it reveals Leonard's own lie to himself as the origin of Leonard's search. Leonard's self-deception is not simply an impediment on the path to the discovery of truth; it is the engine behind the search for truth. The lie to himself creates the mystery that Leonard attempts to solve. It is in this sense that the lie has for Nolan an ontological priority relative to truth. The possibility of truth would not exist without the lie that provides its background. Truth must be torn away from its foundation in deceit.

Throughout the history of cinema, many filmmakers have emphasized the relativity of truth. This can be done with the subjective camera, as in Robert Montgomery's *Lady in the Lake* (1947), or by showing multiple accounts of the same event, which is how Akira Kurosawa constructs *Rashomon* (1950). One might also include video footage within the film, as Michael Haneke does in *Caché* (2005). In contrast to Nolan, these forms of perspectivalism do not impugn the priority of truth but rather insist on its multiplicity and its rootedness in a particular knowing subject. Truth here becomes identified with the capacity to recognize the limitedness of one's vision. As long as one believes in the objectivity of what is seen, one remains deceived. But as soon as one grasps that all knowledge is necessarily perspectival, one accedes to a new form of truth.[2] This type of film redefines truth in order to maintain its ontological priority, which is precisely what Nolan wants to challenge.

The point is not that we are misled by a mistaken idea of truth but that the very conception of truth's priority relative to the lie leaves us unable to recognize the way that deceit structures our reality. In the filmic universe of Christopher Nolan, truth is neither relative nor non-existent. There is truth, but one arrives at it only by passing through the lie. Lies establish the path through which one discovers the truth, and one can make this discovery only by accepting and investing one-self in the lie. A lie establishes a fictional version of events that don't correspond to what is actually happening or what has happened. The problem with our usual conception of truth is that it separates truth from this fiction and views truth as an original state that fiction or de-ceit corrupts. But for Nolan's cinema, the link between truth and fiction always remains clear: if one wants to discover the truth, one must first succumb to the fiction that seems to obscure it.

In each of his films, Nolan follows psychoanalyst Jacques Lacan's well-known axiom that "the non-duped err." The non-duped err because they fail to realize the fictional origin of all truth and thus believe that they can access truth without the detour of mediation. As Lacan notes in his seminar titled "Les non-dupes errent," "The non-duped are two times duped."[3] Not allowing oneself to be duped, demanding the truth directly, leaves one in the dark about both one's own status as a desiring subject and the fictional structure of the social order. Those who refuse to become dupes, who refuse to accept the fiction, ironically abandon the field of truth entirely. Truth exists as a possibility only for those who don't create an absolute distinction between it and the fiction from which it emerges. The fiction has this structural privilege because there is no truth apart from our act of seeking that truth.

Nolan's fascination with the superhero stems from his investment in the primacy and the productivity of the lie. The superhero takes on a false identity to assist in the struggle for justice. Sometimes the myth of the superhero's power has some link to this false identity: Peter Parker has an accident that gives him spider-like powers, and Tony Stark de-velops an iron suit that renders him almost invincible. But most often, the false identity of the superhero has no necessary relation to the superhero's powers. Superman, for instance, is just a guise that Clark Kent adopts when he wants to fight criminality and injustice. In purely physical terms, he might perform all the actions that he performs as Superman while remaining Clark Kent. The Superman identity does not offer him any additional power: at the most, it bequeaths anonymity; at the least, it provides an aesthetic flourish. The superhero's false identity does not appear to be a necessary condition of the superhero's power, and yet it is difficult to imagine a superhero without this false identity. The false identity separates the superhero from the realm of the ordi-

5

nary and thus causes others to look on the superhero differently. What's more, the deceit of the false identity reflects our investment in deceit as such. If superheroes really existed, it would not take much effort to discern their true identity, especially in the case of Superman, and yet spectators accept the idea of the disguise's effectiveness. The superhero's false identity reveals the power of deceit not just for the superhero but also for the audience watching this figure from the outside.

Nolan's first Batman film explicitly delinks Batman's superhero guise from his power. As *Batman Begins* (2005) recounts, Bruce Wayne does have an accident involving bats when he is a young boy. He falls into a cavernous opening, where he stirs up a large group of bats that engulf him. This trauma has a shaping influence on Bruce's life, but it doesn't transform him into Batman. After undergoing a rigorous training regimen in China, Bruce gains the fighting ability that he will employ to act as a superhero. Batman gains his power through physical and mental training, not through being bitten by a bat. Bruce decides to adopt the false identity of Batman not because this training gives him the powers of a bat but because he wants his enemies to experience the fear that he experienced as a young boy.

The identity of the rich playboy Bruce Wayne does not intimidate criminals in the way that the figure of Batman does. As Batman, Bruce gains an additional advantage that has nothing to do with his fighting ability, and this is true of the false identity that every superhero adopts. Batman wins many of his struggles simply because he is Batman, not because of superior strength or cunning.[4] This false identity gives the superhero the illusion of transcendence, and this illusion has the power to reshape the psychic reality of any situation. When confronted with the superhero, the criminal tends to act in a self-destructive manner that ensures the superhero's triumph.

But the deception of the superhero's false identity is not simply a tool for better apprehending criminals. It also captures a truth of the individuals that their actual identity obscures. The fictional Batman is the truth of Bruce Wayne, just as Superman is the truth of Clark Kent. At the end of *Batman Begins*, Rachel Dawes (Katie Holmes) comes to just this realization. After Bruce tries to minimize the importance of the Batman guise, she in turn dismisses the Bruce Wayne identity. She touches Bruce's face and tells him, "No, this is your mask. Your real face is the one criminals now fear." As Rachel grasps in this scene, the illusory identity that Bruce Wayne has created, the superhero figure, becomes his "real face." Batman identifies what is essential about

Bruce—the trauma with the bats that shapes his existence and his ability to confront this trauma. The superhero's false identity is the source of both power and truth, which is why it holds such appeal for Nolan as a filmmaker. The superhero's guise is clearly a deceit, but it points toward a truth of the subject that would otherwise remain completely obscured.

Nolan gravitates toward the superhero for the same reason he is attracted to a formal structure that deviates from a forward-moving chronology and shuffles narrative time. In both cases, truth is inseparable from what misleads us—and this link is constantly at play in the cinema. When we go to the cinema, we allow ourselves to be misled and thus distracted from our everyday lives. But filmic fictions, through their power to deceive, make manifest the truth of the extra-cinematic social reality. In the cinema, a society reveals its repressed desires, its hidden fears, and its implicit ideological imperatives. By highlighting the power of film to deceive and by remaining faithful to film's fictional structure, Christopher Nolan unveils the ethical potential of the cinema.

THE PERILS OF VISITING THE CINEMA

Christopher Nolan's filmic investment in the lie threatens to subject his films to an obvious critique. In fact, one of the most enduring criticisms of film concerns its association with deceit. Even great proponents of cinematic art, such as Hugo Münsterberg and Rudolf Arnheim, recognize a danger when film comes too close to presenting a false sense of reality.[5] Films falsify a sense of reality and thereby dupe spectators into unfounded beliefs that often have pernicious effects in their actual lives. For instance, one leaves the cinema with an idea that a ruthless executive will turn out to have a heart of gold or that every random encounter might actually be a meeting with one's future soul mate. These routine cinematic deceptions help to produce unthinking subjects who accept rather than question the structure of their society and their position in it. Even a critical thinker like Theodor Adorno admits that he finds himself unable to resist this deceptive power. In *Minima Moralia*, he laments, "Every visit to the cinema leaves me, against all my vigilance, stupider and worse."[6] To go to the cinema is to accede at least to some degree to its lies.

Film is famous for its untruth, and this untruth is indissociable from its appeal. We go to the cinema to be deceived, to take the unreal for the real, or to experience the cinematic creation of impossible worlds and situations. In difficult economic times, we head to the movies to experience the improbable fiction that our financial fortune could turn around in an instant if we became, say, the surprise winner of *Who Wants to Be a Millionaire?* due simply to the contingent experiences of our lives. The acclaim that greeted Danny Boyle's *Slumdog Millionaire* (2008), often articulated by otherwise-thoughtful critics and viewers, evinces most clearly the desire for cinematic deception. The film not only encourages us to believe in the possibility of individual escape from economic destitution, but it also portrays Westernization as the means for a parallel escape for an entire nation. These are powerful ideological fictions, and the film's popularity is inseparable from the support that it gives to them. *Slumdog Millionaire* lies in a way that helps contemporary capitalist society to function more smoothly. The difference between Boyle's film and those of Christopher Nolan is that Boyle presents the lie as truth, while Nolan presents truth as the product of a lie. But no matter how a filmmaker deploys deception, it infiltrates all filmmaking through the way that cinema structures our experience.

Special effects add to the cinema's appeal by multiplying its deception. As filmic technology develops, the power of filmmakers to create a convincing image of the world multiplies. Sound, color, and widescreen technology all help to lift barriers in the path of cinematic deceit. Even as critics lament this deceptiveness and rue film's reliance on new special effects such as CGI, the tools that augment filmic deception proliferate further and further into the act of filmmaking. Deception is at once the danger of cinema and its sine qua non.

One of the most common manifestations of cinematic deception is the imaginary reconstruction of history to produce a sense of progress where none should rightly exist. Scholars addressing the relationship between film and history must constantly address this problem. As Robert Rosenstone notes, "The mainstream feature (much like written history) tells the past as a story, with a beginning, a middle, and an end. A tale that leaves you with a moral message and (usually) a feeling of uplift. A tale embedded in a larger view of history that is always progressive. Even if the subject matter is as bleak as the horrors of the Holocaust, the message is that things have gotten or are getting better."[7] The most damning case of this type of lie occurs in Steven Spielberg's *Schindler's List* (1993). Here, a story about the Holocaust becomes a story of salvation, and the darkest moment for European Jews leads, according to the logic of the film itself, to the establishment of a Jewish homeland. Though this is the most egregious example, the distortion of history into a tale of progress is almost ubiquitous in the cinema, and then spectators take the idea of progress as the truth of history. The deceit acquires the quality of truth.

Probably the most powerful legend in the history of cinema is that of spectators screaming in terror and fleeing when the Lumière brothers' *L'arrivée d'un train à La Ciotat* (*Arrival of a Train at La Ciotat*, 1895) was first screened at the Grand Café in Paris. Regardless of whether this legend has any basis in fact, it endures because it speaks to the widespread sense of the precise danger—and, at the same time, the allure—that we associate with the cinema. We fear that under cinema's spell we will take images as more real than reality. This is a danger against which critics from all political stripes have inveighed. Moralists have feared cinematic depictions of activities from smoking to drinking to sex outside marriage because they recognized cinema's ability to give these activities a sense of reality and thus a sense of desirability. The Hays Production Code has its basis in this conception of cinema, and it was created to shape the reality that cinema could present.[8] Just as film deceives us about the train that appears ready to crash into the theater, it also lies about the consequences of smoking, drinking, and sex. Films often show us the night of passion and the pleasures of a cigarette, but they rarely show us the damaging consequences of unintended pregnancy or lung cancer. When they experience these consequences themselves, spectators pay the price for cinematic deception.

The danger exists not just for conservative moralists but also for politically engaged leftists. Hollywood cinema's lies about the absence of poverty, the invisibility of work, and the ubiquity of romantic love have had a perilous effect on American political awareness. When we see characters who never worry about money, who never work, and who always find satisfying love, we don't tend to think about social inequality, the role of labor in the creation of value, or the nefarious social effects of our myopic concentration on romance. Every bit as intensely as the conservative moralist, the leftist political critic of the cinema recognizes the danger of filmic deception and fights against it.

Conservatives recognized that cinematic deceit was politically neutral and could be turned toward conservative ends, which it was with the invention of the Hays Production Code.[9] The Left reacted differently. Leftist and progressive filmmakers have historically adopted various strategies for offsetting or combating cinema's inherent deceitfulness. Leftists have tended to look for ways to wrench truth from cinema's ten-

9

dency to lie. The Italian Neorealists eschewed traditional editing, hired nonprofessional actors, and shot on location—all in an effort to create truthful films. In works like *La chinoise* (1967) and *Le gai savoir* (1969), Jean-Luc Godard abandoned narrative and highlighted the production of the filmic image to avoid falling prey to cinematic deception. Many filmmakers choose the documentary form specifically as an avenue for truth that works against the fiction propagated by narrative cinema. For most of the various camps of alternative filmmakers, the association of deception with the cinema represents a fundamental problem that must be overcome in some fashion. Rather than perpetuating illusions, a politically engaged cinema must dispel them.

The problem is that the deceptions of cinema are inextricable from its place within the capitalist system of production and the reproduction of that system. The contemporary synergy between Hollywood filmmaking and the advertising industry is not a contingent development within cinema but a symptomatic one. As itself a structure of deception, the cinema is the perfect vehicle for indirect advertising through strategies like product placement, and as long as the link with deception remains, cinema will serve as part of the advertising wing of capitalist production.[10] But product placement is just the beginning of the link between cinema and the functioning of capitalist ideology. As Jonathan Beller argues, "Cinema emerges as the development and the intensification of the form of consciousness necessary to the increased mobilization of objects as commodities."[11] Movies help us to treat every object and every person that we encounter as a commodity. They deceive us into a commodified way of seeing that strips us of our capacity to act in order to change the world. In response to the imbrication of cinematic deceit and capitalist production, it seems as if the only possibility for political filmmaking resides in smuggling truth into this deception.[12]

Christopher Nolan does not take this path. He attempts, in contrast, to develop a politically engaged filmmaking that takes up and makes explicit use of cinema's tendency toward the lie.[13] From *Following* onward, his films embrace the deceit inherent in the cinema and even attach an ethical value to this deceit. Nolan initially misleads spectators into accepting a premise that the films later show to be false. This in itself is not all that uncommon. But Nolan's films emphasize the importance of the deception—and submitting to it—for any subsequent discovery of truth. Nolan inverts the traditional priority of truth and deception: the quest for truth originates with a lie, just as the cinematic fiction itself creates a terrain for the discovery of truths.

Characters in Nolan's films who fail to grasp the primacy of deception or fiction are inevitably doomed, like the protagonist of *Following*, who falls into a murderer's frame-up precisely because he believes in the power of truth. And Nolan's heroes, such as Batman or the magicians in *The Prestige* (2006), must take up the mantle of deceit and create a misleading appearance. Nolan shows a transformation occurring through the articulation of a fiction, and this transformation creates value. The fiction produces a sublimation that renders ordinary objects desirable. Without the magicians' deception of the audience, there would be nothing to arouse their desire. Some fiction is necessary to make life worth living at all, and Nolan's films draw attention to this to mark the moment at which value—what gives existence its worth—emerges. They don't encourage lying but rather the recognition of both the role that deceit or fiction has in the creation of value and the recognition of truth's dependence on this creative fiction. This is Nolan's ethic of the lie.

The idea of an ethic of the lie sounds, at first blush, absurd. By promoting such an ethic, one would, so it seems, help to foster a world of universal suspicion and paranoia, in which no one could trust anyone else. This is the kind of world that unrestrained capitalism would produce: claims are made solely to maximize one's profit in every situation, even social or romantic ones. In this world, the used-car salesperson would function as the ideal.[14] But in the end such a world would be unsustainable: if we could not trust the other members of society on some fundamental level, capitalist society could not function (even for the used-car salesperson), since it is based on the faith that others have faith in the value of our money. A world of universal suspicion would represent a complete loss of the social bond in its current form. Though a world of universal suspicion may be a danger attached to Nolan's ethic of the lie, his films focus not on the power of deceit to render us suspicious but on its power to make clear our freedom. In this sense, their concern is not lying as such but a specific dimension of the lie that they associate with the subject's capacity for freedom.

The most famous articulation of an ethic of the lie, in contrast, associates deceit with the flight from freedom. In *The Brothers Karamazov*, Dostoevsky's Grand Inquisitor propagates an ethic of the lie as a way of alleviating the burden of freedom. According to this ethic, because the mass of humanity cannot accept the groundlessness of human existence and the horror of mortality, a few privileged figures of authority provide humanity with a lie that ensures its ignorance and happiness.

The lie serves as a pretext for the abandonment of freedom, a supposed blessing that most experience as a curse. The Grand Inquisitor explains, "Man has no more tormenting care than to find someone to whom he can hand over as quickly as possible that gift of freedom with which the miserable creature is born. But he alone can take over the freedom of men who appeases their conscience."[15] In the Grand Inquisitor's speech, there is an absolute connection between truth, albeit unbearable truth, and freedom. Our inability to handle the truth of the immense burden of freedom leads to the acceptance of the lie that offers happiness. The Grand Inquisitor's ethic of the lie rejects freedom as a widespread possibility. The ethic of the lie developed in Nolan's films works in the opposite direction: they associate the lie with the emergence of freedom rather than its retreat.

In one sense, the link between the lie and freedom seems easy to understand. When we lie, we create a distinction between how we appear to others and how we appear to ourselves, and we thereby establish an interior space of freedom from the demands of the external world. In this way, lying functions as an assertion of one's subjectivity. This is a point that Jacques Lacan makes during a discussion of analytic technique. He notes, "We are necessarily obliged to admit the speaking subject as subject. But why? For one simple reason—because he can lie. That is, he is distinct from what he says."[16] For Lacan, subjectivity resides in the gap that language institutes between the point of enunciation and what one says. Language produces liars. Freedom consists in the irreducibility of the point of enunciation to any statement uttered by the speaking subject.

In *Memento*, the subjectivity of Leonard Shelby emerges not through his apparently earnest quest for his wife's killer. Though Shelby believes that this obsession attests to what most defines him, as spectators we see that this is part of Shelby's own self-deception. The singularity of Shelby's subjectivity appears at the end of the film when he decides to lie to himself and frame Teddy as the killer of his wife. This decision to lie signals his fundamental freedom as a subject. The structure of the film leads to this concluding lie, through which Leonard becomes *causa sui*, the origin of his own being. The lie creates the quest that makes up the film and that gives Leonard his reason for existing. It is through the lie that the subject gives itself the project that separates subjectivity from the rest of being and that makes this separation worthwhile.

Lying doesn't just create a distinction between the subject and what it says; lying also enacts a fundamental separation between the subject and everything else. When we lie, we assert our freedom by detaching ourselves from the world as it is given to us. Truth involves an appeal to what exists and the arrangement of what exists. It enacts fidelity to the existing world and at the same time professes dependence on this world. True statements are statements of acceptance and deference. In the act of lying, however, the subject implicitly takes responsibility for the account it generates, an account that is not based on a given world. The lie creates, and it entails total responsibility because it frees the subject from its dependence on the world. Rather than repeating what one sees or hears (which is what occurs when one tells the truth), the lying subject departs from the given world and invents freely. The fiction that occurs in a narrative is just an elaborate form of the primitive lie. Even if the narrative is based on an actual event, the narrative structure necessarily distorts the event and frees the audience from its constraints. There is freedom in the compression of time, the addition of suspense, the alteration of dialogue, and so on.

Every film frees us from the world outside its fiction, and this freedom is integral to cinematic pleasure. Even if we live in a world where corruption is rampant throughout politics, we can watch *Mr. Smith Goes to Washington* (Frank Capra, 1939) and believe in an authentic political figure who refuses to be bribed. Though ultimately Capra's film works to accommodate viewers to existing social arrangements through its endorsement of the fantasy of the American dream, the experience of the film provides a temporary freedom from corrupt reality outside the cinema. This temporary freedom marks the revolutionary potential of the cinema, and it is housed in the cinema's falsity.[17]

There is little resemblance between the films of Frank Capra and those of Christopher Nolan. Capra uses the cinematic lie to fortify the existing social structure; he places the freedom of the cinematic lie in the service of unfreedom.[18] Nolan, in contrast, draws attention to the lie as such to make spectators aware of their freedom. His films provide not just the temporary freedom that all cinema does, but they also work to create awareness of the primacy of the lie that would sustain freedom outside the cinema.

Nolan illustrates the importance of recognizing the primacy of deception and grasping the wide-ranging implications of its significance. The failure to do so leaves one incapable of understanding how social relations operate. But Nolan does not depict the primacy of deceit to produce a lying and manipulative spectator. Neither Leonard Shelby in *Memento* nor Will Dormer in *Insomnia*—two of Nolan's most conspicu-

13

ous figures of deceit—functions as a model figure. Instead, Nolan's films also reveal how a different attitude toward deceit or fiction can lead to a new conception of ethics, one in which evil is integral to good, just as deception is integral to truth. He shows that cinema can avow its deceptive character and establish an ethical program founded on deception.[19]

NOLAN THE HEGELIAN

Nolan's investment in the fiction does not just emerge full-blown without historical antecedents.[20] The idea of discovering truth through deception appears prominently in film noir, where the noir hero and the spectator often find themselves deceived by the femme fatale. This deception provides a way for film noir to articulate the truth of its society despite the limitations imposed at the time by the Production Code. By insisting on the priority of the lie as the path to truth, Nolan is the most noir of contemporary directors, even when he makes a film, like *Batman Begins* or *The Prestige*, that seems removed from the typical narrative style of film noir. But Nolan takes noir a step further by refusing to position the spectator outside of the hero's state of deception.

In Nolan's films, there is no truth outside the fiction, though there is truth inside it. They show that one arrives at an ethical position by adhering to the fiction and following it to its end point. Each of Nolan's films perpetuates some sort of deception on the spectator. Each is organized around a lie that establishes a fictional world and works to foster the spectator's investment in this world. *Following* reveals how we are constantly trapped by our belief in truth and its capacity for redeeming us. *Memento* depicts a quest for truth based on a lie. *Insomnia* presents itself as a crime thriller, but the detective himself ends up as both the subject and the object of the investigation. *Batman Begins* shows heroism itself as a fiction that we can inhabit. *The Prestige* features a magic act that deceives both the spectator and the characters in the film. *The Dark Knight* shows heroism manifesting itself in the guise of evil. And *Inception* (2010) depicts the fiction of the dream as the realm where one finds the truth of one's desire. These films begin with the fundamental deception of cinema itself—the image passing itself off as reality—and then they push this deception even further. By accepting these deceptions, spectators do not just submit to the cinematic experience that Nolan wants them to have; they work to transform their ethical being.

When we accept the cinematic lie, we invest ourselves wholly in the

14

reality of the world that the film presents. Every film deceives the spectator to some extent by presenting a cinematic fiction as a reality. Even films that endlessly deconstruct themselves conceal their fictional status through the very deconstruction that pretends to avow it. When we take this fiction for reality, we blind ourselves to those around us in the theater and to the edges of the frame; we ignore the world outside the theater and pretend that it doesn't exist. This type of investment represents a fetishistic disavowal: we know very well that the screen isn't reality, but we pretend that it is nonetheless.[21] While film theorists have historically railed against the fetishism of Hollywood cinema and its ideological effects, Nolan sees another side to our embrace of the cinematic lie. By acceding to this lie, we give up the idea of a real world existing elsewhere, and it is this idea, Nolan's films imply, that cripples us as ethical beings.

By creating a radical separation between truth and lie or between fiction and reality, we establish an unrealizable ideal of purity—pure truth or pure reality. This ideal will always require the elimination of the impure to sustain our purity. It is an ideal that depends on the act of exclusion and on the existence of what it excludes, which is why it is both ethically and ontologically untenable. Locating truth within the primacy of the lie, however, enables us to recognize the necessity of the impure, to grasp the impurity of the pure. This provides an alternative to rituals of purification. Existing in the impurity of the pure is existing without a beyond.

In this sense, Nolan's cinema has a profound connection with Hegel's philosophy. Though Hegel is a notoriously difficult German philosopher and Nolan is a largely accessible British filmmaker, they share a philosophical and ethical project. Both take deception as their point of departure while refusing to give in to relativism. Their joint investment in the priority of the lie stems from eschewing any idea of the pure or the beyond. Just as Nolan does in his films, Hegel writes to disabuse his readers of an elsewhere, and he accomplishes this by immersing himself in a series of fictions and tracing their logic to its end point. He never leaps outside the fiction to speak from the standpoint of truth, but instead foregrounds the philosophical movement from one fiction to another. One fiction leads to another when its logic breaks down. It is at the point where the logic of a fiction fails that truth emerges. For Hegel as for Nolan, truth is the failure of the fiction.

Maintaining a position within fictions constitutes the entirety of Hegel's philosophy: the absolute, the end point of this philosophy, is

15

the moment at which one recognizes the inescapability of the fiction as such. One reaches the absolute when one realizes that fiction provides the basis for truth, but one attains this point only by going through a series of fictions that seem to promise a truth external to fictionality. The absolute is not, as the common critique of Hegel has it, the attainment of a transcendent position from which the philosopher might survey the play of all the hitherto-discussed fictions. It is rather the point at which the philosopher must give up the idea of a point external to fictionality. One has to hew to the fiction despite one's investment in truth.

Hegel's *Phenomenology of Spirit* explores a series of false doctrines to discover what their deceptions can teach us about the structure of subjectivity. Even the most deceptive doctrine, sense certainty (or the belief that sense impressions provide the ultimate truth), reveals that the most minimal use of language involves recourse to the universal. Hegel arrives at this truth simply by tracing the logic of sense certainty, which is his starting point in the *Phenomenology* precisely because it is the most deceptive doctrine. We must begin with the greatest deception and work our way from there.

As Hegel shows throughout his philosophy, we discover truth not through separating ourselves from fiction but through fully succumbing to it. The logic of the fiction has a creative power that leads to truth, which is why philosophy—or filmmaking—cannot simply dismiss it. The truth that we find will retain this fictional structure and thus cannot be entirely distinct from the fiction out of which it emerges.[22] Even the transcendent beyond, for Hegel, is part of the world that it transcends and thus not transcendent in the way that we typically understand the idea. This rejection of the transcendent beyond as separated from the ordinary world is an ethical and ontological position that Hegel and Nolan share.

Escaping the idea of an elsewhere or a transcendent beyond is not as simple as exiling all fictions from one's ideal society or abandoning the belief in God. Both Plato and the famous atheist Richard Dawkins, through their flights from fiction and myth, sustain the idea of a reality beyond. For Plato, the beyond is the world of Ideas, and for Dawkins, it is the fully explicable scientific world we have yet to discover.[23] Though Plato famously banishes the poets from his republic as the producers of fictions and Dawkins inveighs against belief in a transcendent deity, they both retain the idea of an elsewhere. An insistence on truth and

THE FICTIONAL CHRISTOPHER NOLAN

the banishment of deception will never take us far enough down the path toward abandoning the idea of a beyond. The abandonment can come only through the acceptance of the primacy of the lie and the fiction, in which truth emerges from within the lie rather than outside it.

In the cinema, the real deception is not that what we see on the screen is reality but that there exists a real world beyond the screen. So when critics upbraid the cinema for presenting a false reality, it is actually these critics themselves who are guilty of perpetuating the idea of a false reality that would exist beyond the fiction. We cannot leave the fiction and enter reality. We live our lives within the fiction, and when we encounter truth, we necessarily do so from within the terrain of some controlling fiction. Though most of us don't spend the entirety of our lives in the movie theater, we do pass our lives on the screen—within the fantasy structure that shapes how we view the world. The point is not that we live within a series of fictional constructions in which there is no truth. Even this commonsensical conception implicitly avows a true point of reference outside from which one can examine the cultural constructions and see them as such. Social constructionism is yet another attempt to escape the fiction by presupposing the existence of a separate realm from which one might examine the social constructions as constructions.

We capitulate to the limitations of the cinematic fantasy structure not because we fail to grasp its fantasy status but precisely because we do. Believing in a real world of real significance beyond the fantasy, we fail to act to change the structures in which we exist. The idea of a truth outside the lie condemns us to live within the lie. We can only escape the lie, paradoxically, if we accept that the lie is all there is, that there is no reality beyond the screen. At this point, the moment at which truth emerges in the fiction becomes visible.

Christopher Nolan immersed himself in cinematic fiction from a young age. At age seven, he began making films with an 8 mm camera. Perhaps it was this early beginning in filmmaking that allowed him to approach cinema not as an illusory alternative to reality but as all there is. Of course, Nolan has a life outside the cinema: he has a spouse, children, and even a purported affection for British literature. But his films reflect a total investment in the completeness of the cinematic fiction. The rejection of an outside to the fiction is the implicit ethic that manifests itself in each of his films.

Without the solace of a reality beyond the screen, we lose the hope

17

that one day we will discover the truth that will completely change our existence. We lose the hope that we will escape the mundane every-dayness of our lives. But at the same time, we grasp the freedom that resides within our everydayness. The terrain of the fiction is the terrain where we struggle. It is the terrain on which all political change occurs. Forcing us to occupy this terrain without alternatives is the cinematic project of Christopher Nolan.

In terms of the conditions of its production, *Following* (1998) stands out among Christopher Nolan's films. It was made on a series of weekends over a year while Nolan and the film's cast and crew worked regular jobs during the week. Constrained by a $6,000 budget, Nolan got along with mostly natural light, 16 mm film stock, and amateur actors. These limitations would seem to preclude any comparison with the $185 million *Dark Knight* (2008). But differences in the conditions of production have not changed Nolan's overriding interest—the use of cinema for the exploration of the lie. Like each of his later films, Nolan's first feature highlights the ontological priority of the lie over the truth. This is apparent even in the opening frames, where Nolan begins with a sequence meant to mislead the spectator.

The opening images of the film are a series of close-ups of an anonymous pair of hands and a group of small objects that we see the hands assemble in a box. In one sense, the sequence hints at a truth that will only become fully evident later in the film. The latex gloves on the hands and the manner in which the items in the box are assembled suggest that someone is carefully arranging the box so that someone else will discover it and find significance in its items. Later, this allows the spectator both to see through the discovery of the hidden box while Bill (Jeremy Theobald) and Cobb (Alex Haw) are searching through an apartment looking for the occupant's secret and also to grasp Bill's error when he finds the hidden box of the woman known only as the Blonde (Lucy Russell). When Cobb announces that almost everyone has such a box and that it holds the secret to the essence of his or her being, we can recall this opening sequence and doubt his claim.

By showing us the box and its carefully chosen items as a construct, the film allows us to be skeptical about what we will subsequently see and thereby offers us an insight into the truth. But in another sense, this truth remains within a larger deception. Using latex gloves in order to leave no trace, we see later that Cobb has designed the box to seduce Bill with the allure of a hidden secret, but the revelation of this fiction

THE SNARE OF TRUTH

FOLLOWING AND THE PERFECT PATSY

is actually part of another fiction that leads to Bill becoming the only suspect in a murder investigation. Cobb did indeed set up the box for Bill to find, but his larger deception depends on Bill becoming aware of this and thereby believing that he has discovered the truth. For both Bill and the spectator, the first images of the film deceive precisely at the moment when they appear to offer an otherwise hidden truth.[1]

As the structure of Nolan's film shows, the truth inevitably works in service of some more fundamental lie, and it is the belief in the ontological priority of truth that blinds us to the way that the lie structures and informs our existence. The film attempts to reveal to us how this blindness functions and how we might find a way out of it. *Following* reveals that truth exists within the structure of a lie. It does this by depicting the complete failure that results from a strict belief in the priority of truth. Bill's practice of following (trailing random strangers in order to learn about their lives) has its basis in his faith in truth—that the truth of someone is hidden somewhere within their secret activities and hidden possessions. He becomes the dupe of Cobb and the Blonde because he invests himself in the project of uncovering the truth they introduce to him. In all these actions, Bill functions as a stand-in for the cinematic spectator who refuses to acquiesce to the primacy of the illusion that film provides and who rather seeks a truth beyond that illusion. *Following* makes clear that there is a truth in and of the illusion that we can understand, but there is no truth beyond it.[2] The belief in this version of truth creates an inescapable trap just like the one that snares Bill at the end of the film.

The conception of truth that the film opposes—and that Bill evinces—is an association of truth with wholeness and independence. Truth, according to this idea, opposes falsity and has nothing to do with it. Truth represents a separate region, integral to itself, that is self-sustaining. When one knows something truthfully, one has an immediate or direct grasp of this truth. This is an attitude that Hegel criticizes in the preface to the *Phenomenology of Spirit*, an attitude that conceives truth as "a minted coin that can be given and pocketed ready-made."[3] One passes from ignorance or deception to truth, but neither ignorance nor deception mediate truth. It exists on its own and can be acquired, just like any other object. Bill's conception of truth is widespread—it is the commonsensical position—but it is also the key to his complete deception. As Nolan's film shows, the standard notion of truth leaves us unfailingly in error.

Following focuses on Bill, an unemployed fledgling writer with little

20

to occupy him. Several shots early in the film depict him spending much of this time walking through crowds and finding people with an interesting look, whom he then decides to follow or shadow in order to learn what is essential about them. Soon, however, a man whom he is following, Cobb, notices him in a café and interrogates Bill about the practice of following. This leads to a partnership between Bill and Cobb, in which they break into apartments, commit minor thefts, and look for hidden items that would reveal the secrets of the people who live there. After Bill falls for a woman, the Blonde, whose apartment they had entered, he begins a romantic relationship with her. She then convinces Bill to break into her former boyfriend's office to steal some money and compromising pictures of her. Unbeknownst to the Blonde, by doing so she helps to frame Bill for her own murder, which Cobb will commit, leaving clues about Bill's guilt and using the same methods that Bill did while breaking into the office. Bill's confession to the police begins and ends the film, and his decision to tell the truth to them provides the key to the case against him. The effectiveness of Cobb's lie, the frame-up of Bill, requires Bill's belief in the ultimate primacy of the truth, and it is this belief that animates Bill's behavior throughout the film and that ultimately dooms him. The problem is the difficulty involved in avowing the ontological priority of the lie.

The central position that confession occupies in *Following* is one of many signals of the film's fundamental affinity with film noir. Perhaps more than any other Nolan film, it is firmly in the noir tradition. Like Walter Neff (Fred MacMurray) at the beginning and end of *Double Indemnity* (Billy Wilder, 1944), Bill confesses the truth in order to right himself with a figure of authority. Walter Neff wants to justify himself in the eyes of Barton Keyes (Edward G. Robinson), and Bill wants to exculpate himself in front of the police. The difference concerns the status of the confession: Neff's revelation of the truth does provide a moment of catharsis for him in which he and Keyes express their mutual love, while Bill's confession of the truth ends up implicating him in the Blonde's murder. This indicates in a microcosm how Nolan moves beyond film noir in his affirmation of the priority of the lie relative to truth. In film noir, there remains a space for truth outside the deception that embroils the noir hero, and this space emerges through the hero's confession, which is often a fixture of the noir style. But Nolan cannot insist on the priority of the lie without running into structural difficulties that film noir, with its ultimate affirmation of truth as a realm separated from deception, can avoid.

21

The most evident barrier to revealing the priority of deception is the liar's paradox. According to this paradox, in the act of depicting the priority of deception, one presents a truth. Consequently, even films that overtly devote themselves to a lie end up presenting the truth about deceit. According to the liar's paradox, one cannot say, "I am lying," while continuing to do so. If the statement is true, then it's false, and if it's false, then it's true. Demonstrating the ontological priority of the lie in a film would appear to run aground on this paradox. A film that proclaims its deceitfulness becomes, even against the intentions of the filmmaker, a cinema of truth. But there is a solution to the liar's paradox, supplied by Jacques Lacan, that enables Nolan to depict the priority of the deceit. Lacan identifies a split within the speaking subject between the subject of the enunciation and the subject of the statement, which means that the one who speaks is not identical with the "I" in the spoken statement. I can truthfully proclaim that "I am a liar" because I am distinct from this spoken "I." In the same way, *Following* can reveal the priority of deceit in the statement without investing itself in the statement's truth.[4]

WE ARE IN WHAT WE SEE

Following depicts the investment in truth functioning within a controlling fiction. This investment manifests itself in the ruling metaphor of the film—the box of secrets. The box of secrets represents what Plato calls the agalma, the secret treasure that the subject has and that attracts the desire of others.[5] According to Nolan's metaphor (which follows Plato's), our interest in others (and in the cinema) derives from the idea of a box of secrets that we believe them to possess—a hidden knowledge of what is most singular about them.[6] When Cobb takes Bill on his first break-in, he introduces the box as the raison d'être of the break-in. The box, like the diary, does not hold ordinary valuables but the little treasures that reveal what a person holds most precious. These treasures represent the owners' hidden desire, the essential kernel of their being. As Cobb explains to Bill, "Everyone has a box. . . . Sort of an unconscious collection, a display. . . . Each thing tells something very intimate about the people. We're very privileged to see it. It's very rare."[7] Seeing the box involves seeing what the Other is when no one is looking. In this sense, it gives the onlooker an impossible perspective on the Other. Cobb builds up the importance of the secret box for both

Bill and the spectator, but, as the film ultimately reveals, he has himself put the various items in the boxes that Bill and he discover. Rather than containing the hidden desire of some stranger, the box is a lie meant to attract Bill's desire and to seduce him.

The illusoriness of the secret box is evident visually at the very moment Cobb proclaims its sublime value. As he is looking through the box, the camera stays focused on him in a medium shot and never reverts to a close-up of the "unconscious collection." The angle of the camera never allows the spectator to make out clearly what the specific objects are. After we see Cobb rifle through the box, he dumps it unceremoniously on the floor. Though he explains this act as a way to let the person know that "someone has seen it" and thereby "make them see all the things they took for granted," the nonchalance evinced in the visual image contradicts this claim. But this justification convinces Bill and puts him on the trail of other secret boxes, in hopes of penetrating the impossible mystery of otherness.

The point is not that the secret box as such does not exist, that there is no hidden kernel of the Other's being, but that even this hidden kernel takes our desire into account. The truth of the Other is a lie meant to seduce us in the way that the idea of the secret box seduces Bill. Even the Other's secret is created with the idea that someone will discover it; there is no such thing as the Other when no subject is looking. Bill falls victim to the power of the box because he fails to think through his own involvement in what he sees. He accepts the world he discovers as a reservoir of truth that simply shows itself rather than as a fiction that he must interpret. His failure is a failure of interpretation.

Bill's failure is also that of the cinematic spectator. The position that Bill takes up when he follows parallels the position of the spectator in the cinema.[8] Cobb is able to seduce Bill into his trap because Bill fails to recognize that the person he is following and the world that he is observing take his presence into account. He is not simply looking at a world waiting to be seen but rather one structured around his act of looking.[9] The objective truth of the world includes within it the subjective fiction that Bill provides when he looks, though he remains completely unaware of the fictional dimension of what he sees. Bill's desires are part of what he sees, shaping his field of vision rather than existing distinct from it. This becomes clearest when the Blonde reveals to Bill toward the end of the film that Cobb had actually been following him. This shocks Bill because he follows without any awareness of his involvement in what he sees. Similarly, the cinematic spectator is structurally blinded to the way that the film includes the position of spectatorship.[10] Like the world that Bill looks at and attempts to figure out, the filmic world is not simply there to be seen; instead, it shows itself to the spectator's look.

Nolan indicates the subject's involvement in what is seen early in the film when Bill's voiceover explains what the act of following entails. He does this through the way he edits together Bill's voiceover and the images that this voiceover narrates. The images during this description show the Blonde coming out of her apartment, and Bill looking up at her from across the street. In the voiceover, Bill states, "Other people are interesting to me. Have you never listened to other people's conversations on the bus or on the Tube, seen people, seen somebody on the street that looks interesting or is behaving slightly . . . oddly or something like that, and wondering what their lives involved, what they do, where they come from, where they go to?" As Bill provides this explanation, the editing in the film makes clear that Bill is not just an observer but also part of what he sees: the film's visuals belie his voiceover account of following.

At first, the narration and the images seem to coordinate, as one would expect. As Bill poses the question about seeing "somebody on the street that looks interesting," the film shows the Blonde walking on the sidewalk and entering a club. But when Bill pauses in the middle of describing the behavior of the person he watches, Nolan cuts to a reverse shot of Bill looking at the woman entering, so that the word "oddly" in his description is not attached visually to the Blonde he is following but to Bill himself—that is, the person who is looking. Through this unexpected cut, the film emphasizes the subjectivity of the follower, not the object being followed. The odd behavior, the peculiarity, is the act of following itself, not what the follower sees. By emphasizing the subjectivity of the follower in this way, the film makes clear that what the follower—or the filmgoer—sees is not simply there to be seen but is also a product of the act of looking. The spectator's way of looking, the desire informing the look, shapes what the spectator sees, even though the spectator cannot see this distortion.

This is one of the moments where Nolan's cinema touches explicitly on Hegel's thought. Hegel wants to recognize our blindness to how desire shapes our look. To this end, he proposes a philosophy in which, as he famously puts it in the *Phenomenology of Spirit*, "everything turns on grasping and expressing the True, not only as *Substance*, but equally as *Subject*."[11] The subject's desire is not independent of the truth that it

24

discovers but rather inextricably linked to that truth. Yet this is the most difficult thing to grasp because the subject can recognize the distortion produced by its desire only through the vehicle of that distortion itself. There is no position outside the distortion where the subject can have direct access to truth, which is why Hegel sees philosophy as the exploration of a series of increasingly complex distortions. Rather than seeking out a position outside, the subject must work through its distortions. Bill fails to do this, but Nolan's film offers the spectator the opportunity to recognize this failure and thereby adopt a different attitude to the distortion. Like Hegel, the spectator of the Nolan film can see how the scene doesn't simply exist on its own but has been set for us.[12]

Bill's blindness to the staging of each scene for his look leads him to believe that his interventions are the result of his own agency rather than of the script laid out for him. For example, when he goes on his first break-in with Cobb, Cobb looks under the doormat for the key and then proceeds to use a pick for the lock after he doesn't find one there. Bill expresses disbelief at the idea of someone leaving a key under the doormat. He wonders, "People don't really to that, do they?"[13] As Cobb works on the lock, Bill searches elsewhere for a hidden spare key and eventually finds one above the door frame. Cobb's exclamation—"Beginner's luck!"—confirms the self-satisfaction that this discovery provokes in Bill, who at this point is convinced of his own ingenuity. But he doesn't see how Cobb's gesture of searching under the doormat induced him to look for the key planted above the door frame by Cobb for him to find. In the shot that shows Bill discovering the key, Nolan depicts him reaching over Cobb so that their bodies partially overlap in the image. This conjuncture in the image parallels the one that Bill fails to notice in the plot. Finding the key is part of Cobb's script that Bill cannot see because he fails to grasp how the world that he sees includes him within it and anticipates his involvement, even though he experiences this involvement as the product of his own free act.[14]

The next break-in that we see in the film reveals the extent of the divorce that Bill experiences between himself and what he sees. After Cobb tells Bill to find a suitable apartment for their subsequent break-in, Bill decides on his own apartment as the target. He hides a key under a doormat and leads Cobb inside after they find it. Bill sets up his own apartment in this way because he wants Cobb to discover the secret of his being that Bill himself doesn't know. This reflects his belief in the complete separation between the seer and the seen: accompanying the insightful Cobb, Bill is convinced that he will see himself from a neutral position, without the distortion that comes from his own act of seeing. He leads Cobb to his own apartment because he believes in the possibility of seeing without the distorting fiction of desire. The insights of Cobb promise a pure truth untainted by illusion.[15] But Cobb, knowing that this is a setup, disappoints Bill with his response.

Initially, Cobb treats Bill's apartment like any other place that they would explore.[16] He looks over Bill's things and evaluates their worth, but he soon begins to attack Bill for his choice of targets. He tells Bill that "there's fuck-all here," complains that the television is "fucking worthless," and concludes that the occupant is "a sad fucker with no social life." When he discovers a UB (a book for unemployment benefits), he picks it up and slaps Bill twice across the face with it. As he walks out of the apartment, Cobb proclaims, "We're not going to take anything. I don't feel like scrounging off some poor dole head." This reaction devastates Bill. Bill set up the break-in to discover the truth of his being, what was most valuable and essential about himself, but Cobb responds by finding nothing valuable and rejecting the very idea of the search. In the final shot of this scene, we see Bill following Cobb down the stairs from his apartment with a disappointed look on his face. The despondency that he displays throughout the scene as Cobb denigrates the apartment's occupant attests to his failure to see himself objectively through a neutral look. Rather than seeing something of value in Bill, the neutral look disdains everything that it sees.

But of course Cobb's look is not a neutral look; he knows that he is looking at Bill's apartment and responds in a way that he knows will disappoint Bill. Doing so—producing this dissatisfaction—further draws Bill into Cobb's plan that ultimately will frame Bill for the murder of the Blonde. But it is not just happenstance that dooms Bill's attempt to see himself from a neutral perspective. Even if Cobb had not known that this was Bill's apartment, even if someone else not trying to frame Bill was looking, Bill would still not be able to see himself in the way he wants to be seen. There is no looking that does not involve desire that distorts it, and Bill's desire for a neutral look will necessarily taint any apparently neutral look that he discovers.

Though Bill fails to perceive his own involvement in what he sees, it becomes clear that what he looks for in the people he follows and in the apartments he breaks into is a part of himself. Bill submerges his own identity and desires when he commits himself to following someone, and he easily assimilates himself to Cobb's project of breaking into various apartments. The film shows him lacking a distinctive presence.

26

And yet all of his actions in the film—the following, the break-ins with Cobb, the romance with the Blonde—have as their aim the discovery of what is essential about himself, the foundation of his being. What he fails to see is that this essence or foundation is not separate from his desiring look but rather inheres in it. What we desire is what we are doing as we are looking for the object of our desire. The truth of our being is not waiting for us to see it; it resides in the distorting fiction of our desire that makes it impossible for us to see the world just as it is.

This does not mean that every vision of the world is relative, that the only truth is relativity itself. Such a verdict sustains the separation of the subject and what is seen that hampers Bill in the film. Identifying the necessary fiction produced by our desiring subjectivity allows us to change the location of truth. It does not exist in the world itself (as objectivism or empiricism would have it) or in the subject (as relativism or subjective idealism would have it). Instead, truth exists in the distortion itself. The truth of our being is in the fictional turn through which we ground the objective world. Though Bill remains completely unaware of this truth throughout *Following*, the film makes a point of his unawareness and thereby foments spectators' recognition of the truth of their spectatorship.

PRESAGING *MEMENTO*

Bill's inability to see the world objectively despite all his efforts has an analogue in the spectator's relationship to the film. Nolan structures the temporality of the film so that the spectator experiences a distortion that appears to hide a truth while actually expressing that truth. That is to say, the film's distorted temporality appears to hide a true linear temporality waiting to be unraveled, but in fact the distorted temporality itself—the form that the distortion takes—holds the key to understanding the film's insistence on the priority of fiction in relation to truth.

As in his subsequent film, *Memento* (2000) (though to a lesser extent), Nolan disrupts typical forward-moving chronology in *Following*. Though the beginning and end of the film mark the chronological starting and ending points, what occurs in between often defies linear ordering. This becomes most noticeable when we see Bill appear with a black eye and cut lip that he never received in prior scenes. Bill's face changes from scene to scene before we actually see the beating itself, which occurs very late in the film. The disruptions of linear chronology are for the most part obvious and don't materially interfere with the spectator's ability to follow the film's story. But Nolan includes these disruptions to place the spectator in exactly the same position that Bill occupies within the film's reality—following a world that appears to hide a deeper truth. For Bill, that truth is the essence of the person he follows, while for the spectator, it is the film's story hidden beneath its nonlinear discourse.[17]

One's first instinct when confronted with a film constructed in a nonchronological order is to mentally restore a linear chronology to the events. Some take this even further by projecting reedited versions of nonchronological films in a proper chronological order. Soon after the release of *Memento*, there were special screenings set up to eliminate the reverse chronology and show the film taking place in a forward-moving temporality. Even if we didn't attend such a special screening or buy a DVD that could play the film chronologically, we undoubtedly performed a similar mental operation, rearranging what we saw in order to make sense of the causal relationships between the events. Without chronology, we cannot think in the traditional terms of causality. The experience of forward-moving time provides the basis for understanding how one event causes another.

In the *Critique of Pure Reason*, Immanuel Kant links our ability to make causal determinations to our ability to think objectively. We can distinguish the objective world from pure subjective illusion because causality (and other categories) governs the former. Without formal rules like causality, we would have no guarantee concerning the objective status of what we were experiencing.[18] Causality, with its basis in chronology, connects our experience to that of everyone else and assures us that we are not living within our own private subjective illusion. As Kant puts it in the Transcendental Analytic of the first *Critique*, "Objective significance is conferred on our representations only insofar as a certain order in their temporal relation is necessary."[19] The causal relations present in linear chronology provide the ultimate assurance: causality functions for Kant as a guarantee of our connection to a world beyond our own desire.

According to the logic of *Following*, it is precisely this step to a purely objective significance that is disallowed. Because there is no linear chronology, there is no traditional causality in the filmic discourse— and thus no objectivity. In this sense, Nolan's film is anti-Kantian: the path to objectivity does not consist in discovering transcendental rules ensuring that we have escaped mere subjective illusion but rather in the subjective origin of the transcendental rules themselves. Just as there is no proper chronology existing beneath the nonlinear chronology the film presents, there is no objective significance that exists outside subjective fiction. Instead, objective significance or truth exists based on a subjective fiction. Finding the truth does not involve escaping the subjective distortion of desire (as Bill believes) but rather working through this distortion and grasping its formative power. The distortion has a truth that becomes visible when we recognize its foundational status.[20]

In order to understand the film, one need not reconstruct the "true" linear chronology. One must instead follow the logic of the connections in the distorted order that Nolan presents them to us. Rather than showing a linear causality tied to the temporality of the clock, he edits the film in a way that stresses the logic of desire. Bill's desire continues in the same path, and this path is constituted through the series of dissatisfactions he encounters. Each movement forward in the narrative represents an attempt to resolve a problem of desire that develops, though these movements defy linear chronology.

For instance, after we see Bill arranging the break-in at his own apartment and the disappointment that results, Nolan cuts to a scene chronologically out of order that shows Bill visiting the Blonde at her apartment after they've become romantically involved. She talks to him about the discomfort she feels about a recent burglary, focusing not on what she has lost but on the feeling of someone seeing her private self. She tells him, "It's the personal stuff that's worse." The attitude that Bill evinces during this conversation demonstrates his interest in the experience of having one's secrets seen. As the Blonde begins talking about the robbery in general, Bill's attention wanders. Nolan shoots him looking around the room and not really paying attention to her. But when she discusses what bothers her—the fact that someone has seen and taken personal things—his expression undergoes a radical transformation, and he begins to look interested in what she has to say.

The inclusion of the scene at the Blonde's apartment sustains the emphasis of the previous scene. The satisfaction that Bill takes in her response to the robbery contrasts with his disappointment after the staged robbery of his own apartment. The conversation with the Blonde presents a solution but at the same time generates another problem that, according to the film's nonchronological logic, the subsequent scene must confront and attempt to solve. Though Bill experiences the thrill of the secret essence of the Blonde's being when she recounts her feeling about a stranger accessing it, this secret remains vague and without any content until the next scene, which shows Cobb and Bill breaking into the Blonde's apartment. Even though the actual break-in scene occurs chronologically before the conversation between Bill and the Blonde about the break-in, it comes afterward in the film because it depicts an attempted solution to the problem evident in the prior scene.

Unraveling the narrative development of *Following* requires identifying the logic of desire that structures it, not determining the linear chronology that it hides. The idea of a hidden linear chronology—a story waiting to be deciphered from the filmic discourse—represents a lure for the spectator, just as the secret essence of a person represents a lure for Bill. His mistake is not so much the act of following itself but the belief that following will lead to a truth independent of what he sees when he follows. Bill is trapped by the logic of linear chronology in the same way as the noir hero. Both believe that the future will bring them an object that they don't already have rather than sustaining the desire that they already do have. When he is following, Bill sees all there is to see: the secrets of the people he follows are not hidden away within a box in their apartments but present in the places they go, the things they say, and the gestures they make. The truth of their subjectivity exists in the quotidian fictions they inhabit. *Following* allows us as spectators to see this truth through its depiction of Bill's utter blindness to it.

READING FOR THE TRUTH

In contrast to Bill, Cobb shows himself capable of grasping how truth manifests itself in the form of a lie. Though Cobb is certainly the film's villain, he also represents the site where knowledge is located in the film. While the film aligns our sympathies with Bill and his desire, it establishes Cobb as exemplary in his approach to fictionality and truth. This approach allows him to frame Bill for the Blonde's murder without leaving any trace of his own involvement. The key to knowing the truth derives from grasping that truth exists in the way that the lie is articulated.

Through Bill's first interaction with Cobb, the film establishes that lying does not present a barrier to truth but rather a pathway to it. After he notices Bill following him, Cobb approaches Bill in a café and sits down across from him at a table. He then interrogates Bill and quickly gathers the essential information about him, even though Bill lies to Cobb throughout the conversation. The way that Bill lies displays his intentions and desires in a way that statements of truth would not. He tells Cobb, "I wasn't following you. I saw you with your bag. I just thought you looked interesting." This is a direct lie. Bill was following Cobb, and he confesses this truth through his manner of lying. The way that the film shows Bill speaking undermines everything he says. The whole time that he speaks, Bill looks down and then can barely enunciate the final word "interesting." These physical manifestations of shame permit Cobb to read the truth behind his lie and to conclude that Bill has been following him.

This revelation of the truth through the manner of telling the lie continues throughout the conversation and throughout Bill's entire relationship with Cobb. After denying that he is pursuing Cobb out of a sexual interest, Bill lies again: "To tell you the truth, I thought you were this guy that I was at school with." Here, Bill's insistence that he is telling the truth acts as an index of his deception. If he were not lying, he wouldn't have to add that he is telling the truth.[21] Then, when Cobb questions Bill about his ultimate motivations, Bill exposes the truth through his hesitation:

Cobb: There's some burning ambition inside you, isn't there? Something of the starving artist in you, no?
Bill: No.
Cobb: No?
Bill: No.
Cobb: You're a painter?
Bill: No.
Cobb: Photos?
Bill: No.
Cobb: You're a writer?
Bill: No.
Cobb: Writer, eh?
Bill: No.

Cobb quickly gleans that Bill imagines himself as a writer when, in contrast to his denials about being a painter or a photographer, he pauses before denying it, and then when Cobb repeats the question, the tone in Bill's voice changes, expressing an excess of denial. The visual image and the audio track in the film assert a truth through their contrast with the lie in the dialogue. But it is the lie that creates the possibility of this contrast; it has a fecundity that the truth doesn't have. Every time Bill attempts to lie, Cobb discovers a truth of Bill's character that he would otherwise not have known. The lie functions as a mode of access to the truth, and it is Cobb, the film's villain, who recognizes this.

Reading the truth through another's lies—Cobb's approach to Bill—is an everyday practice that most of us engage in. In his attempt to demonstrate the penetration of psychoanalytic principles into our daily interactions, *The Psychopathology of Everyday Life*, Freud contends that we constantly interpret the slips, pauses, expressions, and gestures of our interlocutors in order to discover the truth that their words hide. He notes, "It can in fact be said quite generally that everyone is continually practising psychical analysis on his neighbours and consequently learns to know them better than they know themselves."[22] This quotidian version of psychoanalysis permits us to understand what others desire when their words work to veil their desire, and as a result, we can respond to their desire rather than the public fiction they present.

We often don't know significant details of our friends' lives—their political views, their religious beliefs, and so on—because we focus on knowing their desire. Most conversations are not efforts to uncover information about the lives of our interlocutors but to see where their desire resides. Our lack of knowledge of the other aspects of our friends' lives can thus be the sign of true friendship. Without this ability to read the desire of others through their words, we would constantly find ourselves the victims of the crudest deceptions and cruelest disappointments. We would mistake disinterest for caring, civility for concern, and even love for friendship. The capacity for reading the truth through the lie is essential for our being in the world, and *Following* aims to highlight its importance.

The ability to read the truth through another's lies does not simply uncover the truth that the person hides from the world. It also can uncover the truth that the person hides from her- or himself. In the act of creating a public fiction to cover our private thoughts and desires, we expose to others thoughts and desires unbeknownst to ourselves.[23] The truth manifested in the unintentional gestures that accompany our lies is a truth that others know before we do. As Freud points out, "Actions carried out unintentionally must inevitably become the source of misunderstandings in human relations. The agent, who knows nothing of there being an intention connected with these actions, does not feel that they are chargeable to him and does not hold himself responsible for them. The second party, on the other hand, since he regularly bases his conclusions as to the agent's intentions and sentiments on such actions among others, knows more of the other's psychical process than that person himself is ready to admit or believes he has communicated."[24] Through all of our unintentional actions, we reveal more of ourselves to others than we do to ourselves. No matter how well we lie to ourselves, the truth of our desire necessarily manifests itself to others.[25]

The ontological priority of the fiction in relation to truth has a parallel in the priority of the Other relative to the subject. Others know the truth of the subject before the subject does because this truth reveals itself through various errors and gestures that the subject performs unconsciously. The idea of a meaning behind what we say necessarily blinds us to all the ways that we say something other than what we consciously mean.[26] Through our effort to communicate a meaning to others, we expose to them the unconscious truth of desire. They have access to this truth before we do, if they know how to interpret the fiction that we present. If they want to understand what we are saying, they must interpret the desire that animates the fiction, which is what the psychoanalyst attempts to do.[27]

Through the way that he structures *Following*, Nolan establishes this interpretive imperative as a model for cinematic spectatorship. The proper spectator of the film must see the truth of the desire articulated by the filmic fiction. This is not the truth of the filmic story; one does not arrive at it by figuring out the plot or solving the mystery that the film presents. It is instead the truth of the filmic discourse itself. The structure of every filmic discourse exposes a desire, and this is the desire that animates the film. By focusing on this desire, the spectator can discover the unconscious truth of the social order itself.

THE NEGATION OF NOIR

The fundamental mode of deception is the act of revealing the truth. This type of deception occurs all the time in the cinema, especially in twist films, which rely on a surprise ending to reorient spectators' perception of what they have just seen. The twist reveals the lie that has occurred throughout the film by introducing new information that makes the spectator aware of this deception. For instance, *The Village* (M. Night Shyamalan, 2004) concludes with the revelation that the film takes place in the contemporary world despite the premodern setting

33

that it presents to spectators. The awareness of this truth forces spectators to reinterpret everything that they have seen and to understand how the film has deceived them. One leaves the film with a sense of having separated the truth of the film from its deceptive appearance. But this involves an even greater deceit. The twist film appears to affirm the priority of the deception, but the final revelation of truth locates the deception within the structure of truth, thereby obscuring the priority of the fiction.[28]

Like *The Village* and other twist films, *Following* concludes with a revelation that forces spectators to reevaluate everything that they have seen. After robbing the Blonde's ex-boyfriend and discovering that the pictures of her were not at all compromising, Bill goes to her apartment to confront her. She proceeds to divulge the truth of the scheme, revealing that Bill has served as Cobb's patsy. During a break-in, she explains, Cobb discovered the body of a murdered woman and the police suspected him. By having the Blonde convince Bill to break in using the technique and using the claw hammer as his weapon, Cobb is able to divert suspicion away from himself and onto Bill. The Blonde reveals that Cobb was actually following Bill at the moment when Bill thought he was following Cobb, and that their break-ins were staged. She avows that even the romance between Bill and herself was part of the trap. Nolan shoots the Blonde's revelation in a darkened scene that takes place at her apartment—an intimate setting that suggests the revelation of a long-hidden truth, which is confirmed by her free and mocking manner. This confession, like the revelation at the end of *The Village* that the setting is the contemporary world, forces a reinterpretation of the earlier events of the film.

The story that the Blonde gives to Bill functions in the film as the revelation of the truth, but this revelation turns out to be, unbeknownst to even the Blonde herself, yet another deception. Hence, unlike in *The Village*, here we see the triumph of the lie over truth, and when Bill attempts to confess the truth to the police at the end of the film, he assures the ultimate victory of Cobb's fiction, which frames him not for the murder of an old woman but for that of the Blonde, killed later by Cobb himself.[29] Bill's response to what he believes to be truth with the revelation of truth effectively enacts a self-condemnation. His misrecognition of the Blonde's revelation for the revelation of truth leaves him completely at the mercy of Cobb's manipulation. Nolan's hero is effectively guilty—not for the murder that the police attribute to him, but for his investment in an idea of truth distinct from fiction.

34

The Blonde's confession in her half-lit apartment suggests the history of similar confessions in film noir. Like Phyllis Dietrichson (Barbara Stanwyck) confessing to Walter Neff (Fred MacMurray) that she simply used him and never loved him amid the chiaroscuro lighting that half-illuminates her house or like Kathie Moffat (Jane Greer) revealing to Jeff Bailey (Robert Mitchum) the truth of her perfidy against the background of dusk setting on a lake, the Blonde's explanation of the plot that ensnared Bill occurs in an amalgam of light and darkness.[30] Nolan's use of side lighting often leaves half of the image dark and the other half bright, sometimes even dividing characters in two. By echoing the lighting patterns used during the femme fatale's confession of truth and by replicating the dynamics of these confessions with Bill and the Blonde, Nolan aligns the Blonde's explanation with the revelation of truth. Admitting that Cobb hatched the plot, she tells Bill, "It was for a friend. The police think he did something, and he didn't. So he needs a decoy, another likely suspect, someone caught robbing a place using the same way he does it, his methods. . . . He broke into a place a couple of weeks ago. He found an old lady bashed to death. He ran off. Someone saw him. Couple of days later the police called him in for questioning. They think he killed her." By establishing Bill as his patsy, Cobb will exculpate himself in the eyes of the police. Like the noir hero, Bill finds himself in an impossible position after hearing this truth.

As the Blonde reveals Cobb's plan to Bill, he becomes angry and decides to reveal everything to the police, despite the crimes—including breaking and entering and robbery—in which this revelation would implicate him. Though he knows that a confession will have negative ramifications for himself, he is also convinced that the truth will function as the final word. He claims, "I'm going to tell them everything. They'll believe me because it's the truth." When the Blonde points out that she will simply lie when the police question her, Bill responds, "Your lies won't stand up to the truth." But Bill's conviction that the truth will be decisive is itself part of Cobb's plan. The Blonde's version of the plan, while correctly noting that Cobb was using Bill, is yet another deceit. Even though it appears in the form of a confession of truth and even though Nolan signals its truth value cinematically (through the echoes of film noir), the revelation functions as the final trap for Bill. Because Bill expects to find a hidden truth, Cobb provides one for him, and his response to this truth—offering the police his own version of the truth—ends up confirming Cobb's lie.

If Bill had not gone to the police to confess the truth, Cobb's plan—

killing the Blonde for her ex-boyfriend and pinning the murder on Bill—would not have been assured of success. Bill's confession about robbing the ex-boyfriend and about his involvement with the Blonde tied him to her and to her murder. Since the police can find no trace of Cobb's existence, all of Bill's stories about him and his plot strike them as fanciful. The plot works perfectly because Bill believes that appearances are hiding something. The avocation that he explains at the beginning of the film—following—is predicated on the idea of a hidden truth and a failure to see truth in appearances themselves, which makes him the perfect patsy for Cobb. His explanation of this hobby in voiceover itself evinces his failure and its parallel in cinematic spectatorship.

One of the most common repositories for truth in classical cinema is the voiceover. The voiceover most often provides an objective account of the filmic situation, and even when it is subjective, as in film noir, it typically functions as a confession revealing the truth of what has occurred. It articulates truth because it remains in a position of authority outside the image. As Kaja Silverman notes in her discussion of the cinematic voice, "Interiority implies discursive dependency, and exteriority discursive authority."[31] Both the external position of the voiceover relative to the image and the film's narrative facilitates its identification with truth, and this identification is taken up in *Following*.

The film begins with Bill's voiceover description of the act of following, which is, we learn, part of his confession to the police. This confession also concludes the film. The voiceover status and the confessional mode of Bill's speech have the effect of underlining its truth for the spectator. And in fact, Bill is speaking the truth, but his truth serves not to exculpate him but to confirm Cobb's deception. At the end of the film, deception triumphs over truth, and it does so because the belief in truth obscures how a fiction establishes the coordinates of the struggle between Bill and Cobb. Bill's investment in truth leaves him defenseless against the machinations of Cobb, who understands the structural priority of the lie.

Like almost every film, *Following* leaves the spectator with a true version of the events it depicts. We are not left uncertain about what has happened or unable to judge who has done what. In this sense, it ends in a traditional way. But it does show that the truth has no power as long as it is simply opposed to the lie. Cobb's lie shapes the narrative trajectory, and Bill's attempt to tell the truth does nothing but augment the lie's efficacy. The effectiveness of Cobb's lie depends on the expectation of Bill's desire to confess the truth to the police. Bill believes that, even though it implicates him in certain crimes, the truth will set him free. As Nolan shows through the opposed fates of Bill and Cobb—Cobb gets away with murder, and Bill ends up framed for a crime he didn't commit—Bill's faith in the power of truth is misplaced. Bill follows a path to his own destruction because of this belief in truth and the corresponding failure to grasp the priority of the lie. *Following* depicts Bill's error and aligns it with the parallel error of the typical cinematic spectator in order to demand a different type of spectatorship and a different type of subjectivity.

The deception of the cinema does not consist in spectators accepting the imaginary filmic world as true. It does not consist in falling for the cinematic illusion. Instead, the deception operates in the other direction, in the dismissal of the cinematic illusion and the belief that truth resides outside this illusion. Bill functions in the film as a stand-in for the deceived cinematic spectator. Cobb is able to victimize Bill in *Following* because Bill believes in the possibility of a truth existing beyond appearance rather than within it. Similarly, cinematic spectators become deceived spectators only insofar as they fail to see the truth of the cinematic illusion itself. The spectators that Nolan's first film demands are those who seek the truth of the deception, not the truth behind it. His next film moves further down the same path and calls into question another central assumption of cinematic spectatorship.

After the film festival success of *Following* (1998), Christopher Nolan managed to procure a significant budgetary increase for his next film. Armed with studio support and a $4.5 million budget, Nolan could shoot *Memento* (2000) on a standard shooting schedule rather than sporadically on weekends over a year's time. The film also marks his move from London to Los Angeles and his first step into the Hollywood system. And yet it retains the feel of an independent film, despite the increased budget and the relatively well-known cast (though this would probably not be the case if Brad Pitt had not passed on the lead role). What gives *Memento* the aura of an independent film, more than the sparse sets or the use of black-and-white photography, is Nolan's use of reverse chronology in the narrative structure. Though many contemporary films jumble time and some reverse chronology, like Quentin Tarantino's *Pulp Fiction* (1994) or Wong Kar Wai's *2046* (2004), none does so with as many scenes as *Memento*. Its narrative structure forces the spectator to take a new approach to making sense of what happens, and in doing so, it exposes the fundamental deception inherent in spectatorship itself.

The fundamental deception of spectatorship is its association with knowledge. At the cinema, spectators experience themselves as subjects of knowledge with an innate curiosity about the world who want to know more about what they are seeing. They view the cinematic images on the screen as a separate world that they increasingly come to understand throughout the course of a film. One comes to a film relatively ignorant of the events it will depict, and through the course of the screening, one gradually acquires knowledge. Films parcel out knowledge in different ways, and as David Bordwell (among other narrative theorists) has shown, we can even categorize films according to how they distribute knowledge to spectators. Art-cinema narration, for example, presents knowledge tinged with ambiguity, and for such films, this ambiguity is a sign of artistic success.[1] Hollywood films, in contrast, distribute knowledge more straightforwardly. But both forms of narration (and most others) tend to emphasize spectators' relationship

MEMENTO AND THE DESIRE
NOT TO KNOW

to knowledge as the fundamental stake in the viewing experience. Similarly, the heroes of most films move from a state of relative ignorance to a state of knowledge as spectators follow this trajectory.

Even other films that employ a nonlinear narrative often heed to the trajectory from ignorance to knowledge that structures most films. In *Pulp Fiction*, for instance, the jumbled temporality creates an intellectual puzzle for the spectator to solve. The spectator begins with uncertainty about when the events of the film occur, but the conclusion of the film allows the spectator to figure out the correct chronology and thereby arrive at knowledge. In this sense, *Pulp Fiction* resembles what Bordwell calls art-cinema narration more than classical narration, though it nonetheless continues to posit the spectator as a subject of knowledge, to envision the spectator's aim as the accumulation of knowledge about the events in the film.[2]

The move from ignorance to knowledge occurs across genres. In romances, characters begin without realizing their love for someone else, and the films conclude with the revelation of this love. In mysteries, detectives seek the solution to a crime that initially has no clear answer. Even in action films, heroes most often start the films unaware of the crisis they will confront or what sort of villainy they must defeat (or how they will defeat it). As films give more information to spectators, characters within the films gain more knowledge as well. Just as most films conceive of the spectator as a subject of knowledge, they conceive of their heroes as subjects of knowledge in the same vein. The idea of the subject as a subject of knowledge predominates equally outside the cinema, and it provides the basis for subjects' failure to notice their own involvement in what they see. The subject of knowledge begins in a state of ignorance and approaches the world as an object of inquiry that exists prior to and apart from that inquiry. This subject desires, but its desire is always a desire to know more. The model for this type of subject is the pure scientist concerned only with scientific discovery to the exclusion of all mundane concerns (money, fashion, gossip, and so on). Though we don't all consider ourselves pure scientists in this manner, we do approach the world as subjects of knowledge insofar as we tend to picture ourselves as simply wanting to know things that appear unrelated to us, even if it is a question of our interest in the lurid behavior of celebrities.

Memento shows, however, that we are not simply subjects of knowledge seeking to learn about the world in front of us but subjects of desire invested in this world through our desire. The conception of the

40

subject of knowledge constructs a barrier between itself and its world: this subject never sees how the world takes it into account through the world's very structure. Contra what the subject of knowledge necessarily believes, the world is not just there to be seen by a knowing subject but is already structured around the subject's look when the subject sees it for the first time. It is in this sense that the subject is always a subject of desire rather than simply a subject of knowledge. The subject of desire invests itself and thus shapes what it knows; it distorts the apparently external world.

For the subject of knowledge, the basic questions are those of truth and falsity. Either a representation corresponds to what it claims to be, or it doesn't.[3] As this subject sees it, one can avoid deception and uncover truth. Deception is a contingent, empirical phenomenon. For the subject of desire, on the other hand, deception is written into the structure of subjectivity and its relation to the world. The subject doesn't desire knowledge about the world but desires satisfaction, and knowledge often interferes with this satisfaction, which leads the subject of desire to avoid it. Though there is truth, there is no neutral truth, no truth that doesn't involve the distortion of subjectivity. One accesses truth through distortion or through deception, not by avoiding it altogether. According to this way of thinking, the greatest deception involves believing that one can function as a pure subject of knowledge.

Cinema is perhaps the most fertile terrain for the myth of the subject of knowledge. It allows spectators to hide themselves in the dark and sit at a distance from the screen in order to sustain the idea of ontological separation.[4] No matter what happens on the screen, it happens apart from the subjectivity of the spectator. Even films that entice spectators to identify with what happens on the screen, like most Hollywood films, nonetheless leave their spectators fundamentally separated from what they see. The unity of the spectator and the screen image is false. Spectators never experience themselves implicated or trapped in the screen. In order to make such an experience possible in the cinema, a film must interrupt the reign of the subject of knowledge by forging the awareness among spectators that they are subjects of desire.

This type of transformation—the turn from a focus on knowledge to a focus on desire—animates Nolan's second feature film. *Memento* represents the ultimate cinematic achievement in establishing a character and the spectator as apparent subjects of knowledge and then exposing the subject of desire that the subject of knowledge masks. Though the denouement of the film leaves the spectator in the dark concerning

41

several key facts that constitute its underlying story, it nonetheless gives the spectator enough information to understand everything about the relationship of the hero, Leonard Shelby (Guy Pearce), to his desire, and by doing so, it facilitates the deduction of a story that it otherwise obscures.

Leonard suffers from a disorder he calls anterograde amnesia, which means that he has been unable to form new memories since sustaining a head trauma when an intruder (or intruders) broke into their home and attacked him and his wife. *Memento* depicts Leonard in pursuit of vengeance for his wife's rape and murder. Though he killed one intruder during the assault, he is convinced that a second assailant clubbed him on the head and murdered his wife. Nolan divides the film into two parts—one that proceeds in reverse chronological order through roughly five-minute segments that end where the previous segment began, and another interspersed in the former that moves forward and primarily depicts Leonard talking on the phone in his hotel room. The part of the film that moves in reverse chronology is in color, and the part that moves forward in time is in black and white.[5] The two timelines meet at the end of the film: just after Leonard believes that he kills his wife's murderer, Jimmy Grants (Larry Holden), the film stock almost imperceptibly shifts from black and white to color.[6] This complex temporal structure allows the film to offer an unprecedented meditation on the relationship between time and knowledge.

From the perspective of the subject of knowledge, time appears as being increasingly filled up with additional knowledge. For this subject, the present is lacking, and the future seems pregnant with the possibility of filling the lack. The future embodies completion for the lacking subject. The subject begins in ignorance—it views the past as a time of even greater ignorance—and hopes to gain knowledge in the future. There is an inherent progressivity in the conception of the subject as a subject of knowledge. The innocent and ignorant baby becomes the wise old woman or man. This conception of subjectivity informs the history of modern philosophy and provides the basis for all the theorizations of time emanating from that philosophy, even those that present themselves as departing from the philosophical tradition.

At the core of Martin Heidegger's project of overcoming metaphysics is the effort to break with the conception of the subject as a subject of knowledge.[7] His rejection of the term "subject" altogether in favor of "Dasein" stems in part from the association of subjectivity with the pure act of knowing. In addition, Heidegger critiques Edmund Husserl's notion of intentionality for sustaining the subject on the plane of knowledge rather than recognizing the priority of being relative to knowing. It is mood—specifically anxiety—rather than knowledge that reveals being. As Heidegger notes, "In the clear night of the nothing of anxiety the original openness of beings as such arises: that they are beings—and not nothing."[8] If we focus solely on knowing, we will apprehend beings but not their being, the being of beings. For Heidegger, the subject of knowledge represents the basis for philosophy's flight from being.

And yet, Heidegger's conception of temporality, which is the foundation of his thought and his interpretation of being—he interprets being through temporality—remains within the confines of the conception of the subject as a subject of knowledge. The subject of knowledge views the future as the site for the accumulation of knowledge. The subject of knowledge takes its bearing from a future in which it will know what it doesn't know in the present. Similarly, Heidegger views the temporality of Dasein as oriented around its future. The incessant forward movement of time locks Dasein into a futural temporality, and any avoidance of time's focus on the future is, in Heidegger's view, inauthentic. In *Being and Time*, he states this without any ambiguity: "*The primary phenomenon of primordial and authentic temporality is the future.*"[9] This orientation toward the future marks the lingering effect of the subject of knowledge in Heidegger's thought. His attempt to conceive of Dasein immersed completely in the world rather than sustain a subject removed from and thinking about the world is not radical enough.[10] A theory of time that prioritizes the future in the way that Heidegger's does inherently takes the subject of knowledge as its point of departure.

Memento points to a different alternative because its structure is organized around first establishing and then undermining the idea of the subject of knowledge for the spectator. The film creates the image of Leonard as a subject of knowledge—a subject bent on discovering the truth whatever the costs to himself personally, a subject devoted to the truth for its own sake—and then the end of the film reveals him to be a subject of desire. As the conclusion of *Memento* makes clear, though Leonard may be consciously sure that he pursues truth, he is unconsciously working to avoid knowledge rather than acquire it. A path of sustaining desire underwrites the seemingly autonomous quest for knowledge that the film depicts.

43

The unique structure of *Memento* allows the spectator to experience a radical revaluation of Leonard's character at the end of the film. Of course, numerous films conclude with a revelation that changes the spectator's estimation of a character. The conclusion of David Fincher's *Fight Club* (1999) reveals that Tyler Durden (Brad Pitt) is not a separate character but actually the double of the unnamed hero and narrator of the film (Edward Norton). In light of this delayed knowledge, the spectator must reconstruct the film's story and reevaluate the actions of Durden and the narrator in order to make proper sense of the film. The revelation that occurs at the end of *Memento* appears less momentous than the one that concludes *Fight Club*, but it is one of the most radical in the history of cinema. We don't discover that Leonard is really someone else or actually dead, but the film does show that the satisfaction of desire, not desire for knowledge, has animated his investigation. Where we saw Leonard pursuing a quest for knowledge, the conclusion makes clear that he was following the path of desire, a path that evinces an active disregard for knowledge.

Throughout most of the film, Leonard appears, despite his inability to make new memories, as a subject of knowledge. In fact, Leonard's condition renders him the ideal subject of knowledge. Unlike subjects who can remember, he must, like Descartes, assume that "some malicious demon of the utmost power and cunning has employed all his energies in order to deceive [him]."[11] That is, the film shows Leonard practicing a version of the Cartesian skeptical method in order to arrive at certainty concerning the facts surrounding his wife's death. Like Descartes, he can't trust the opinions offered by others or even the apparent certainties of his own experience.

In order to conduct an investigation without the ability to remember, Leonard must doubt everyone he meets. For most people, this process of doubt could at least end with themselves. They could rely of their own recollections and have certainty about these. But when he eats lunch with Teddy (Joe Pantoliano), his primary interlocutor in the film (and the man Leonard kills for his wife's murder in the opening shot of the film), Leonard correctly points out the flaws with an investigation that relies on memory. He says,

> Memory is not perfect. It's not even that good. Ask the police. Eyewitness testimony is unreliable. The cops don't catch a killer by sitting

around and remembering stuff. They collect facts. They make notes, and they draw conclusions. Facts, not memories, that's how you investigate. I know, it's what I used to do. Look, memory can change the shape of a room; it can change the color of a car. And memories can be distorted. They're just an interpretation; they're not a record. And they're irrelevant if you have the facts.

Leonard's commitment to the verifiable facts is in one sense a product of necessity: he lacks the ability to rely on memory as an alternative. But in another sense, it indicates his exemplary status as a subject of knowledge. For Leonard, true knowledge is possible through a skeptical method that employs doubt in order to arrive at certainty. The unreliability of memory rules it out as a tool in the project of knowledge. The true knowledge seeker must eliminate the crutch of memory, just as Leonard must.

But even at this relatively early point in the film, Christopher Nolan's editing of Leonard's description of his skeptical method to Teddy hints at the truth that this method hides. Nolan shoots the first half of the speech not as one might expect with an over-the-shoulder shot of Leonard juxtaposed with reverse shots of Teddy listening but with a straight-on medium-long shot of the two sitting side by side at the counter of a diner. This type of shot bespeaks an objective presentation of the characters: though Leonard is speaking, we don't see the scene from the clearly subjective perspective of either character (or another character). The straight-on shot corresponds to Leonard's method, which relies on apparently objective evidence rather than subjective memories. But at the precise moment when Leonard proclaims "Facts, not memories," the film cuts to a close-up of him speaking. This cut suggests the subjective nature of the seemingly objective facts—the presence of the subject of desire lurking behind the subject of knowledge. The timing and contrast of the close-up allow it to signify a turn away from the objective world and objective facts, in contrast to what Leonard is saying.[12] The film's conclusion will subsequently confirm this suggestion. Before that, however, *Memento* shows where the pursuit of knowledge leads Leonard.

As the film proceeds, it shows various ways in which the quest for knowledge might be derailed. Despite his skeptical method, Leonard's inability to remember allows the people with whom he interacts to deceive him and thereby misdirect his investigation, even though he takes Polaroid pictures of those with whom he interacts. The deception becomes most conspicuous in the case of Natalie (Carrie-Anne Moss), who

45

manipulates Leonard in order to advance her own interests. When she first shows up in the film waiting for Leonard in a diner, Natalie seems to be his ally in the search to find his wife's killer. Not only does she provide Leonard with information about the identity of John G., the purported name of his wife's killer, but the two of them also share a sense of intimacy, which is evident when Natalie asks Leonard to remember and describe his wife for her. As she leaves Leonard, she says to him affectionately, "You know what we have in common? We are both survivors. You take care, Leonard." This declaration hints at the existence of an established bond between them that the spectator has not yet witnessed. Furthermore, on the back of his Polaroid of Natalie, Leonard has written, "She has also lost someone. She will help you out of pity." This statement seems to provide the final confirmation that Natalie is someone that both Leonard and the spectator can trust.

Later, however, the developments in the film completely change the spectator's relationship to Natalie. It becomes clear that she knows Leonard has probably murdered her boyfriend, Jimmy, and that she views him as nothing but a tool that she can use. Because Jimmy's associates assume that she and Jimmy have stolen the money that they were going to use for a supposed drug deal with Teddy, Natalie finds herself in jeopardy, and she looks to Leonard, who is staying at her home, to resolve her difficulties. When she sees him as she returns home, none of the earlier (or later in diegetic time) tenderness that she displays toward him manifests itself.

She asks Leonard to kill Jimmy's associate Dodd for her, and when he refuses, she launches into a verbal assault against him and his wife. The venom expressed in the exchange makes clear that she has no attachment to Leonard and that she cannot be trusted:

Natalie: You pathetic piece of shit. I can say whatever the fuck I want, and you won't have a fucking clue, you fucking retard.
Leonard: Shut your mouth.
Natalie: You know what, I'm going to use you. I'm telling you now because I'm going to enjoy it so much more because I know that you could stop me if you weren't such a fucking freak. Did you lose your pen? That's too bad, freak. Otherwise you could write yourself a little note about how much Natalie hates your retarded guts and I called your wife a "fucking whore."
Leonard: Don't say another fucking word.
Natalie: About your whore of a wife. I've read about your condition,

Leonard. You know what one of the causes of short-term memory loss is? Venereal disease. Maybe your cunt of a fucking wife sucked one too many diseased cocks and turned you into a fucking retard. You sad, sad freak. I can say whatever the fuck I want, and you won't remember. We'll still be best friends, or maybe even lovers.[13]

When Natalie describes Leonard's "whore of a wife," he grabs her mouth, and then when she suggests they might become lovers at the end of the exchange, he completely loses his temper and punches her in the face. Natalie subsequently uses her injuries to prompt Leonard into going after Dodd for her. After Leonard punches her, Natalie goes to her car, waits a few minutes, and then returns to the house, proclaiming that Dodd has beaten her up. This impels Leonard to promise to take care of Dodd for her. In this way, the film exposes the character that appears the most trustworthy—Natalie—as one that merits no trust at all. This marks a clear failure in Leonard's method of skeptical doubt and reliance on facts. His doubt does not prevent him from trusting someone who enjoys reviling him in the most violent manner.[14]

The problem with Leonard's method parallels that of the hero in film noir. The noir hero can easily be duped because this figure suspects everything, even—or especially—that which is not suspicious. As a result, everyone and everything has a secret meaning that the noir hero can decipher, and thus everyone and everything becomes seductive—which is why the Swede (Burt Lancaster) falls into the trap laid by Kitty Collins (Ava Gardner) in Robert Siodmak's *The Killers* (1946) or why Christopher Cross (Edward G. Robinson) ends up destitute as a result of his pursuit of Kitty March (Joan Bennett) in Fritz Lang's *Scarlet Street* (1945). From the perspective of the noir hero, the femme fatale always seems to be hiding a secret, and the idea of this secret seduces the hero. Like the noir hero, Leonard, as Hugh Manon puts it, "fails to fail to suspect at each point of encounter."[15] The procedure of skeptical doubt suspects everything but its own suspicion, and this results in gaps in the knowledge it produces.

But the aim of *Memento* is not just to show the potential obstacles in the path of the subject of knowledge. It is rather to show that the subject of knowledge doesn't exist. The film ends when the narrative moving backward in time and the one moving forward converge with Leonard's murder of Natalie's boyfriend, the drug dealer Jimmy Grants. The transition point at which the two narratives meet occurs just after Leonard kills Jimmy and takes a picture of his dead body. As the Polaroid photograph is gradually developing in close-up, the film changes almost imperceptibly from black and white to color, which provides the indication of a transition to the narrative line moving backward chronologically. Unlike the other transitions between the two distinct narrative lines, this one occurs not through a cut, a fade, or another clear marker of a break, but through a change in film stock that doesn't interrupt the flow of images at all. It is easy to watch the film and not even realize that the film stock has undergone a transition. By blending the two narratives together at the end, Nolan creates a sense of continuity where the spectator had hitherto experienced discontinuity and thus breaks down the opposition between the two narrative lines.

Until this final sequence, the two narrative lines serve two distinct purposes in the film. The narrative that moves backward in time depicts the actions that Leonard goes through in the search for his wife's killer. Even though it moves in a reverse chronology, it is the narrative line most identifiable as a narrative since it shows events happening. The line that moves forward in time, on the other hand, exists to provide the spectator with information about Leonard and his condition. It consists almost solely of Leonard talking on the telephone and describing his work as an insurance investigator probing the case of Sammy Jankis (Stephen Tobolowsky), who, according to Leonard's account, also suffered from the same ailment, anterograde amnesia. Leonard's verbal descriptions of Sammy's condition and his own—and the corresponding visual images that the film includes—offers the spectator background knowledge with which to better understand Leonard's actions in the other narrative line. The role of the forward-moving narrative in the structure of the film appears distinct from that of the backward-moving narrative: it provides knowledge rather than depicting actions.

By associating the forward-moving narrative with knowledge, Nolan exposes the theoretical link between temporality and knowledge. The subject of knowledge is a temporal subject looking toward a future in which it will eliminate ignorance with more knowledge. For this subject, the future has a privileged position because it is identified with knowledge itself. The more time passes in the forward-moving narrative line, the more knowledge conquers ignorance. But this conquest does not survive the end of the film.

The conclusion of *Memento* breaks down the barrier between the two narratives and in this way subverts the privileged status of knowledge. By initially separating the part of the film that imparts knowledge from the part of the film that depicts actions, Christopher Nolan establishes knowledge as a pure and unassailable domain. Both Leonard's search for knowledge and the spectator's appear to be just that: an effort to know for the sake of knowledge itself, divorced from any relation to desire. When the two narrative lines come together at the end of the film with an imperceptible transition rather than a distinguishing cut, the purity of the subject of knowledge begins to come into question. The conclusion of the film thoroughly eviscerates this subject and replaces it with the subject of desire.

This becomes especially apparent through the actions that Leonard performs after he kills Jimmy. Teddy arrives at the abandoned building just after the killing, and Leonard confronts Teddy about the event and with his fear that he has killed the wrong guy. Teddy then offers Leonard a long explanation that undermines both Leonard's self-understanding and the spectator's view of him and his quest. Teddy suggests that his wife survived the assault and that she, not Sammy's wife, was diabetic. He hints that she allowed Leonard to kill her with insulin in the way that Leonard tells himself that Sammy's wife did.

After debunking Leonard's story about Sammy and about the murder of his wife, Teddy explains that Leonard's quest for the second attacker ended a year earlier. He says,

> Look, Lenny, I was the cop assigned to your wife's case. I believed you. I thought you deserved a chance for revenge. I'm the guy who helped you find the other guy in your bathroom that night, the guy that cracked your skull and fucked your wife. We found him. You killed him. But you didn't remember, so I helped you start looking again, looking for the guy you already killed. . . . I gave you a reason to live, and you were more than happy to help. You don't want the truth. . . . Cheer up, there's plenty of John G.s for us to find. All you do is moan. I'm the one who has to live with what you've done. I'm the one that put it all together. You, you wander around, you play detective. You live in a dream, kid. A dead wife to pine for, a sense of purpose to your life, a romantic quest that you wouldn't end, even if I wasn't in the picture.

Teddy's story offers a reasonable resolution of the events in the film. It permits the spectator to fit the details of the filmic discourse together into a coherent story. And yet, the knowledge that one gains is not conclusive.[16]

The end of *Memento* doesn't provide the answers through Teddy's rev-

49

elations—it isn't clear to what extent his explanation is credible—but through the depiction of Leonard's actions after he hears this explanation. He takes Teddy's keys and throws them into some tall weeds in order to occupy Teddy and give himself time to act. He gets into his truck and proceeds to create a deception for himself about Teddy. Leonard's voiceover says, "I'm not a killer. I'm just someone who wanted to make things right. Can I just let myself forget what you've told me? Can I just let myself forget what you've made me do? You think I just want another puzzle to solve, another John G. to look for? You're a John G. So you can be my John G. Do I lie to myself to be happy? In your case, Teddy, yes I will." As we hear Leonard's voice, we see him write, "Don't believe his lies," on the back of Teddy's photograph, burn up the pictures of the dead Jimmy Grants and of himself smiling after an earlier killing, and write, "Tattoo: Fact 6 / Car License / SG13 71U," on an index card. These actions trigger the events that lead to the killing of Teddy that opens the film, and Leonard does them in order not to know the truth and to give himself a false problem to solve.

Even though neither Leonard nor the spectator can be sure about Teddy's reliability, we do know that Leonard has no reason to suppose that Teddy is the second assailant or that he is necessarily a liar. When he implicates Teddy, he shows no suspicion of Teddy and admits that he is lying to himself. Leonard chooses to lie to himself rather than seek the truth, and this lie is the foundation for all the apparent truth seeking that occurs earlier (later chronologically) in the film. Through Leonard's actions in his truck and the attitude evinced in his voiceover, we can identify him as a subject of desire rather than a subject of knowledge. He acts not in order to gain knowledge but in order to follow the path of his desire, and he even avoids knowledge in order to remain on this path.

Memento establishes Leonard initially as a seeming subject of knowledge and concludes by revealing him to be a subject of desire in order to both illustrate and subvert the hold that the conception of the subject of knowledge has. We believe that subjects are knowledge-seeking beings because we don't see the originary lie that the illusion of the quest for knowledge obscures. We don't see, in other words, why someone seeks knowledge but only the act of doing so, and we don't see how this quest is organized around a desire not to know. We assume an inherent curiosity attached to subjectivity—especially visible in children—because the desire underlying this curiosity is unconscious both for the subject itself and for observers.

50

Rather than an innate curiosity, subjects have what Jacques Lacan calls a passion for ignorance. Whatever knowledge they gain must be obtained within the context of this passion. Some knowledge becomes possible only insofar as it sustains a more fundamental ignorance in another form. The existence of the unconscious is the expression of the desire not to know. As Lacan points out, "The unconscious is the fact that being, by speaking, enjoys, and . . . wants to know nothing more about it."[17] We can't be subjects of knowledge because our enjoyment depends on remaining hidden and violating some real or imagined restriction. If we reconciled our enjoyment with our knowledge, we would eliminate the possibility of enjoying, which is impossible. The best that we can do is to understand this gap, to understand ourselves as subjects of desire in the way that *Memento* attempts to show.

Most films try to sustain the spectator's sense of being a subject of knowledge in order to avoid calling the predominant modes of enjoyment into question. For the spectator of the typical film, even the existence of the subject of desire remains unconscious. But *Memento* reveals that there is another way of understanding subjectivity, even if no one can directly know unconscious desire. Leonard appears to be a subject of knowledge insofar as he acts for the same reasons that the spectators watching him imagine themselves to act. The lie that ends the film and leads to Teddy's murder reveals how misleading this understanding of Leonard and this self-understanding of the spectator turn out to be.

Just as the film begins by establishing Leonard as the subject of knowledge and concludes by undermining this ideal, it also performs the same gesture toward the spectator. One watches *Memento* the way one watches any detective film: the beginning creates a mystery that the end will solve, and the film implicitly attaches the ideal of complete satisfaction to the solution.[18] But the reverse chronology of *Memento* pushes this narrative logic to its end point. While the typical detective film works backward to the original crime through the detective's investigation, *Memento* moves backward to this origin through its very discursive structure. It thereby offers the allure of the spectator actually seeing the crime that other detective films can only present through the detective's reconstruction.[19] This is why Mary Ann Doane criticizes the film for its ultimate affirmation of linear temporality. She says,

Although the film begins with a striking sequence of reversed motion, in which blood returns to a body, a bullet flies back to a gun, the gun is reinserted in a belt, etc., this reversal is not sustained throughout

51

the film and, indeed, acts as a trope for the backward movement of the film's narrative as a whole, which unfolds, in the tradition of the detective story, to reveal the critical event allowing an understanding of the character's destiny. For the most part, the fragmentation and reordering of time in this film is supported by a basic irreversibility of movement.[20]

The reverse chronology bears within it the promise of the direct experience of the crime itself, the traumatic origin of every detective film, transforming *Memento* into the ultimate film of this genre. The film's spectator follows the narrative structure into the past but with the hope consistent with an orientation toward the future. The origin seems to function here as the ultimate future.

The end of the film disappoints the expectation that the film's narrative structure creates. The spectator does finally see the origin of the chain of events that leads Leonard to kill Teddy in the film's opening shot, but this origin is not the traumatic event itself, which is what Doane's reading fails to register. It is Leonard's decision to have a tattoo made that would mislead himself and result in his future certainty that Teddy was the murderer of his wife. Rather than witnessing the truth of the origin, the spectator witnesses the original lie. As Anna Kornbluh points out, the film works by "mobilizing in the spectator the desire to decide whodunit and, simultaneously, rendering this desire not only impossible to fulfill, but *false*, and as such, *irrelevant*. It is as if the spectator is forced to experience from within the disintegration of an ideological universe: the film's texture undermines its own explicit project."[21] One watches *Memento* with the desire to know the original crime, but the end of the film shows that this original crime, if it exists at all, has nothing to do with the events depicted. Here again, we see Nolan's affinity with film noir. The common critique of film noir concerns its failures on the level of plot: often, as in Howard Hawks's *The Big Sleep* (1946), it is not even possible to deduce who has committed an important crime. The point in film noir, as in *Memento*, is not the solution but the desire that animates the search for it. But Nolan's film takes this further than classical noir by completely marginalizing the crime. Leonard's lie to himself, not the initial murder, is the sole and unique origin of the events we see before the final segment of the narrative.

This is not to say that the film completely abandons the idea of truth altogether. Melissa Clarke contends that "there is certainly no universal truth awaiting either Leonard or the audience at the end of

Memento. There is no way to verify either the real vs. the imaginary or any of the many questions as to the true vs. the false."[22] As long as one remains within the domain of knowledge, Clarke is correct. But the film does allow the spectator to access another kind of truth. The truth that the film exposes is not the truth of knowledge but the truth of desire, which a lie inaugurates. One cannot simply dismiss the lie for its untruthfulness. It is the creative moment in the film, the source of the narrative itself. Figuring out the film implies figuring out not the truth that it hides but its foundational lie. In this way, *Memento* repositions the spectator of the detective film, moving this figure from the role of knowledge seeker to that of desire seeker. Unlike the knowledge seeker, the desire seeker looks to present actions for truth rather than to future revelations. The truth for the desire seeker is always already manifesting itself in the ways that the subject comports itself.

TIME AND FANTASY

Uncovering the truth of desire is the explicit project of Sigmund Freud, and the truth of desire involves a specific relation to time. Many of the most famous dreams that Freud recounts involve the fantasy of reversing time and thereby changing the past. The dream on which Freud founded the interpretation of dreams, the dream of Irma's injection, is one example. According to Freud's interpretation of his own dream, it allows him to transform an unsuccessful analysis from the past. Through its depiction of Irma's case, the dream exculpates Freud in multiple ways for the treatment's failure.[23] As he describes the dream and its alterations of reality, "Irma's pains could be satisfactorily explained by her widowhood . . . which *I* had no means of altering. Irma's pains had been caused by Otto giving her an incautious injection of an unsuitable drug—a thing *I* should never have done. Irma's pains were the result of an injection with a dirty needle, like my old lady's phlebitis—whereas *I* never did any harm with my injections."[24] By constructing a dream that returns to a past failure, Freud fantasizes the failure working out differently, in a way that erases his responsibility for it. Though fantasy sometimes envisions an expected future, more often it delves into the past. And even the futures it imagines are not purely futural but recycled and transformed remnants from the past.

Fantasy violates the temporality of the clock. Through its constant reshaping of the past, fantasy defies the forward movement of time and

53

rejects the seemingly ontological fact that the past is over and done. Fantasy allows the subject to turn back the clock and experience the past again in an alternate form. It would thus seem as if the narrative line in *Memento* that moves backward in time would correspond to the experience of fantasy. Though all films necessarily employ fantasy in their address to spectators, the structure of *Memento* seems to go further in this direction than the typical film, which presents fantasy in the form of a realized future rather than a revisited past. According to this interpretation, the backward movement of the film would represent the movement of fantasy par excellence. The film would offer the spectator the fantasy of overcoming time and returning to a lost origin.

But this is not what *Memento* provides for the spectator. Rather than showing fantasy as the vehicle through which one might conquer time, the film reveals that chronological time itself is the product of fantasy. This becomes most apparent through the link that the film makes between the forward-moving narrative line and the clear interpellations of Leonard's fantasies into the plot. Nolan primarily shoots Leonard's fantasies and memories with black-and-white film stock, just like the forward-moving narrative line, which suggests a similar ontological status for each. But the film stock is not the only clue linking the forward-moving narrative line to the fantasmatic interpellations.

The primary function of the forward-moving narrative line is to provide the details of the Sammy Jankis story. It is the one story, other than the account of his wife's rape and murder, that Leonard tells, and it functions to orient both Leonard and the spectator relative to his condition. The message "Remember Sammy Jankis" between the thumb and forefinger of Leonard's left hand is his most visible tattoo. Each time that he loses track of what has happened to him, this tattoo serves as a reminder. And yet, one could imagine other possible reminders that would serve equally well or even better. Though the story of Sammy Jankis helps Leonard to grasp more fully his condition, it does not help him pursue his investigation or navigate the world in which he finds himself. Sammy did not develop a system for coping with the ailment that they share; at best, he serves as a negative example. But even as such, he isn't particularly instructive or useful for Leonard. In this light, it is not exactly clear why the reference to Sammy Jankis has such a prominent place in Leonard's psyche and in the film.

The doubt that Teddy casts on the Sammy Jankis story at the end of the film—with his revelation that Sammy was a faker and his insinuation that Leonard's wife, not Sammy's, was the diabetic who allowed herself to be killed by her husband—calls the role of the story in *Memento* further into question. If Teddy is telling the truth about Sammy, then Leonard is using the story as a fantasy screen to obscure the trauma of his own involvement in the death of his wife. Unable to represent his guilt directly, he does so via the mediation of a fantasy in which Sammy Jankis kills his wife in precisely the same way. But even if Teddy is lying and the Sammy Jankis story is true, it nonetheless functions as a fantasy for Leonard and for the spectator because of the structural position that it occupies: it fills in the gaps in the filmic discourse and allows the narrative to cohere.[25]

By associating the forward-moving narrative line with fantasy and with shielding the subject from a traumatic recognition, Nolan lays bare the fantasmatic nature of chronological time itself. The idea that time moves forward chronologically represents the ultimate expression of fantasy that serves to protect the subject from the structure of its desire, which resists the movement of time. Even though the forward movement of time brings the horror of eventual death, it more fundamentally offers the possibility of compensation for an originary and unredeemable loss that initiates the subject's desire. The subject experiences loss for the first time not when it confronts the idea of its own death, but when it emerges as a subject.[26] Subjectivity is the product of a traumatic loss of the privileged object that no amount of time can alleviate. The subject can only access its own death through what Heidegger calls anticipatory resoluteness, which means that some distance remains between this loss and the subject itself. But the loss of the privileged object constitutes the being of the subject as such. No subject can escape or attenuate this loss, though the turn to chronological time marks the primary attempt to do so.

At first glance, Leonard appears to have a different relationship to chronology than most other subjects. His condition, anterograde amnesia, prevents him from making new memories and leaves him stuck in a perpetual present. Though this is an actual disorder that affects victims of head trauma, its significance for the film bears no relation to its real-world referent. Instead, anterograde amnesia offers Nolan the opportunity to depict an experience of temporality that the healthy subject lives without fully grasping. Leonard's condition is thus not an isolated anomaly but a window into a truer understanding of temporality. The depiction of his (relative) inability to form new memories reveals that time itself is not a primordial structure into which the subject is thrown, as Heidegger would have it, but a defense against the experience of trauma.

55

Unlike those of us who can produce new memories, Leonard's inability to do so leaves him constantly confronting the structure of desire. As Leonard burns his wife's things in an attempt to forget the trauma of her death, he says to himself, "I can't remember to forget you." He remains caught in the wake of a traumatic loss that he can't overcome and to which he perpetually returns. Anterograde amnesia forces Leonard to endure the lost object as such, but Leonard wants to escape from the constant encounter with the lost object in the way that other subjects do. Leonard seeks the typical refuge of time itself, but his condition renders him incapable of actually accessing a forward-moving temporality.

The film also makes it impossible for the spectator to escape the loop of desire. On the one hand, the film promises a satisfying look at the traumatic origin in the manner of the detective film. But on the other, it subjects the spectator to a series of discrete episodes, each of which promises a solution that it subsequently defers.[27] Each segment of the film's backward-moving narrative line promises to explain the former segment, but the explanation proffered never provides a complete answer. A new lacuna is introduced, requiring a further narrative segment to provide the missing explanation until the film reaches an end point with Leonard's lie to himself about Teddy's involvement in his wife's murder. At no point in the film does narrative movement constitute progress toward truth.

The apparent movement forward toward the truth of the traumatic origin (which is a movement backward in chronological time) never actually advances in the direction of truth but instead circulates around a fundamental lie. Desiring subjectivity makes its way through failure rather than success, and its temporality involves the repetition of that failure. The apparent successes of progress serve a repeated failure. Though this path offers no hope for the subject, it does provide access to a satisfaction that the eternal hopefulness of knowledge can never realize.

A TWO-TIMED MARRIAGE

Memento establishes a contrast between the temporality of knowledge that Leonard exemplifies and the structure of desire to which it alludes more obliquely. It associates the latter structure with Leonard's unnamed wife (Jorja Fox), who appears only in sequences demarcated as Leonard's memories or fantasies. Ironically, the film reveals this alternate structure at the moment when Leonard is most dramatically ensconced in temporality—as he attempts to move forward by burning the mementos that remain from his wife (a stuffed animal, her favorite book, and other personal items). He destroys these because he believes in the possibility of a future that will be different, a future that will provide a solution to the experience of the lost object.

Leonard's entire existence is organized around the idea of moving on, of being able to escape the hold of a traumatic past. After bringing a prostitute to his hotel room to act out the scene of his wife's attack (as he has done numerous times before), Leonard drives to a deserted industrial area where he finds old pieces of wood that he uses to build a fire to burn his wife's things. This scene could easily have taken place in the country, where Leonard could have built a fire with even less risk of being disturbed. But Nolan sets it in a dilapidated industrial part of a city to provide a larger point of comparison for Leonard's mode of temporality. Leonard's attempt to escape his own traumatic past has its objective correlative in the concrete slabs and rotted boards that populate the scene.

Like Leonard, capitalist society believes in the possibility of the future. The waste it leaves behind in this quest, like the dead bodies that Leonard accumulates in his attempt to move on, is the inescapable product of the quest itself. Despite the vehemence of the effort, the traumatic past remains ever present. The future never provides the missing satisfaction—neither for capitalist society nor for Leonard. Dissatisfaction with the new commodity will leave the consumer with an insatiable lust for the next commodity, and an inability to remember the vengeance of his wife will leave Leonard continually pursuing it. No possible image of future success could erase the constitutive trauma and arrest the repetition.

But it is possible to reject the lure of temporality. After Leonard arrives at the industrial area to burn his wife's things, we see a brief flashback sequence that offers the most extended insight into the relationship between Leonard and his wife. In this sequence, a fundamental difference in their approach to time emerges. Leonard, as the rest of the film also shows, proves himself a subject devoted to the future and to whatever new object the future might bring. His wife, in contrast, is able to enjoy repetition for its own sake, without the hope of attaining something new, and she does so by immersing herself within a fiction. A book that Leonard burns triggers a memory in which they argue about the book. In their conversation, the difference between them becomes apparent:

> Leonard: How can you read that?
> Leonard's wife: It's good.
> Leonard: Yeah, but you read it like a thousand times.
> Leonard's wife: I enjoy it.
> Leonard: I always thought the pleasure of a book was in wanting to know what happens next.
> Leonard's wife: Don't be a prick. I'm not reading it to annoy you. I enjoy it. Just let me read, please.

Leonard's insistence on the pleasure of an unexpected future contrasts here with his wife's enjoyment through repetition of a story that she knows will not surprise her. Each character articulates a mode of subjectivity that has an ethical core to it. For Leonard's wife, the enjoyment of repetition is an end in itself that requires no other justification. In this sense, it provides a meaning for existence. Leonard, for his part, attaches a teleology to actions. One acts in order to bring about a pleasurable end that transcends the action, and without this pleasurable end, the action itself is meaningless. According to Leonard's way of thinking, meaning must lie in a transcendent realm.

The fact that Leonard and his wife use contrasting terms to describe the activity of reading serves to underline the point. While Leonard describes the *pleasure* he associates with reading, his wife sees the act of reading this particular book as something to *enjoy*. Pleasure, as Leonard theorizes, comes at the conclusion of an activity as the payoff for performing it. Enjoyment, in contrast, derives from the activity itself. One enjoys without the prospect of a future pleasure that will outstrip the present experience. The repetition occurs without hope for a truth outside the fiction.

Just before the conversation, we see Leonard sitting in front of the fire and holding the book. As he opens it and smells the pages, there is a very brief flashback to his wife reading the book in her bed. In this shot (which lasts less than a second), the book appears in close-up as she is reading it. What stands out here is the prominence of the object. Even though Leonard is thinking about his wife, the image places her at the margins of the paperback book, which it foregrounds. This arrangement suggests the importance of the book not for Leonard—he subsequently burns it—but for his wife.[28] Unlike Leonard, for whom objects are tools that he uses to achieve a hitherto missing satisfaction, his wife treats the object as an end itself. She enjoys it for its own sake rather than for its utility.[29] She stands out as a subject of desire in contrast to Leonard as a subject of knowledge.

In the shots of the conversation between Leonard and his wife, we see enjoyment registered on Leonard's wife's face as she reads. The film cuts between close-ups of her intently reading while responding to Leonard and medium shots of Leonard dressing while questioning her. The contrast between how the two characters are filmed in this scene suggests the difference in their modes of subjectivity. Leonard is preparing to go to work, readying himself for a future activity (which he will perform for the sake of the future), while his wife repeats an activity that has played out many times in the past and that implies no prospect of a different future. The film affirms the mode of subjectivity exhibited by Leonard's wife through its negative depiction of his project for revenge. Leonard's quest for vengeance bespeaks a failure to grasp the structure of desire, and his quest fails in the same way that knowledge always does.

A TIME FOR REVENGE

An affirmation of the subject of desire eliminates the logical apparatus that supports an economy of vengeance. Revenge as a motivation for aggressive action and violence depends on the idea of a future truth that will redeem the past. An aggrieved party pursues vengeance because the action promises some degree of restitution for the loss suffered. By forcing the offender to suffer in kind, one compensates for the loss through the joy that derives from watching the offender suffer. In *Memento*, Leonard feels as if the murderer of his wife has taken everything of value from him, and he demands some form of repayment. Even if the compensation remains inadequate in the face of the loss, it nonetheless represents a partial restoration. In this way, revenge allows the vengeance seeker to invest in the future and to believe that it holds the promise of the lost—and therefore privileged—object. The very idea of revenge depends on a linear conception of temporality oriented toward the future, a conception that belongs to the subject of knowledge.

The degree to which spectators share this temporality marks the degree to which revenge seems justified, at least to some extent. The idea of a raped and murdered wife is a classic Hollywood revenge motive, and

Memento initially encourages the spectator to accept Leonard's project for vengeance as understandable and even ethical. No one in the film questions his right to pursue his wife's killer—in fact, other characters are ready to aid him in this pursuit, though they manipulate him for their own ends as they do so—and the film's content does not register any ethical qualms about the practice of vengeance. The end of the film does reveal that on at least two occasions Leonard has avenged himself on the wrong person. This calls the project into question empirically but not ontologically. It may simply be an ethically supportable project poorly executed. It is the form of *Memento*, however, and its thematization of time, that gives the lie to revenge as such.

If the logic of revenge depends on a future uncovering of truth that can offer recompense for the past, the film shows that such a future does not exist. Rather than moving in a linear direction, the narrative of *Memento* encircles a trauma that cannot even be properly named, let alone transcended. This encircling is the movement of the subject of desire, in contrast to the forward movement of the subject of knowledge. If the trauma has a constitutive status for the subject, no subsequent act of vengeance can deliver the subject from the trauma, which means that the forward movement of the subject of knowledge is impossible. No truth can repair the loss that constitutes subjectivity. Revenge is an attempt to escape that from which there is no escape, and the ultimate result of revenge is always a violent return to the inescapable trauma. But as *Memento* shows, the logic of revenge is not a natural phenomenon with which one must struggle but fully a product of the temporality associated with the project of knowledge.

For most, revenge appears as part of the order of things, and only society or law allows for its transcendence. According to René Girard, for instance, reciprocal violence is the fundamental social fact that every society must address in order to create stability. There is no facile end to violence because the only solution to violence is more violence, which creates an unending cycle of revenge. As Girard notes, "Only violence can put an end to violence, and that is why violence is self-propagating. Everyone wants to strike the last blow, and reprisal can thus follow reprisal without any true conclusion ever being reached."[30] According to this way of thinking, there is an inevitable tendency toward violence, and no one is willing to let violence go unanswered, which leads to unending vengeance. Here, punishment is not justice so much as authorized vengeance or yet another step in the cycle of reciprocal violence. Though he never says as much directly, Girard assumes (and most would follow him in this assumption) that a proclivity toward violence exists in the subject and that this proclivity overrides all others.[31]

Contra Girard, *Memento* insists that the cycle of reciprocal violence stems not from the violent nature of humanity but from a large-scale investment in the temporality of knowledge that envisions the future as the site for the accumulation of knowledge, as the site for the possibility of redress or compensation. The problem isn't vengeance itself or the tendency toward violence but the mode of subjectivity that underwrites the belief in vengeance as a satisfying answer. Without the investment in the future as a reservoir of ultimate truth, vengeance would lose its animating force. Of course, violence would still meet with violent reprisals, but the idea of achieving a future compensation for a violent injury would disappear—and with it, the logical justification for revenge. Outside the temporality of knowledge and its investment in the future, justice becomes a way of affirming the singularity of the subject rather than reducing it to a balance sheet of gain and loss.

Leonard becomes a murderer not because the lost object traps him, but because he attempts to transcend loss and achieve a goal. This goal is revenge. As Garry Gillard notes, "The notion of 'revenge' provides one of the keys to approaching the film in generic terms."[32] It is a revenge film that undermines the logic of the revenge film, just as it is a detective film that undermines the logic of the detective film. Leonard believes that killing the murderer of his wife will restore part of what has been lost, even if he will be unable to remember the act of vengeance. But Leonard's inability to remember renders his act of vengeance meaningless, as Natalie points out to him. If the avenger can't remember the act of vengeance, the promised compensation for the loss is itself lost. As Leonard's conversation with Teddy at the end of the film makes clear, he assumes that the monumental nature of the act will make some impression on him, even if he forgets it. But Leonard's inability to know with certainty whether Teddy is telling the truth when he says that Leonard has already had his revenge shows this assumption to be completely erroneous. Leonard's lack of memory concerning the act of vengeance reveals the complete futility of the act. His dead wife can't know about it, he can't remember it, and no one else in the film cares. Even the spectator finds no satisfaction in the act of vengeance because it occurs—if in fact there was a second assailant and Leonard actually found the right person—a year before the events in the film take place. *Memento* permits no one to find satisfaction in the act of vengeance.

The spectator's lack of satisfaction in Leonard's revenge separates *Me-*

mento from almost all other revenge films. Most films of this type build up to the act of vengeance and foreground the spectator's enjoyment of it. The examples are almost too numerous to mention, but they include *Dirty Harry* (Don Siegel, 1971), *Coffy* (Jack Hill, 1973), *Rocky III* (Sylvester Stallone, 1983), *Lethal Weapon 2* (Richard Donner, 1989), *Tomorrow Never Dies* (Roger Spottiswoode, 1997), *Kill Bill: Vol. 2* (Quentin Tarantino, 2004), and *Taken* (Pierre Morel, 2008).[33] In each of these films and many similar ones, the spectator's satisfaction reaches its peak with the hero's act of vengeance, which promises compensation for a previous loss. This type of film has such popularity not so much because revenge has such a wide appeal but because the revenge depicted affirms a mode of temporality that spectators are desperate to embrace. *Memento* denies the satisfaction of revenge by never allowing the spectator to know with any certainty who the correct target is or if there even is a correct target. As the film develops it, this uncertainty cannot be resolved with more facts. The facts that would provide the basis for revenge are missing because the film displays an active indifference toward them.

The purported acts of vengeance that the film does depict—the killing of Teddy at the beginning of the film and of Jimmy Grants at the end—are erroneous. The film's conclusion makes clear that neither Teddy nor Jimmy Grants had anything to do with the murder of Leonard's wife, and though neither is an attractive character, their deaths seem senseless rather than justified. The killings that the film shows, far from being acts of revenge, tend more in the direction of murder. In fact, William Little sees Leonard as a version of the serial killer. He says, "Leonard bears many marks of a serial killer, one of which, of course, is that he repeatedly kills relative strangers. More specifically, he targets these others solely on the basis that they conform to a type; each one is identified as 'John G.,' the apparent name of his wife's murderer."[34] Even if one doesn't go as far as Little, one still cannot experience Leonard's quest in the film as just. His desire for vengeance, as Teddy points out to him, provides a reason for him to go on, but it has nothing to do with achieving justice.

But Leonard is not simply an anomalous individual unable to exact revenge due to his condition. All subjects are in the same boat. Everyone exists with a structure of desire through which they repeat a constitutive experience of loss, and no future act of vengeance can avenge this primordial loss. Leonard's attempt to do so renders him exemplary, but the film's structure makes clear that he is a negative example.

62

In addition to providing the vengeance seeker with a sense of recompense for a prior loss, revenge promises to restore justice to the society itself, which the unpunished crime has thrown out of balance. This is why Oedipus self-destructively pursues his investigation into the killing of Laius and why Leonard can't stop his own quest. Leonard continues his pursuit of his wife's killer because he believes that the act of vengeance will be registered somewhere by someone, even if no one but him sees it and even if he can't remember it. He implicitly believes in an Other—God, some faceless authority, society as such, the natural world, or some similar figure—as the source for justice and justification.[35] This belief in an Other as the ultimate and infallible arbiter traps Leonard, just as it does the typical subject.

Though the Other exists as a force binding subjects together, it does not exist as a substantial identity capable of providing a final scale of justice. This nonexistence of the Other leaves subjects on their own when it comes to finding justice and being ethical.[36] Ethics comes down to the subject's relation to its own desire rather than the achievement of redress or balance in the eyes of a nonexistent Other. But *Memento* depicts a subject who cannot escape the idea of society as the source for justice and thus cannot discover an ethics based on his own desire. By endeavoring to escape in order to find justice outside repetition, one succumbs, like Leonard, to the repetition of injustice.[37] He begins to resemble a serial killer because he can't affirm the inescapability of his defining experience of traumatic loss. The effort to get beyond the trauma by redressing the social imbalance it occasioned leaves him both unfree and unethical.

Throughout the film, Leonard is unable to avow the lack of support in society for the subject's ethical being. He believes that the meaning of his actions lies in social recognition, a recognition that will exist even if no one sees these actions or has knowledge of them. In this way, Leonard serves as the perfect model for an ideologically interpellated subject because his condition has stripped away all the seemingly natural justifications for believing in a substantive link between himself and society. When talking with Natalie in the diner, Leonard says, "My wife deserves vengeance. It doesn't make any difference whether I know about it. Just because there are things I don't remember doesn't make my actions meaningless. The world doesn't just disappear when

63

you close your eyes, does it? Anyway, maybe I'll take a photograph to remind myself, get another freaky tattoo." Leonard's statement about the unimportance of his own knowledge indicates his implicit belief in an entity that will know its truth and will register the importance of the event. For him, truth is transcendent and exists beyond the knowing subject, even as it animates the quest of this subject.

At the end of the film, Leonard makes a similar profession about the world. As he drives away from Teddy to have Teddy's license plate number tattooed on his leg, through his voiceover he says, "I have to believe in a world outside my own mind. I have to believe that my actions still have meaning, even if I can't remember them. I have to believe that when my eyes are closed, the world's still there. Do I believe the world's still there? Is it still out there? Yeah. We all need mirrors to remind ourselves who we are. I'm no different. Now, where was I?" As he asks himself if the world is still there, we see an apparent flashback of Leonard in bed with his wife while his body is covered with tattoos, including one (nonexistent until this moment) on his left breast, where his wife's hand is lying, that says, "I've done it." This image calls into question the veracity of all of Leonard's memories and suggests that Teddy has provided a more credible version of the events than Leonard has. Leonard needs to believe in a world existing outside of his positing activity because this belief rescues him from the singularity of his desiring subjectivity, in which he is fundamentally alone.

On two occasions in the film, Leonard asks himself about the persistence of the world when one closes one's eyes. Of course, only children believe that the world disappears when their eyes are closed, but the question resonates for Leonard because of the nature of his condition. *Memento* suggests that contrary to the commonsensical belief the world remains when one's eyes are closed, the world is dependent on the subject's activity for support and that truth derives not from the world as an independently existing entity but through the subject's act of positing it. Truth emerges from within the subjective fiction rather than completely apart from it. This is not to say that the film affirms the subjective idealism of a thinker like George Berkeley, who sees nothing existing outside ideas. Instead, it suggests that the subject's act of giving itself a project—the act of sublimation, of making the ordinary into the transcendent—endows the world with meaning and creates the possibility for truth. In this sense, when one metaphorically closes one's eyes and no longer invests oneself in anything in the world, the

64

world does cease to exist. The ultimate fantasy is not that the world ends when I die but that it goes on without me. Leonard's belief that the world persists when his eyes are closed is the result of his devotion to a privileging of knowledge, and this privileging of knowledge fosters dependence.

Because his condition foregrounds his status as a desiring subject, Leonard should be able to free himself from the illusion of knowledge. The fact that he can't form new memories should free him from his dependence on how the social order views him or his acts since he knows that this judgment will mean nothing to him. But Leonard can't accede to the structure made evident by his condition. Being thrust into the structure of desire leads Leonard to insist all the more on the refuge of the subject of knowledge and the idea of making a lasting impression on the social order as the ultimate arbiter of justice. By presenting the spectator with this image of a subject of desire devoted to seeing himself as a subject of knowledge, *Memento* reveals the power that the image of the subject of knowledge has over those of us able to remember. The film uses Leonard's anomalous condition to shed light on the complete dominance of the prevailing conception of the subject of knowledge by highlighting its presence even in someone who can't experience gaining knowledge. Though he will never be able to register any new knowledge, Leonard is the slave of its promise.

The subject of knowledge is a hopeful subject, a subject invested in future possibilities, but it is precisely this investment in the future that is the source of the subject's dependence. Belief in future possibilities allows the social order to constantly hold the subject hostage. As long as the subject believes in the possibility of discovering a solution to the problem of loss in a future truth, the social order holds all the cards insofar as it contains all alternate possibilities. The subject sacrifices itself and its freedom at the altar of the future truth.

But while the project of knowledge fosters the subject's dependence, the transition to the structure of desire frees the subject from this dependence. The structure of desire involves a constant striving, but this striving occurs for its own sake. The satisfaction of desire derives from work itself, not from what the work accomplishes. The subject who recognizes the structure of desire as its own proper structure becomes the free subject—free not to do whatever it wants, but free to act from within its own singularity and without any external support. This freedom marks subjectivity as such, but it only comes to those who have given up the illusion that the subject is one of knowledge and accede to the existential priority of fiction. By showing the spectator a subject of desire lurking beneath a seemingly perfect subject of knowledge, *Memento* aims at undermining the prioritizing of truth that derives from this latter form of subjectivity, and thereby freeing the spectator from the trap that the cinema has historically perpetuated.

The critical and popular breakthrough of *Memento* (2000) gave Christopher Nolan the opportunity to enter the Hollywood system, and this opportunity produced *Insomnia* (2002). Nolan had ten times more money to make *Insomnia* than he had to make *Memento* ($46 million versus $4.5 million), and this budget allowed him to hire more well-known actors and to shoot in more extravagant locations. Nolan's turn to the Hollywood system also resulted in a much more conventional film than either *Following* (1998) or *Memento*. While reviewers in general responded positively to the film, even many of those who appreciated it saw a decrease in boldness in relation to Nolan's previous feature. Writing for the *Village Voice*, Dennis Lim put this most succinctly. He claimed that "while the icy dexterity of the technique places *Insomnia* ahead of virtually all the studio competition (a chase sequence over and under floating logs is superb), it must count as a disappointment when the most promising mindfuck director of the last few years goes on to make a movie that's basically a triumph of location scouting."[1] Though others were not so harsh, a recognition of the relative typicality of Nolan's third film became the consensus, not just among critics but also among Nolan's fans.[2] Though *Insomnia* may be a compelling film in their minds, it is nonetheless in the territory of a standard thriller.

Part of the idea that the film is not groundbreaking in the way that *Memento* is stems from the conditions of its production. Like Brad Silberling's *City of Angels* (1998) or Cameron Crowe's *Vanilla Sky* (2001), *Insomnia* is a Hollywood remake of a successful foreign film.[3] Typically, Hollywood takes a foreign original, in this case Norwegian director Erik Skjoldbjaerg's *Insomnia* (1997), that attracted a large following, and it dilutes the edginess and grittiness of the original in order to render the film more acceptable to a mainstream American audience. It is difficult to think of a case in which the remake becomes more disturbing or ambitious than the original. Even instances where a director remakes his or her own film, such as George Sluizer's *The Vanishing* (1993) or Takashi Shimizu's *The Grudge* (2004), most often compromise the radicality of

THE DIRTY COP

INSOMNIA AND THE ART OF DETECTION

THREE

the original, as occurs in the case of both Sluizer and Shimizu. Sluizer's follow-up to his Dutch original illustrates the logic of the American remake in shocking clarity. While *Spoorloos* (*The Vanishing*, 1988) concludes with the protagonist, Rex Hofman (Gene Bervoets), buried alive, the remake ends with the rescue of the parallel character, Jeff Harriman (Kiefer Sutherland). Inescapable trauma in the original becomes the possibility for redemptive action in the remake. This is the tradition of the American remake in which, one would assume, Nolan's film is located.

And many aspects of *Insomnia* appear to confirm that it belongs in this tradition. Nolan transforms the unrelenting pessimism of Skjoldbjaerg's film into what resembles a standard moralistic thriller. The original version shows the descent of police detective Jonas Engström (Stellan Skarsgård) into criminality as a result of shooting his partner and his inability to sleep. After the shooting, Jonas begins to act much more despicably than Will Dormer (Al Pacino) does in the remake. In order to divert suspicion away from himself in the shooting of his partner, Jonas shoots a live dog and retrieves the bullet to substitute for the bullet from the autopsy; in the remake, Will shoots a dead dog. Skjoldbjaerg's film shows Jonas attempting to rape a woman, while Nolan's film depicts Will opening himself to and connecting emotionally with the parallel character. Finally, the original ends with the detective escaping justice while Nolan's film concludes with his punishment through death. These are the type of changes that one expects from a Hollywood remake—describing them makes it seem as if Nolan is responding to the long-defunct Production Code—and they hint at a series of ideological compromises impugning the remake. But Nolan manages to use these apparent compromises to forge a film as challenging as the original, though in a fundamentally different way. In fact, one should not compare the two films. Despite the shared source material, their concerns diverge radically.

As in the original, in the remake a police detective goes to an extreme location to investigate a murder. While under investigation by the internal affairs division in Los Angeles, Will Dormer and his partner, Hap Eckhart (Martin Donovan), fly to Nightmute, Alaska, to assist an old friend, Charlie Nyback (Paul Dooley), who is the police chief there. They come to investigate a girl's murder, and during the pursuit of the murderer, Will shoots and kills Hap. Though it appears to be accidental, Will lies about the killing, attributing it to the girl's murderer, Walter Finch (Robin Williams).[4] At the end of the film, Will and Finch kill each other, as local police officer Ellie Burr (Hilary Swank) learns the truth of Hap's shooting.

Though Nolan's remake of *Insomnia* may retreat from the bleakness of the original, it also opens up an idea that the original doesn't—the role that the lie plays in the search for truth. As Nolan conceives it in the film, the lie provides the basis for the investigation into truth. No one would be able to discover any truth without recourse to deception. Though many other detective films depict detectives using lies to discover the truth—it is difficult to imagine a single film where a detective manages to be completely honest and effective at the same time—*Insomnia* goes further than any other in thematizing the necessity of the lie and making the detective's lie its focal point.[5]

The necessity of the lie in the investigation of truth stems from the lie's structural priority in relation to truth. Truth is not a primary assertion but emerges only through contradicting a falsehood. As Jacques Lacan puts it, "The truth is founded only . . . on the supposition of the false: it is contradiction. It is founded only on the no. Its enunciation is only the denunciation of the non-truth."[6] Without a falsehood to denounce, one would have no way of distinguishing the truth. This limitation of truth grants the lie a structural priority, and this priority makes itself felt in every search for truth.

The irony that underlies *Insomnia* is that its exploration of the lie occurs within a summertime arctic setting that allows for no darkness. Since Plato, Western philosophy and common sense alike have aligned the process of coming to truth with movement toward light and have aligned deception with darkness. The Allegory of the Cave from the beginning of Book VII of the *Republic* locates illusion in the cave with the bound prisoners watching shadows on the wall and truth in the bright light of the external world to which the philosopher escapes. Truth, as Plato sees it, operates like light. Though it initially blinds us in the same way that a burst of light does, it ultimately allows us to see clearly instead of indistinctly. Though later thinkers in the philosophical tradition departed significantly from Plato, this controlling metaphor identifying truth and light retained its hold. Even common sense supports this equation of truth and light. Without some form of darkness, deceit would seem to be impossible because it depends on the capacity to hide. When everything is in the light, then we believe that we can see the whole truth.[7]

But the absence of darkness in *Insomnia* does not lead to the universal revelation of truth. Instead, it produces an increase and a foregrounding of deceit. In Los Angeles, Will could continue his police work while keeping his deceit hidden. Even if Hap confesses to the LA internal affairs agents about his partner's past deeds, it is not at all clear from the film that Will's lie back home would be exposed. As Hap relates his decision to strike a deal, he claims that, as a good cop, Will has no reason to worry. Though Will disputes this, Nolan offers no definite indication to the contrary. But in the unending daylight of Nightmute, Will expands his proclivity to deceive. His lies become excessive, whereas in Los Angeles they remained under control. His lie about Hap's death leads to his undoing and ultimately to Ellie's discovery of his culpability. Light enhances lying rather than simply exposing truth, though this enhancement of the lie ultimately reveals the truth. As J. L. A. Garcia notes in a discussion of *Insomnia* as a story of redemption, light doesn't provide insight but instead increases confusion: "Several times during the movie, we come across a bright glare, which might eventually facilitate vision but at first only blinds and dizzies both the characters and us viewers."[8] Nolan's use of light in the film reverses the usual associations of light with knowledge and clarity.

Insomnia attempts to readjust our understanding of the relationship between truth and lie. On the one hand, the film seems to suggest that the truth will always manifest itself. Will Dormer's superior sends him from Los Angeles to Alaska for respite from the internal affairs investigation plaguing Will and threatening his career. But instead of offering Will a temporary escape, Alaska becomes the site where Will inadvertently admits the truth of the accusations against him. On the other hand, this truth emerges through a lie. Without Will's decision to lie about shooting and killing his partner, the fact that he had planted evidence in a previous case might not have come to light. Will's lies not only lead to capturing and convicting criminals, but his lie about shooting Hap leads to the revelation of his own guilt.

THE NECESSARY LIE

By associating Will Dormer with deceit, Nolan is not simply exploring police corruption. Will's deception is that of a model police officer. From the opening, the film works to establish Will as a committed and serious detective and thus to illustrate that his actions are part of effective police work. During the plane ride to Nightmute, Hap reads the newspaper while Will studies evidence from the murder case. When Hap laments the lack of any signs of civilization in the area, Will reminds him that they are not vacationing; when Hap tells him to "Cheer up," Will shows him a picture of the dead girl and says, "Tell that to her, partner." Just as the initial plane ride establishes Will's seriousness as a detective, the arrival in Nightmute makes evident his skill. Local police officer Ellie Burr expresses her respect for Will the moment she sees him, and the depth of her adulation gives Will a legendary status at the beginning of the film. She recites all of his famous cases and even notices the pronounced scar on his neck that was the result of a murderer cutting him. Furthermore, Nolan chooses Al Pacino for the role of Will Dormer, an actor with a history of playing police heroes above reproach in such films as *Serpico* (Sidney Lumet, 1973) and *Heat* (Michael Mann, 1995).[9] By opening the film with numerous suggestions of Will's credentials as a police detective, Nolan transforms him into an archetype. Will is not the flawed, too-human detective from many contemporary police dramas.[10] His failings are, instead, intrinsic to detection itself and ultimately inseparable from it. Or one might say that *Insomnia* does not depict a good cop gone bad but rather the necessary badness of the good cop.

The early scenes of the investigation in Nightmute support the initial impression that the film establishes concerning Will's prowess as a detective. Even though he has read the report on the body, he wants to see it nonetheless and is able to discover what the local investigators missed. Then, when searching the room of the murder victim, Kay Connell (Crystal Lowe), he finds an expensive dress that he links to an admirer. When he makes this link, the film cuts quickly to Ellie, who smiles at the display of investigative skill. Though this display of skill takes place after the allusion to the internal affairs investigation, the knowledge about that investigation does not mitigate its impressiveness. Upon his arrival in Nightmute, Will continually provokes astonishment at his investigative ability.[11] Whatever his faults may be, they are not the faults of a corrupt police officer or one who cannot do his job. They are the faults contained within the ideal itself.

This emphasis in Nolan's remake becomes especially evident when we contrast it with Skjoldbjaerg's original. In the Norwegian version of the film, the detective, Jonas Engström, begins to act more and more like a criminal as the film progresses. Whereas Will Dormer continues to try to apprehend Finch (and at the same time exculpate himself), Jonas ceases to act like a police detective after the shooting of his partner. His actions in the film contrast with his role as a police officer rather than deriving from it, as they do in Will's case. Though the beginning of Skjoldbjaerg's film presents Jonas without the difficulty of the internal affairs investigation that plagues Will, his actions subsequent to the shooting of his partner evince his complete divorce from his vocation. Skjoldbjaerg's original film reveals the incapacity of an empirical individual to embody the ideal of the police detective; Nolan's remake depicts the necessary fault within the ideal itself.[12] The internal affairs investigation that Nolan adds to his version provides Will a motive for shooting Hap (who has decided to strike a deal and potentially incriminate Will), but it also links deception with good police work.

On their first night in Nightmute, Hap confronts Will with his pending deal with internal affairs. Even though Hap has no plans to implicate Will in his testimony, Will insists that the deal would represent a complete betrayal. In Will's mind, the betrayal would not simply be personal but professional: it would do violence to the people that their investigations work to protect. Though one might argue that Will's professional plea to Hap hides a personal one, that he is just trying to save his career in the most effective way he can, what is telling about the exchange is that Will's first thought is the professional damage that Hap's testimony would do; the consideration of personal damage comes later and seems unimportant to him. The discussion between Hap and Will allows Nolan to stress the ethical nature of Will's position, even as it involves a defense of lying:

> Will: He's putting the squeeze on you to get to me. It's very simple, Hap.
> Hap: But you're clean, Will.
> Will: I'm a good cop, yeah, but there's always something they can use, you know, to get at your credibility, you know that. Have you any idea what this could do? Just think about all my cases, all the cases dependent on my word, my judgment. All those fuckers are back on the street. Now you think about that. That's what you do.
> Hap: That's bullshit. They got nothing on you because there's nothing to get.
> Will: Dobbs. . . . What about Dobbs?
> Hap: That's different.
> Will: It's different?
> Hap: Yeah, because even Warfield doesn't want shit like Dobbs back on the street.
> Will: It's a house of cards, man. Once it starts, it's just going to tumble, all of it.

Hap: That's a chance I've gotta take, pal. I've got family, Will.

Will: Don't give me that family shit.

Hap: Warfield made it clear. I get probation.

Will: We're cops, man. This is not about us. This is about all the people who depend on us. People with families. I spent my life doing this. My life . . . you're going to destroy it. Like that. Why? Why? So some IA prick gets one step closer to being chief of police or playing golf with the mayor or whatever the fuck else he's after.

Hap: You finished? Sorry, I gotta cut a deal.

For Will, the credibility of police detectives is essential to their effectiveness, and yet he realizes that an inquiry can always impugn this credibility. When he tells Hap that "there's always something they can use," he acknowledges the centrality of the lie in the work of detection.

The role of the necessary lie in effective police work becomes evident soon after this discussion with Hap. The discovery of the book bag of the murder victim near an isolated cabin offers the police an additional clue about the identity of her killer. But the bag and its contents alone provide nothing decisive. Knowledge of its existence, however, allows Will the opportunity to set a trap for the killer. He instructs the local police not to reveal that the bag has been found, but rather to release a statement that they are looking for the bag that they know Kay had when she was last seen. This statement, he believes, will draw the killer to the cabin in an effort to recover and destroy the evidence.

After Will sends the local police out to return the bag, he looks at Hap, who smiles at the cleverness of Will's plan. The film cuts back from Hap to Will, and Will turns to Charlie in order to express second thoughts about the plan. Remembering Hap's deal with the internal affairs investigation, Will recognizes that this ploy might be seen as suspicious. He voices his doubts, and immediately Hap and Charlie try to reassure him. After he rebuffs Hap's attempted consolation, we see Charlie put his hand on Will's shoulder and remind him that "someone out there just beat a seventeen-year-old girl to death. Your job is to find him." Hap seconds this sentiment, and the next scene of the police staking out the cabin reveals implicitly that Will has agreed to go along.

Will's expression of doubt in this scene seems completely perfunctory. It is more an attempt to insult his partner than a sincere concern that the operation is somehow reproachable. Nonetheless, the link that Will makes between his earlier planting of evidence and returning Kay's bag to the cabin is revelatory. In both cases, a lie by the police is nec-

73

essary to catch and convict the criminal. With the bag, the lie appears to be wholly justified; no spectator would question that this is simply clever detective work and not entrapment. But justified or not, the lie, as the film shows, is necessary for discovering the identity of the murderer. Rather than showing Will and Hap simply searching for clues that eventually lead them to the murderer, Nolan includes the discovery of the bag and Will's plan to use it in order to highlight the role that the lie plays in the police's search for truth. There is no truth that can be completely divorced from the lie, which is not to say that there is no truth.

THE UNNECESSARY LIE

After the pursuit of Finch at the cabin, Will opts to lie again, this time to cover up the fact that he shot Hap. Unlike the lie that Will employs to prove the guilt of Dobbs or the lie about Kay's bag that he uses to trap Finch, this lie serves a personal rather than professional function. He lies here in order to avoid implicating himself in Hap's death. But there is another crucial difference between this lie and the earlier ones: nothing necessitates it. Even for self-protection, there is no clear reason for Will to lie in this situation. The dense fog in the area hampered visibility and would fully justify the claim that the shooting had been accidental, even if Will had in fact shot Hap purposely. By lying about Hap's shooting, Will begins the process of his own confession. It represents the first step toward avowing the truth.

The lie about the shooting plays a fundamental role in exposing Will's guilt in planting evidence in the earlier case and Finch's guilt in the murder of Kay Connell. Will's lie functions as the vehicle through which truth becomes evident. The lie leads Will to discover that Finch is the murderer and to reveal his own guilt to Ellie. Even the apparently unnecessary lie plays a crucial role in the justice of the film. Will's lie about Hap's death gives Finch a hold over him. Finch saw the event. He initiates contact with Will and arranges to meet him because he knows that Will has killed his partner and subsequently lied about it. Motivated by the idea that he and Will are working together to implicate Kay's boyfriend in her killing, Finch describes the murder to Will in great detail. This insight into the crime comes as a direct result of Will's lie about the shooting. Without this, Finch would not have reached out to him in the way that he does, and his guilt would not have been readily apparent. Here, the film makes evident the productivity of the lie.

Nolan portrays the shooting in a way that creates ambiguity about Will's intention. A few scenes before the shooting, we see the confrontation between Hap and Will concerning Hap's decision to strike a deal with the internal affairs investigation, and we witness Will's cold treatment of Hap when he learns that Hap can't be talked out of his confession. Will's hostility toward Hap continues unrelentingly after this initial discussion. And as they are staking out the cabin just before Finch arrives, Hap's offer to Will of a cup of coffee receives nothing but a silent stare. This background of ill feelings serves to cast doubt on Will's shooting of Hap. Nolan furthers this sense of suspicion by showing Will change to his backup gun just before shooting Hap and by depicting Hap's dying belief that Will had shot him intentionally.

But the film offers no conclusive evidence of Will's culpability. After Finch shoots one of the local police officers in the leg, Will pursues him on the rocky beach through the dense fog. At no point does Will or the spectator see Finch's face clearly, and throughout the crosscut chase sequence Finch remains only partially visible. Nolan shoots Will's pursuit from a variety of angles, violating the 180-degree rule and disorienting the spectator in the fog along with Will. This disorientation contributes to Will's decision to shoot, but when he does shoot, the film offers no indication that he is shooting his partner rather than Finch. We see the image of a man in the fog from Will's perspective, and this man appears to be the same one that Will has been chasing. Though the film doesn't clearly show Will shooting Hap intentionally, nothing indicates definitively that it was an accident either. This central ambiguity of the film leads to the central lie of the film.[13]

The sense of ambiguity that the scene instills in the spectator—the impossibility of knowing whether Will kills Hap intentionally or accidentally—mirrors Will's own sense of ambiguity. The film makes it clear that Will himself doesn't really know whether he intended to kill Hap, and it is this uncertainty that leads Will to lie. The lie is correlative to doubt rather than certainty.

Will's relationship to the lie about the shooting of Hap is much different than his relationship to his earlier lies. While he evinces no shame about lying to implicate the child-murderer Dobbs, he barely articulates his lie about Hap's shooting. Charlie reviews what happened in the fog, and we see a close-up of Will's silent reaction to this description of the events. After a quick cut to Charlie asking for confirmation, another close-up of Will shows him nodding his head in agreement. This is the extent of his lie, and later he evinces an ambivalent relationship to it, even though he knows that revealing the truth at that point would destroy his life.

The film makes it clear that Will is not simply interested in saving his own career by covering up his role in Hap's death. Even though he takes great pains to eliminate evidence that would implicate him, he refuses to sign Ellie's report on the incident that places the blame on Finch (and thereby exculpates himself). Though she is ready to end her investigation, he tells her, "Be sure of all your facts before you file this thing. It's your name on the report." This admonition ultimately leads Ellie to discover the discrepancy in Will's account of the shooting and to conclude that he was actually the shooter. By urging her to review the facts of the case, Will undermines his own self-interest, but at the same time, he evinces his fealty to the detective's attitude of universal suspicion. The ethical nature of Will's commitment to this suspicion will not allow him to abandon it even when he himself is the target.[14]

The subject's capacity for self-destruction, which Will evinces even in his dialogue with Ellie, is what allows the subject to escape its foundational lie. Through self-destruction, one discovers the truth of one's subjectivity. As Hegel puts it in the *Phenomenology of Spirit*, the subject "wins to its truth only when, in utter dismemberment, it finds itself."[15] Subjectivity emerges through a fiction, but truth comes when this fiction self-destructs. The subject finds truth at the moment when it recognizes its identity with what appears most foreign to it and thus what signals its destruction. This is the path that Hegel traces in the *Phenomenology* and that Nolan depicts Will taking in *Insomnia*.

In the sequence immediately following the interaction between Ellie and Will, Nolan cuts between Will trying to sleep in his hotel room and Ellie going over the evidence from the case once again. We see Will taping shut the window shade (to keep the omnipresent light out of the room) and lying on his bed unable to sleep. Images of Hap and of a bloodied white fabric alternate with images of him awake in the hotel room. We see Ellie, in contrast, falling asleep while looking over the pictures from the shooting. As she wakes up from dozing off, Ellie discovers Will's lie about the shooting. She says to herself, "He couldn't have come from there." At the end of the film, Ellie puts together the clues and concludes that Will is guilty of shooting his partner, but the initial insight into the truth comes at this moment, and Nolan links it to the moment when Ellie falls asleep. By depicting Ellie coming to the truth just as she dozes off, Nolan again reverses the traditional link between light and truth. Like Freud, Nolan locates truth in sleep—the time in which consciousness loses some of its control over the unconscious desire of the subject. In this sequence, he also associates Will's deceit with his inability to sleep. Along with the light from outside, his guilt renders him incapable of falling asleep. But the light also exposes the lie, while truth comes with sleep and darkness.

Will's self-destructiveness in pursuit of the investigation becomes evident again when the police bring Finch in for questioning. Finch's answers point toward the guilt of Kay's boyfriend, Randy, but during the questioning, Will aggressively works to direct suspicion back to Finch himself. Nolan shoots their interaction in a shot/reverse shot sequence with Will looking down on Finch in an intimidating manner. Will asks him about his reluctance to come forward and about the details of his relationship with Kay. This questioning visibly discomfits Finch and as a result threatens to expose Will's lie. At the conclusion of the questioning, Will explodes in rage and says, "You just wanted to fuck her, didn't you?" From the reactions of the other police officers, it is clear that this outburst casts more suspicion on Will than it does on Finch. Throughout the investigation, Will covers his own guilt, but at the same time his actions bring this guilt to light, and it is his decision to lie about Hap's shooting that drives this movement toward the revelation of truth. This lie functions as the basis of the truth that the film uncovers.

THE EVOLUTION OF DETECTION

The relationship between *Insomnia* and film noir holds the key to properly understanding the ontology of the lie that it proffers. The kinship stems from the film's detection plot and the personal involvement of the detective in the case that he is investigating. Whereas the classical detective (such as Poe's Auguste Dupin and Doyle's Sherlock Holmes) maintains a distance from the case and solves it through ratiocination, the noir detective immerses him- or herself in the case (perhaps by falling in love with the client) and solves it by way of this intense involvement. The distance of the classical detective corresponds to a realist conception of the universe that does not account for the subject. The facts of the case simply present themselves, and anyone with the proper deductive skills could solve the case. The pleasure for the reader or the viewer of a story of classical detection resides in figuring out the case alongside the detective. The subjectivity of the detective does not bear on the solution. In contrast, the subjectivity of the noir detective is intimately linked to the solution of the case, and consequently the pleasure of watching a film noir (or reading a noir detective novel) does not derive so much from figuring out the mystery but from immersing oneself in the criminal underworld along with the detective.

The subjective turn in film noir manifests itself most obviously in extreme techniques or narrative developments, such as the exclusive use of the subjective camera in Robert Montgomery's *Lady in the Lake* (1947), the hero investigating his own murder in Rudolph Maté's *D.O.A.* (1950), or the detective discovering that he himself is the murderer he pursues in John Farrow's *The Big Clock* (1948) or Alan Parker's *Angel Heart* (1987). Even when noir doesn't go to such extremes, it always portrays the detective as integral to the solution rather than external to it, as is the case with classical detection. In order to solve the crime, most often noir heroes must discover something about themselves, which will provide the key to solving the case.

In *Insomnia*, Will Dormer proclaims himself a classical detective. This becomes most apparent when Walter Finch arranges a meeting with him on a ferry. In a typical noir fashion, Finch tries to draw a parallel between himself as criminal and Will as detective.[16] By pointing out this parallel, Finch hopes to seduce Will into a plot that would direct suspicion away from both of them. But Will completely rejects the idea that he shares something with Finch or that Finch's psychology is of any interest to him. He tells Finch, "You don't get it do you, Finch? You're my job. You're what I'm paid to do. You're about as mysterious to me as a blocked toilet is to a fucking plumber. Reasons for doing what you did? Who gives a fuck?" In this emphatic assertion, Will attempts to display his distance from Finch and the case, which is why he emphasizes that he is paid to investigate. The classical detective, from Auguste Dupin on, is always paid and always insists on being paid. The remuneration attests to—and actually works to ensure—the absence of any personal involvement on the part of the detective. The acceptance of money for the job assures everyone involved that the case involved nothing personal on the part of the detective. In clear contrast to the classical detective, the noir detective never receives payment, and if a client offers payment, the noir detective necessarily refuses it. Accepting money would demean the detective's personal stake in the case. Despite Will's assertion of his concern for money and his denial of any personal investment, the case does involve him, and his assertion to the contrary is nothing but an effort to hide this fact.[17]

Unlike the genuine classical detective, Will feels compelled to assert his lack of personal investment in the case and his distance from the criminal. The classical detective wouldn't make such an assertion because the distance would never be in doubt.[18] But for Will, his own doubt about his distance from the criminal (and the crime)—actually, his knowledge that he is implicated through the shooting—underlies the assertion to the contrary. The position from which Will speaks contradicts the substance of what he says, or the fact of the enunciation itself belies the content of the statement. Nolan highlights this contradiction through the way he shoots the interaction between Will and Finch just after Will proclaims his lack of interest in Finch's motivations.

After Will rejects Finch's attempt at self-justification, Finch brings up Will's shooting of Hap and questions the intent behind it. Then he walks away. When Will follows him and resumes the conversation in another part of the ferry, Finch proposes working together to frame Kay's boyfriend for the murder. As he describes this plan, we see a lengthy close-up of Will and Finch talking to each other with a green pole dividing them in the middle of the image. Though they each remain on one side of the pole, their faces almost touch at times during the conversation. At one point, Will even puts his lips against the pole and seems almost to kiss it. Nolan uses the pole as a sign of the division that exists between the two but also as a mark of their connection. Whereas Nolan shot Will's proclamation of distance from Finch in a standard shot/reverse shot manner, here he allows both characters to occupy the same frame for a long, uninterrupted close-up. The shared close-up signals an almost-romantic bond between them, even in the aftermath of Will's attempt to deny any connection whatsoever. Though Will is simply playing along in order to trap Finch at some future point, doing so requires and stems from his personal involvement in the case. He shows himself in this scene to be on the side of the noir detective rather than that of the classical one.[19]

Furthermore, the construction of its plot seems also to locate *Insomnia* securely within the tradition of film noir. Will Dormer's personal involvement in the case mirrors that of Sam Spade (Humphrey Bogart) in *The Maltese Falcon* (John Huston, 1941) or Mark McPherson (Dana Andrews) in *Laura* (Otto Preminger, 1944). The investigation is about him as much as it is about the criminal under investigation. And yet, one would be loath to call *Insomnia* a film noir simply because the film's mise-en-scène so defies this label. Much more than by its plot, a film noir is defined by its mise-en-scène: an inner city setting, the seductive look of the femme fatale, and almost ubiquitous low-key lighting.[20] Film noir is, as the name suggests, fundamentally dark. Often the entire film takes place at night, and darkness is essential to its aesthetic structure. *Insomnia*, in contrast, includes no night scenes. Not only does Nolan not shoot at night, but he sets the film in the middle of the Alaskan summer, when night simply does not exist. Reviewer Peter Rainer notes that "*Insomnia* is a noir with the lights turned on."[21] The absence of darkness in the film contributes to Will's inability to sleep (and thus the title), but it distances the film from the aesthetic tendency of film noir. Though the plot of *Insomnia* is certainly noir, the aesthetic is completely divorced from a noir aesthetic, which is what most critics and viewers use to define the noir style. The turn away from the noir aesthetic while sustaining a noir-style plot and detective indicates the complex relationship to film noir that Nolan establishes in *Insomnia*.[22] He revolutionizes this revolutionary form.

The importance of noir lies in the subjective turn that it effects. Film noir performs a kind of Copernican revolution of the classical detection form. Just as Copernicus overturned the Ptolemaic system by focusing on the movement of his own standpoint rather than that of the object being seen—and by locating truth in that movement (and illusion in the apparent movement of the object)—noir isolates the crime's solution in the subjectivity of the detective rather than in the objectivity of the crime.[23] With the emergence of film noir, truth in detection does not become relative, but it does become dependent on the subject pursuing it.

Christopher Nolan pushes film noir's Copernican revolution one step further in *Insomnia*. Film noir locates the solution in the truth of the knowing subject rather than that of the known object. *Insomnia* locates the solution in the lie of the knowing subject.[24] Will becomes personally involved in the case when, in pursuit of Walter Finch, he shoots his partner and subsequently lies to cover up his role in the shooting. From this point on, the stakes in Will's investigation of Finch change: rather than simply apprehending a murderer, Will must manage to do so in a way that doesn't implicate himself in the killing of his partner. Finch's knowledge of Will's lie places Will in an almost-impossible position. If he catches Finch, Finch will reveal the truth of Hap's shooting, and if he kills Finch without justification, he will bring further suspicion on himself.

The revolutionary step of *Insomnia* begins with the first image of the film, which appears during the credit sequence as the film's title comes up. Nolan shows an extreme close-up of a white weaved fabric becoming red as blood spreads through it. After this shot of blood soaking a

80

garment, he cuts to a traveling shot of the Alaskan wilderness, which we will subsequently conclude to be from the plane that contains Will and Hap coming to investigate the murder of Kay Connell. The image blurs and turns white, slowly becoming the white weaved fabric of the first shot, which again becomes stained with blood. This alternation repeats and ends with the image of blood dripping on a white shirt cuff and an unidentified man—seemingly a criminal having just committed a crime—trying to rub away the bloodstain. The credit sequence ends at this point, and the film cuts to Will Dormer waking up in the plane. An external shot locates the plane in the Alaskan wilderness that was visible during the credits.

The opening credit sequence appears to move back and forth between the scene of the crime and the arrival of the investigators. It ends with what seems to be a quick cut from the criminal wiping away blood to the investigator (Will) perusing photographs of the dead girl. This type of linkage through editing occurs often. It is not unusual for a detective film to cut from scenes of the investigator to images of the crime. This occurs famously in Jonathan Demme's *Silence of the Lambs* (1991), for instance, when Demme juxtaposes scenes of Clarice Starling (Jodie Foster) searching for the suspect, Jame Gumb (Ted Levine), with scenes of the latter interacting with the woman he has kidnapped. The opening of *Insomnia* seems to operate fully in this tradition of detective film editing. We subsequently learn, however, that the blood staining the white fabric, contrary to our initial impression, has nothing to do with the crime that Will is coming to investigate. Though it isn't apparent at the time, the shots of the blood staining the white fabric are of Will planting evidence at the house of a suspect in an earlier crime. The image of the criminal wiping away the blood on his cuff was actually an image of Will in the process of framing a suspect.

By initially suggesting that the bloodied white fabric is part of the crime being investigated rather than an object in the history of the investigator, *Insomnia* establishes a sense of objectivity that it will then undermine. As in film noir, what appears to exist as an objective incident—the commission of a crime by an anonymous criminal, say—becomes a subjective one: the investigating detective's criminal act. Here, the bloody white shirt belongs to the detective and not to the criminal. But this twist shows how Nolan pushes this dynamic further than the typical film noir does. The solution to the crime is not to be found in the truth of the detective but rather in his lie. Nolan begins the film by juxtaposing shots of the detective framing an earlier suspect while he

81

travels to the next case. This editing structure places the entire emphasis of the investigation on the detective. His lie is at once its own form
of criminality and the basis for the investigation of all criminality.[25]

Nolan does not simply show the centrality of the detective's lie. The
structure of the credit sequence perpetuates a similar deception in the
film's relationship to the spectator. The juxtaposition of the bloodied
white fabric and the plane flying over the Alaskan wilderness leads the
spectator to associate the fabric with the crime that Will is going to
investigate, not with his own act of fabricating evidence. In this way,
Nolan links the necessary lie of the police investigation with the deceptiveness of cinema (and specifically cinematic editing). Cinema lies
just like the police detective, but this lie (like that of the detective)
is integral to its ability to arrive at the truth. Whereas *Memento* shows
us that the pursuit of truth hides a desire to sustain the lie, *Insomnia*
reveals that the lie provides the key to arriving at truth.

Ironically, Nolan brings film noir out of the darkness in order to show
that there is no repressed truth of the subject that we can find if we
delve deep enough into the dark recesses of the subject's unconscious or
the society's underside. Instead, there is a repressed lie, a foundational
fiction that organizes the subject's being and provides the basis for its
truths. Being aware of this fiction does not eliminate it (or the need
for it), but it does allow us to recognize its necessity—and recognizing
the necessity of the foundational lie transforms the ground of our social
interactions. As Nolan conceives it, propagating this transformation is
the cinema's fundamental task.

THE UNIVERSAL GUILT OF THE POLICE

One can imagine a leftist attack on *Insomnia* for its implicit claim that
the police must lie and fabricate evidence in order to do their job effectively. In fact, one doesn't even need to imagine such an attack
because it actually exists. In her review of the film, Joanne Laurier
decries *Insomnia* as "yet another hackneyed film about a hard-working,
diligent police officer who is being hamstrung by juridical restrictions
in his pursuit of the perverts and criminals who hold society hostage.
Although Nolan has Dormer wrestle with the morality of police misconduct, the arguments against the latter are formal and weak. In the end,
the audience is led to feel that everything Dormer has done [and] does
is understandable, even necessary."[26] In a sense, Laurier's critique is

correct. One experiences Dormer's turn to deception as a necessary part of police investigation, and this serves to blunt the criticism of police abuses. *Insomnia* is an apology for the lies of Will Dormer insofar as it emphasizes their necessity.

But a critique like Laurier's is completely misguided precisely because the film reveals the deception as necessary. A film that showed deceit as the personal failing of a single police officer (or even of the entire police force) would leave the purity of police detection itself intact. The responsibility for deception would reside within the individual or group, not in the structure of detection, and we could watch it with the assurance that the bad apples could be removed and the system could then prosper justly.[27] By implicating the structure of detection, Nolan's film demands not simply that we rid the police force of a few bad apples but that we fundamentally rethink our attitude toward policing. Of course, *Insomnia* does not suggest that an awareness of the necessary lie would require us to do away with policing altogether. It envisions a world where criminality requires a police force. The point is neither that we must ignore police deception because it is necessary for justice, nor that we must cease trying to police criminality because such policing necessarily involves deception; rather, we must interpret every investigation—and the evidence it obtains—through the prism of the lie.

The exaggerated contempt that Will evinces toward Warfield, the internal affairs investigator, derives from his understanding of the integral nature of the lie in police work and the outside investigator's inability to understand this. When Warfield phones Will after Hap's death, he announces his suspicion about the circumstances of the shooting. Nolan confines the visuals of this conversation to Will's end of it and leaves Warfield as a disembodied and aggressive voice, which serves to alienate the spectator from Warfield's position. We see Will talking on the phone in a series of close-ups, with cuts to hotel manager Rachel Clement (Maura Tierney) looking concerned by the amount of invective in Will's voice. Though Warfield wants to talk to Will about Hap's shooting, Will immediately turns the conversation to the position of the internal affairs investigator as such. At one point, he tells Warfield, "You're always sitting safe behind some fucking desk reading your bullshit reports, and that is why I have nothing but contempt for you. You and all the assholes like you risk nothing and spend all day sucking the marrow out of real cops when you never had the balls to be one yourself." As he finishes this statement, we see Will hang up the phone without allowing Warfield to respond, an act that serves to punctuate his claim. When the phone slams down, the film cuts to a shot of Rachel, who looks down and blinks, thereby registering the force of Will's contempt. Though we see Will acting with hostility, the film nonetheless presents him more sympathetically than his accuser.

Will does not detest Warfield in particular, and his venom does not stem from the fact that the investigation targets him personally. As his phone conversation with Warfield and earlier discussion with Hap both indicate, his objection to internal affairs is much more philosophical: investigating instances of police deception or misconduct threatens the essence of detection, which has its basis in the necessary lie. In order to solve even simple cases, the detective must create a deception that entices guilty parties to reveal themselves. Very few suspects openly confess their guilt, and in these cases no detective is necessary. But in the vast majority of cases, a detective must mislead the suspect by pretending to have evidence, by feigning understanding and compassion, or by some other means. Such deceits are integral to the process of the detection, which would be unimaginable without them.[28] Nonetheless, they remain deceptive and lead to the kind of abuses that Will perpetuates in *Insomnia* and even worse.

Insomnia ends with the revelation of truth. The conclusion of the film depicts Will's repudiation of the lie that framed Dobbs. Just before he prepares to leave Nightmute, he confesses planting evidence in the Dobbs case to Rachel Clement in his hotel room. He tells her, "The second I met this guy Dobbs, I knew he was guilty. That's what I do. I assign guilt. You find the evidence, figure out who did it, then you go get them and put them away. This time there wasn't enough evidence." As Will relates planting the evidence, Nolan cuts to the images of the dripping blood on the white shirt, which have been inserted intermittently since the beginning of the film. The return of these images at this point finally reveals their connection with Will and his fabrication of evidence in the earlier case. Here, the film makes clear that Will's investigation of Kay Connell's murder has been all along an investigation of his own lie. The juxtaposition of images in the opening credit sequence illustrated, it is now clear, the scene of Will's own crime in conjunction with his trip to investigate Finch's crime.

In his conversation with Rachel, Will gradually comes to recognize that he cannot justify the lie to convict Dobbs. He concludes his description of what he did by saying to her, "The end justifies the means, right?" Rachel refuses to exonerate or condemn Will, though the doubt in his voice and his actions at the end of the film indicate that he no longer accepts this consequentialist argument. Will ends up indicting himself for his actions both in the Dobbs case and in the shooting of his partner, and as he dies at the end of the film from a gunfight with Finch, he refuses to allow Ellie to discard the shell from his backup gun that she found on the beach (which proves his culpability). As he resists her urge to destroy evidence and protect his reputation, he tells her, "Don't lose your way." This admonition to Ellie serves also as a tacit rejection of his own decision to manufacture evidence.[29]

In the Dobbs case, Will took the detective's necessary lie too far, but based on this overreaching, the film does not offer a full condemnation of police deception. Deceit is the foundation of detection and the royal road to truth. Even the revelation of the lie in the Dobbs case requires Will's lie about shooting his partner in order to come to the surface. If Will had not covered up his shooting of Hap, he would not have confessed that he planted evidence to prove Dobbs's guilt. Guilt over the shooting, fostered by the lie about his role in it, leads Will to sleeplessness and to confession. The affirmation of truth that concludes the film depends on a lie that enables it. We can discover truth only through the lie.

Understanding this doesn't destroy truth or render it completely relative. The effect of *Insomnia* is not the relativization of truth but a reformulation of the relationship between the lie and truth. By foregrounding the necessary lie throughout but ending with the revelation of truth, *Insomnia* affirms a commitment to truth but at the same time reveals the necessity of tarrying with the lie in order to arrive at truth. One can never escape deception because it forms the basis of our inquiry into truth. The recognition of the priority of the lie allows us to reimagine truth in the form of a fiction.

When Christopher Nolan won the opportunity to make *Insomnia* in 2002, he received the advantages that come with being an up-and-coming Hollywood director. The film's budget afforded him expensive location shooting, top stars like Al Pacino and Robin Williams, and prominent advertising. But it was *Batman Begins* (2005), with a budget almost triple that of *Insomnia*, that fully catapulted Nolan into the middle of the Hollywood system. *Insomnia* was the Hollywood film of an independent director; *Batman Begins* left behind all traces of Nolan's independent origins.[1] Not only did he work with much more money than before, but he also took on an established film franchise in a popular contemporary genre. While a move in this direction offers increased opportunity, it simultaneously limits a director's freedom. Superhero films carry with them certain audience expectations that directors must meet if they hope to be successful, and these expectations are even more pronounced in the Batman series. Nolan benefited, however, from the moribund status of the franchise.[2] The failure of *Batman & Robin* (Joel Schumacher, 1997) led to a temporary hiatus in the production of Batman films, which allowed Nolan to reconceive the origin of Batman and thereby remake the series anew.[3]

The result is a film that challenges the idea of the superhero as such. Batman has always stood out from other superheroes because he lacks a superpower. He doesn't have the strength of Superman, the speed of Flash, the size of Hulk, or the agility of Spider-Man. He also lacks a device that would render him almost invincible, like the ring of Green Lantern, the metal bodysuit of Iron Man, or the invisibility of Sue Storm in the Fantastic Four. Batman is strong but only in human terms. He has a powerful arsenal of weapons, but none that enables him to perform fantastic acts. As a result, Batman has always been the superhero closest to humanity, and this provides one of the bases for his popularity. If the figure of Superman creates a superheroic ideal that people can only admire from afar, Batman brings the superhero back down to earth. In this sense, Batman embodies what Hegel might call the speculative identity of the heroic and the ordinary. He shows that the superhero is only the result of a fictional mask that the ordinary person puts on, and he

THE BANAL SUPERHERO
THE POLITICIZED REALISM OF *BATMAN BEGINS*

FOUR

demonstrates the power of this fiction.[4] The association of Batman with the power of fiction clearly attracts Christopher Nolan's attention, and he constructs his film version in a way that emphasizes this fictionality.

Nolan's version of Batman stands out from all other superhero films because of the stress that he places on the ordinariness of the superhero's powers. He devotes fully half the film to the depiction of the intense training among the League of Shadows that prepares Bruce Wayne (Christian Bale) physically to become Batman and to the depiction of how Bruce discovered or commissioned the tools that Batman uses. Neither his body nor his various tools simply appear, ready to be used. The film emphasizes again and again that everything has been specifically produced through ordinary means of production, even when the result is somewhat extraordinary (like the Batmobile). In this way, Nolan remains true to the idiosyncratic status of Batman among superheroes and at the same time creates a film that highlights the structural importance of the fiction in the establishment of heroism.

By emphasizing that Batman is just an ordinary person who has thrust himself into the position of the superhero, Nolan illustrates the fictional status of the superhero: the only thing that separates the ordinary person from the superhero is the fiction that the superhero adopts in the act of becoming a superhero. Relegating the superhero to a fiction does not denigrate the superhero but rather allows ordinary people to recognize their own capacity for being heroic. *Batman Begins* thus functions as a plea for everyone to take up a fiction in the way that Bruce Wayne does. It shows the radical otherness of the superhero as attainable and in doing so puts the burden of the superhero on everyone watching the film.

Batman Begins leaves Batman within the ordinary even when he becomes a superhero. The film thus presents heroism as a path available to all if they could embrace a fiction—not necessarily that of a superhero, of course—that would free them from their situation. As Jacques Lacan notes in his discussion of Antigone's heroism, "In each of us the path of the hero is traced, and it is precisely as an ordinary man that one follows it to the end."[5] Nolan displays this idea through his depiction of Batman, a character who remains ordinary and yet follows the "path of the hero" to the end.

Batman Begins opens with a scene that stresses Batman's ordinariness: a young Bruce Wayne (Gus Lewis) is playing with a young Rachel Dawes (Emma Lockhart) in the gardens outside his house. After Bruce falls into a hole during their game, the film reveals that this has been a dream sequence, as he wakes up in his twenties in a Chinese prison, where he singlehandedly defeats a group of seven men attacking him. A man who introduces himself as Henri Ducard (Liam Neeson) retrieves Bruce from the prison and trains him to be a leader in the League of Shadows, a vigilante organization led by Ra's Al Ghul (Ken Watanabe). When Bruce learns that the organization will try to destroy his hometown of Gotham, he sets fire to the mountaintop fortress, which kills Ra's Al Ghul, and flees back to the United States, where he takes up the alter identity of Batman to fight crime in Gotham. The conclusion of the film reveals that Ra's Al Ghul did not perish in the fire, but that he is actually the man who claimed to be Henri Ducard. A final showdown with Ra's results when he attempts to release a drug that produces psychosis in the Gotham air in order to eliminate the criminality and corruption that has overrun the city.

Batman's ultimate struggle in the film is against other vigilante figures who believe that they are seeking justice. The film's depiction of Ra's and his need to purify society shows the danger of one who privileges truth over the lie. Ra's wants the purity of truth, and he will destroy all of Gotham to attain that purity. But he is not above using deception against Bruce (appearing as Henri Ducard) in order to advance his plan. When truth or purity functions as the final cause, it always serves to justify a multitude of lies and impurities.[6] The great danger is not so much the criminal as it is the hero who would fill in the gap in the social order because doing so coincides with destroying that order in the attempt to save it.[7]

The superhero occupies a distinct place in the public's psyche. Superheroes are never traditional authority figures but instead reside in the gap in the social order that traditional authority necessarily leaves vacant. That is, they occupy the space of fantasy. Inhabiting the gap in the social order, superheroes are fantasmatic figures without parallel. The fantasy of Superman allows us, for instance, to imagine a complement to the traditional authority of the police, one who is able to make up for all the deficiencies of this traditional authority. He can respond more quickly to crises, he can confront threats that exceed normal human powers, and he can avoid the danger of corruption. Superman doesn't fall victim to any of the problems or limitations that ensnare traditional authority. Batman works in the same way. When a case is too difficult for Gotham Police Lieutenant James Gordon to solve, he illuminates the Bat-Signal in order receive help from the law's complementary figure. Through recourse to such a fantasy, any blank space or gap in the social order disappears.

The danger of the superhero fantasy, like all fantasies, is that it will promulgate belief in a non-lacking social order, one without a gap—or that someone or something exists to fill that gap. At the same time, however, the fantasy has the capacity to highlight the existence of this gap by showing the superhero occupying it. The superhero embodies the split political valence of fantasy—its conservative tendency to hide the lack in the social order and its radical tendency to expose this failure. Fantasy functions conservatively when it allows the subject to distance itself from the fantasy object and to experience this object as wholly Other. This occurs in the case of Superman, a figure whose near perfection contrasts with the subject's own lack. But fantasy functions radically when it forces the subject to see itself in the fantasy object, to identify with this object.[8] Through this identification, the subject recognizes itself in the gap of the social order, not some omnipotent figure of otherness.

Most of the time, however, we posit an omnipotent figure of otherness in this gap. That is to say, fantasy often functions conservatively. Whenever we encounter contradictions or failures of meaning within the social order, we believe that some hidden authority can resolve the problem. Whether it is God, experts, the laws of the market, or an imaginary superhero, a force can heal all social fractures and preserve the idea of a fully meaningful order. By positing the gap in the social order as remediable, subjects implicitly accept this order as it is given.

The key to the politicization of the subject—and to all subjectivity—lies in the readiness of the subject to assume the gap within the social order, to see itself in the form of this gap. It is only in this way that the subject transcends the order that founds it. As Joan Copjec points out in *Read My Desire*, "It is not the law, but the fault in the law—the desire that the law cannot ultimately conceal—that is assumed by the subject as its own. The subject, in taking up the burden of the law's guilt, goes beyond the law."[9] What Copjec calls "the fault in the law" is the law's inability to authorize itself, its ungrounded status, which functions as the law's unsurpassable limit. Most superhero films work to distance the spectator from the superhero and thereby distance the subject from the fault in the law. The superhero fills the gap as a figure of hyperbolic otherness. Even Batman serves this function in the films from the 1980s and 1990s. In contrast, through the depiction of Batman in *Batman Begins*, Christopher Nolan attempts to place the spectator in this latter position, one in which the subject resides with Batman in the gap of the social order.

The film also presents a heroic alternative to Batman in the form of his father, Thomas Wayne (Linus Roache). Though Thomas dies early in the film, his stature as an ethical being serves as a constant reference point for Bruce and others. When Bruce appears to stray from an ethical path, Alfred (Michael Caine) reminds him of the importance of his father's legacy; when the chief of Wayne Enterprises invests the corporation in the manufacture of weapons, this is seen as a violation of Thomas Wayne's intentions for the company. Thomas Wayne stands for integrity and compassion. He is the ultimate embodiment of enlightened authority or liberal humanism in the film. Unlike Bruce, who puts on a mask and decides to operate in the gap that authority leaves, Thomas denies the constitutive nature of this gap and works to fill it.[10] He believes that his inventiveness and money can produce social harmony and thereby eliminate all social antagonism. As Thomas Wayne and enlightened authority in general views it, progress leads society toward the good—a social order without gaps.

In contrast to the superhero, enlightened authority doesn't have to present itself in the guise of a fiction or a fantasy. Instead, it bases itself on the truth of its position and on the force of its scientific knowledge of the world. Enlightened authority's link to truth allows it to avoid all disguises.[11] It solves difficulties by dissolving the misconceptions that form their basis or by acting decisively, as Thomas does whenever he appears in the film. We first see him during a flashback that occurs during Bruce's training with the League of Shadows as Henri asks Bruce what he fears. The film returns to the opening sequence, where Bruce has fallen in a deep hole. Almost instantly, we see a shot of hundreds of bats rapidly flying past Bruce as he lies in the hole. But in a subsequent shot from the hole, looking upward to the light, the film depicts Bruce's father climbing down with a rope in order to rescue him. Thomas pulls Bruce out of the hole and carries him into his bedroom, telling Alfred along the way that he would personally set the bone so that no trip to the hospital would be necessary.

The way that Nolan shoots the rescue makes clear that Thomas functions as an enlightened authority that inserts itself in the holes of the social fabric. Thomas climbs down out of the light into the hole, and while doing so, he fills the hole visually. When he finally arrives at the bottom of the hole, he emerges out of the darkness to comfort Bruce, and Nolan lights his face in order to emphasize what Thomas represents. Thomas not only heroically rescues his son and fixes his injury, but he also displays a perfect equanimity at all times, even in extreme situations. This equanimity stems from his knowledge of the truth, which he evinces the day after Bruce's fall. When Bruce awakens from a nightmare, Thomas comes to comfort him. He says, "The bats again? You know why they attacked you, don't you? They were afraid of you. . . . All creatures feel fear." Bruce asks, "Even the scary ones?" Thomas responds, "Especially the scary ones." Through this dialogue, Thomas Wayne paints a reasonable world for his son, one in which scary creatures themselves feel fear and in which our knowledge about fear allows us to overcome it. Nothing throws the world of Thomas Wayne off balance in a way that he cannot fix, either with his knowledge or with his wealth or with his surgical skill.

The sequence shows perfectly the abject failure of enlightened authority when it comes to dealing with trauma. Rather than addressing the trauma as such and allowing it to remain a trauma (albeit one that Bruce could come to relate to), Thomas quickly tries to eliminate the trauma with knowledge: the bats are not a genuine threat but attack only out of fear. As enlightened authority conceives it, there is no real evil that we must confront, only a series of misplaced fears and a general lack of knowledge.[12]

Throughout the flashback to Bruce's childhood from the League of Shadows mountaintop training center, Thomas Wayne reveals himself to be the perfect figure of enlightened authority. When he first appears, he rescues Bruce; then as Bruce is recovering he calms Bruce's fears about the bats; then he describes building a public transportation system to help those less fortunate in the city; and finally, even as he and his wife are dying from a thief's bullets, he assures Bruce that there is nothing to fear. Thomas can provide constant reassurance because he does not acknowledge any constitutive gap within the social order. With the proper enlightenment, Thomas believes, authority can account for every gap.

To this end, Thomas's new public transportation system can revitalize the Gotham downtown and rescue the city from the economic downturn, which is the source of the rampant criminality. As they are riding on the train, Bruce asks, "Did you build this train, Dad?" Thomas explains, "Gotham's been good to our family. But the city's been suffering. People less fortunate than us have been enduring very hard times. So we built a new, cheap public transportation system to unite the city, and at the center, Wayne Tower." Thomas views the public transportation system not only as a way to accomplish good ends with his wealth, but also as a path to unity. With cheap public transportation, all the space of Gotham will be included. The train is part of a vision of social harmony achieved through progress.

In an otherwise dark film, this scene on the train is brightly lit throughout. After the conversation, Nolan includes an outside shot of the train as it passes through downtown. The sun reflects off the windows of the skyscrapers that surround the train. The luminous shot seems to be an effect of Thomas Wayne's power to realize his enlightened authority. Though he doesn't create the sun, he does help to refashion the city so that the sun will shine everywhere. He aims to produce a city without fissures and without darkness. Every problem, for Thomas Wayne, has a clear cause and a clear solution. With the proper knowledge, we can solve these problems. Thomas describes to Bruce a world that makes sense, where a sufficient reason informs everything that occurs. Thomas protects Bruce (and the entire city) through his knowledge and the truth that he accesses.

But the protection that Thomas offers fails in the last instance. Though his enlightened benevolence helps to bring the city out of its economic downturn, it cannot stop a subsequent slide into criminality once he is no longer present. This is because his understanding of the world as one of sufficient reason fails to account for the appeal of criminality. One doesn't always turn to crime out of economic necessity but sometimes, perhaps most often, for the enjoyment that crime provides. There is an excess in crime, even in the crime of necessity, that defies all attempts to explain it in terms of a strict calculus of reasons, and this is what Thomas Wayne's enlightened view of the world cannot understand or account for.[13]

Thomas Wayne makes exactly the same mistake that Enlightenment thinkers make in Hegel's account of the struggle between Enlightenment and religious faith. The Enlightenment reduces all actions to a calculus of ends, which means it cannot understand the senseless sacrifices demanded and made by faith. Nor can the Enlightenment understand the appeal of criminality, which, like faith, enjoins us to sacrifice without a calculated goal.[14] Thomas would never imagine the need for Batman because his world has no place for criminals who simply enjoy their criminality.

In fact, Thomas's view of the world cannot even account for himself. Though he eases Bruce's fears by explaining the truth to him, his power of protection finally depends on a deception, which becomes clear on the night he dies. While attending the opera with his parents, Bruce becomes troubled by certain scenes that remind him of the bats, prompting him to ask his father to leave during the performance. Once outside, Bruce's mother (Sara Stewart) asks why he wanted to leave, and when

Bruce hesitates, his father lies in order to take responsibility for their departure, saying that he needed some air. As he says this, we see him wink at Bruce, confirming the deceit and the agreement to hide the truth from his mother. Thomas's gesture here is one of kindness: he saves Bruce from the humiliation of admitting his fear to his mother. But at the same time, it reveals that his ability to protect Bruce relies on his capacity for generating a convincing fiction, not on the truth.

Of course, what Thomas tells Bruce about bats, in contrast to what he tells Martha about the opera, is true. He certainly does not always rely on deception. But this scene—the only time he lies in the film—reveals his willingness to resort to deception for the sake of protection and thereby exposes what Thomas actually values. Protecting Bruce (or the city of Gotham) is more important to him than the truth, despite his enlightened position. Truth telling is important for Thomas not in itself but insofar as it serves to provide reassurance or protection. Thomas's own enjoyment is wrapped up in being a figure of reassuring authority, but he is blind to this, just as he is blind to the enjoyment of criminality. By showing this deception occurring just before his death, the film underlines the inadequacy of enlightened authority and its explanation of the world.

In contrast to the truth telling of his father, Bruce, through the figure of Batman, will turn to fiction in order to fight criminality. As Nolan's film makes clear, Bruce recognizes the limitations of truth and of sufficient reason, which is why he decides to don a mask. The mask allows him to occupy a position of excess from which to fight the excess in crime. As Batman, Bruce avows his own enjoyment in a way that his father never did, and he also avows the necessity of the constitutive gap within the social order. Batman resides in that gap, testifying to its persistence rather than filling it.

THE FICTIONAL SUPERHERO

Through its depiction of Batman and his struggle against injustice, *Batman Begins* directly criticizes the enlightened liberalism of Thomas Wayne. Batman's effectiveness stems from his ability to marry the ideals of his father with the necessity for deception that he learns from Ra's Al Ghul. Ra's teaches Bruce that the fight against injustice requires excess, and he trains Bruce to become an excessive figure in order to lead this combat. Excess takes the form of deception and trickery. As Ra's points

94

out the fecklessness of Thomas Wayne and his insistence on truth, he offers Bruce a different path that privileges deception as the most important weapon. Unlike truth, deception motivates change.

Through the figure of Ra's, the film demonstrates that the truth of deception or fiction lies in its power to change the world. When Ra's (disguised as Henri Ducard) first confronts Bruce in the Chinese prison and offers him entrance into the League of Shadows, he invites Bruce to transform himself into a fictional entity. He tells him, "If you make yourself more than just a man, if you devote yourself to an ideal, and if they can't stop you, then you become something else entirely." Bruce asks, "Which is?" And Ra's responds, "A legend, Mr. Wayne." As he says this, through an effect of side lighting, we see half of his face almost completely darkened. This image underlines the importance of the fiction that Ra's articulates. Rather than seeing Ra's completely lit, Nolan shows him with half of his face darkened to reveal the role of disguise and deception in the part that Bruce must play. By attaining fictional status and becoming a legend, one achieves the capacity to effect revolutionary change.

Later, even as Bruce has burned down the League of Shadows training center and rejected its political program, he nonetheless decides to transform himself into a legend just as Ra's had suggested. On the plane flying back to Gotham, he describes his plan to Alfred. He says, "People need dramatic examples to shake them out of apathy, and I can't do that as Bruce Wayne. As a man, I'm flesh and blood, I can be ignored, I can be destroyed. As a symbol, I can be incorruptible, I can be everlasting." Ra's foresees that Bruce must become a legend, and Bruce decides, after rejecting Ra's, to make himself into a symbol. The film presents this turn toward adopting a fiction as necessary because, as both Ra's and Bruce emphasize, a fiction—either a "legend" or a "symbol"—has a transformative power that an ordinary human being lacks. A fiction has the capacity to mobilize people through the image of sublimity that ordinariness cannot approach. The image of the transcendent attracts and even comes to embody our form of enjoyment. We enjoy through the sublime figure, not through the ordinary human being, which is why the sublime figure can lead us toward a radical transformation.

By dedicating himself to becoming a symbol, Bruce heeds the advice that Ra's gives him. But he nonetheless rejects the political position embodied by the League of Shadows. During the training, there is no clear statement of this position, but when Bruce's training ends, Ra's presents him with a final test and a description of their first act, both of which prompt Bruce's recoil and illuminate the gulf that separates the political philosophies of Bruce and the League of Shadows. As Ra's informs Bruce of the plan to destroy Gotham, he tells him that he must execute a local murderer that they have apprehended in order to prove his "commitment to justice." Bruce rejects the idea that his hometown is so corrupt that it must be destroyed, and he refuses categorically to play the part of an executioner. At this point, the film, through Bruce's refusal to act, affirms the liberalism of Thomas Wayne. When Bruce says that he wants the man tried in a court and that he wants time to reform Gotham, he sounds very much like his father. But his reasons for rejecting the politics of the League of Shadows are not his father's, and it later becomes clear that it is actually the League of Shadows that is closer to the political philosophy of Thomas Wayne, not Bruce.

The film presents two seemingly dissimilar political acts—the execution of the murderer and the destruction of Gotham—at the same time, which has the effect of linking them philosophically. At the end of Bruce's training, the false Ra's Al Ghul explains why Bruce must execute the murderer, and in the process, he reveals the mission to destroy Gotham. The false Ra's says to Bruce, "You cannot lead these men unless you are prepared to do what is necessary to defeat evil." Bruce asks, "And where would I be leading these men?" Ra's answers, "Gotham. As Gotham's favored son you will be ideally placed to strike at the heart of criminality. . . . Gotham's time has come. Like Constantinople or Rome before it, the city has become a breeding ground for suffering and injustice. It is beyond saving and must be allowed to die. . . . Gotham must be destroyed." After the false Ra's says this, Bruce reiterates his refusal to become an executioner, but Henri (the actual Ra's) makes clear that there is no choice as he holds a sword out for Bruce to use. Nolan here melds the command to execute the criminal with the injunction to destroy Gotham. When Bruce burns down the training center, it isn't entirely clear whether he is doing so in response to the demand that he execute the murderer or in order to thwart the plan to destroy Gotham. But to reject one is to reject the other insofar as both actions stem from the same political philosophy, and the film depicts Bruce rejecting this philosophy more than either action.

For Bruce (and for the film), the fight against injustice does not seek to restore an earlier state of justice or harmonious balance. Whatever justice we achieve must be forged out of and through injustice, which is always the necessary starting point for struggle. The problem with Ra's and the League of Shadows, as the film makes evident, is related to the problem with Thomas Wayne's enlightened liberalism. Like Thomas, Ra's believes that a true harmonious order is possible and that our activity can restore this order that once existed. Though Thomas and Ra's disagree about the means, they share the same goal. The same is not true for Batman, for whom ethical being resides in the effort to create justice out of injustice, to foment a revolutionary change. His focus is not on the type of society this change will produce—the film never mentions a vision of a better future—but on the struggle that works to inaugurate it. The means of this struggle become, in the film's conception, an ethical end in itself.[15]

Though Bruce refuses to take up a position of leadership in the League of Shadows and he rejects the teaching of Ra's, he does embrace the organization's emphasis on the necessity of adopting a fiction, except he takes the fiction much further than the league itself does. This attests to the philosophical difference between Bruce and the League of Shadows, and to the difference between Bruce and his father. The difference manifests itself most plainly when Ra's arrives in Gotham and confronts Batman for the first time. After Ra's burns Wayne Manor and leaves Bruce for dead, he begins the operation of destroying Gotham. While he is loading the vaporizing weapon onto the train, Batman interrupts him. Nolan films this scene by first registering the shock of Batman's appearance on the face of Ra's. As he hears the screams of people increase in volume, he turns around, and in a close-up we see his face indicate that what he sees defies his expectations. The subsequent reverse shot shows Batman swooping down and landing on the platform. The first words that Ra's speaks to Batman suggest the philosophical difference between them. He says, "Well, well, you took my advice about theatricality a bit . . . literally." For Ra's, theatricality and deception function as a means that one must use to restore order when a situation has become too excessive. From this perspective, Batman is too theatrical, too involved in the deception that he creates. Ethical activity must resort to deception, but its final goal is always the restoration of truth and order. One must not get carried away with the fiction.

For Bruce, in contrast, ethical activity lies in the excess of the fiction itself. As Ra's knows, this ethical excess is necessary for confronting the excess embodied in criminality. One must adopt a fictional deception in order to conquer the many ruses and corruptions of criminals. But Bruce takes it further than Ra's, treating the fiction as an end in itself. Of course, Batman exists in order to fight crime and injustice, but the excessiveness of the fiction allows Batman to become a sublime figure

97

around which people can unite to change their world. He represents a mobilizing fiction, and the film shows that it is by taking up such fictions that we can attain an ethical position beyond that of Thomas Wayne's enlightened liberalism or the league's revolutionary purity.[16] This ethical position is not habitable only by Batman but can be adopted by all those who invest themselves in a transformative fiction.

THE PRODUCTION OF BATMAN

What separates Christopher Nolan's version of Batman from the one incarnated in Tim Burton's 1989 film *Batman*—and from almost every other superhero film—is the attention that Nolan's film pays to constructing a realistic origin for all of Batman's abilities and devices.[17] Nolan retains most of Batman's primary fantastic devices from the comic books—his Batmobile, his Batcave, his masked helmet—but he provides reasonable explanations for all of them. The Batmobile is a prototype developed for the army by Wayne Enterprises; the Batcave is a secret area under Wayne Manor used for the Underground Railroad; and Bruce designs the helmet himself and purchases it via mail order. Nolan even adds new fantasmatic touches to the comic book character: Batman can now glide through the air thanks to a cape that stiffens with an electric charge, and he wears a Kevlar vest that protects him from bullets. We see how he obtains both of these devices from Lucius Fox (Morgan Freeman), who helped to develop them for the military on behalf of Wayne Enterprises. The film spends a great deal of its running time providing this type of explanation. At every point where the film depicts Batman having a superpower or outrageous capacity, it shows how he acquired it, which has the effect of demythologizing Batman and his powers.

Not only does *Batman Begins* show the realistic origin of all Batman's seemingly magical equipment, it also spends much time detailing the intense training that he has with the League of Shadows that prepares him to become Batman. Throughout the beginning of the film, we see sequences of Bruce training with a group of ninjas, learning to swordfight with Ra's, and learning to face his greatest fears with the aid of a hallucinogen. The lengthy first part of the film before Bruce becomes Batman works to normalize all of Batman's actions in the second part of the film. When he takes on eight villains at once and overcomes all of them, we understand where this capacity originates.

Typically, showing the construction of a figure of power has the effect

98

of subverting that power. This is the case with Michel Foucault's archaeology of medicine, for instance. By showing the origin of the doctor's social authority, Foucault could undermine its givenness and thereby challenge its legitimacy. The investigation of the origin of the doctor's authority in *The Birth of the Clinic* allows him to equate the rational authority of the doctor with the irrational authority of the priest, an equation that becomes convincing only in light of this investigation and calls into question the doctor's social authority.[18] One might imagine that Christopher Nolan performs a similar operation in *Batman Begins*: revealing the superhero as a construction in order to thwart the fantasmatic power that this figure has over us.

If this is the idea behind the film, however, one must count it as one of the most colossal failures of all time. Most of the millions of spectators who saw Nolan's film came away even more convinced of the sublimity of the superhero, despite the realism in Batman's depiction. In fact, the film and its response appears to offer proof of Slavoj Žižek's anti-constructivist claim that revealing the origins of authority figures has the effect of augmenting their authority rather than subverting it. A more human Batman is, ironically, a more unassailable Batman.[19] When we continue to experience his sublimity, it becomes all the more mysterious when we know its mundane origins.[20] The difference persists, and yet the constructivist has taken away any possible explanation for it. Rather than undermining the power of authority, constructivism serves to augment it.

But Nolan's film does not depict the construction of Batman in order to liberate us from the illusion of his power, so it does not fail at this task. Instead, it shows the realistic origin of his powers and his devices in order to make clear the ordinary subject's proximity to him, not his proximity to the ordinary subject. Whereas most constructivist texts aim at lessening the sublime effect of an authority figure, *Batman Begins* tries to multiply the sublimity by extending it to ordinary subjects. The point of its constructivism is not to demythologize Batman but to allow others to mythologize themselves. The film proclaims that the path of the fiction is open to anyone.

WHY CHRISTOPHER NOLAN IS NOT LUDWIG WITTGENSTEIN

The barrier between the superhero and the ordinary person is sustained by the idea that there is something essential about the superhero that

99

the ordinary person doesn't have. *Batman Begins* thoroughly rejects this idea. There is no essential core of the superhero that separates him or her from everyone else. The heroic decision that Bruce Wayne makes is, as the film shows, a decision open to everyone. This is because, as the film conceives it, the truth of a subject does not reside hidden within that subject but is constantly being expressed through the subject's acts—and any subject can act like Batman. Thus, in order to become a superhero, one need only act like one.

The film advances this idea through Rachel's interaction with Bruce when he returns to Gotham. Initially, she is disappointed in him. When she sees Bruce outside a hotel acting the part of a millionaire playboy while the city is falling apart, she chides him, and he responds haltingly, "All this, it's not me. Inside, I am, I am more." After Bruce says this, in the background we hear the two women whom he came with yelling for him to come join them. Seeing the kind of life that Bruce is leading, Rachel rejects his logic, telling him, "Bruce, deep down you may still be that same great kid you used to be. But it's not who you are underneath, it's what you do that defines you." When she says this, she turns her back on Bruce and walks into the hotel. The film cuts from the shot of her walking away to a close-up of a disturbed look on Bruce's face. Her statement stings him because, though Rachel doesn't properly see him, he can only make this clear through action.

Rachel's statement comes to serve as something like the film's mantra when Bruce, as Batman, later repeats the sentiment back to her. After the initial release of the gas, a group of drugged people prepare to attack Rachel and a young boy she is protecting. Batman swoops down and lifts them onto a roof and out of danger. Just before he leaves to stop Ra's from releasing more of the gas, Rachel says, "You could die. At least tell me your name." Rather than answering, he reformulates what she had earlier said to him: "It's not who I am underneath, but what I do that defines me." As Batman says this, he is kneeling on the ledge of the roof, ready to glide away, and the film cuts to a reverse shot of Rachel registering recognition and saying, "Bruce?" The irony of this statement is that Batman declares the unimportance of who he is under the mask in order to tell Rachel who he is under the mask.

The film's effort to emphasize doing instead of being follows in the path of the major movements of twentieth-century thought. Two of the most important strains of philosophy in the twentieth century worked to relocate truth in what we do rather than in some hidden domain of meaning. Though Jean-Paul Sartre and Ludwig Wittgenstein did not agree about much, they did share an investment in this realignment of the position of truth. For Sartrean existentialism, there is no truth of the subject outside what it does, which leads Sartre to contend, "The act is everything."[21] Through our actions, we constitute our being, which is why Sartre sees the subject as unavoidably free. We define ourselves not by what nature or culture has given us but by how we act in the face of that givenness. Our acts bespeak our truth.

The act, as Sartre sees it, enables us to transcend our being and become what we aren't, which is, paradoxically, the truth of our being. As long as we remain in the private world of contemplation, in contrast, who we are defines us because we have no opportunity to break from it. Though there are numerous social and natural barriers to the free act, the act always has the possibility of transcending these barriers and thereby asserting the subject's freedom. Even in the most tightly controlled situation, there are possibilities for the transcendent act. In Sartre's description of the subject in *Search for a Method*, he notes, "Man defines himself by his project. This material being perpetually goes beyond the condition which is made for him; he reveals and determines his situation by transcending it in order to objectify himself—by work, action, or gesture."[22] The act accesses the truth of the subject by allowing the subject to transcend the situation that hitherto defines it.

From the opposite side of the philosophical spectrum, Wittgenstein places truth not outside language but in our particular utterances within language. For Wittgenstein's philosophy of language, there is no deep truth of what we say outside the particular act of saying it. As he puts it, "The meaning of a phrase is for us characterized by the use we make of it. The meaning is not a mental accompaniment to the expression."[23] Consequently, if we want to understand an idea or a word, we need only pay attention to how that idea or word is used. The use, as Wittgenstein sees it, is the definition.

Though Sartre and Wittgenstein transform the understanding of truth in the direction of an act, the former advances an idea of transcendence that the latter would reject. Because truth exists in use or action, there is no transcendence for Wittgenstein, whereas for Sartre every use goes beyond—transcends—the prescriptions for use laid out by the situation. Nonetheless, what is important about these two approaches is that they preserve an idea of truth while dissociating it from an immutable essence. Nolan's film follows in this tradition.

But it also departs from it. Though *Batman Begins* places an emphasis on what one does rather than what one is in the manner of Sartre or Wittgenstein, it breaks from both lines of thought in its equation of the act with a fiction. When Bruce acts, he always does so in the guise of Batman, and it is this fiction that allows him to act. The fictionality of the act allows the subject to act beyond itself—not just to affirm its truth but also to go beyond itself. Contra Sartre, the subject's act can lead to transcendence only if is rooted in a fiction. *Batman Begins* links transcendence to the lie inherent in Batman's mask. The lie enables one to accomplish what one is not otherwise able to accomplish with the truth. The lie breaks from the givens of the situation and introduces heretofore unthought-of possibilities.[24] The fiction is the truth of the subject that exists outside itself.

This becomes clear in the film's penultimate scene, where Rachel re-affirms the idea that the fiction that Bruce has adopted articulates his true self. We see Bruce at the ruins of what was Wayne Manor, where he is boarding up the hole where he fell as a boy. While he is hammering in the foreground, we see Rachel emerge out of focus in the background. She walks toward Bruce, and they kiss. Then she points out to him that his fictional identity as Batman is in fact his true identity. After Bruce dismisses the mask as "just as symbol," she touches his face and says, "No, this is your mask. Your real face is the one criminals now fear. The man I loved, the man who vanished, he never came back at all. But maybe he's still out there somewhere. Maybe someday when Gotham no longer needs Batman, I'll see him again." Rachel's complex statement offers key insight into the central idea of the film. She identifies Bruce's "real face" as that of Batman, but she also notes that this fiction has allowed Bruce to become more than he was. The sublime fiction of Batman is the truth of Bruce Wayne, but it is a truth irreducible to him as a subject.

What *Batman Begins* reveals is that the distortion of the fiction creates a truth that doesn't exist prior to the fiction. When one invests oneself in a fiction, one becomes something other than what one was. The fiction has the power to transform not only those who encounter it but also the one who perpetuates it. By emphasizing the fictionality of Batman's fiction, Nolan's film renders Batman's position accessible for the spectator. The ethical challenge that the film lays down is that of being adequate to our own fictions.

102

It was possible that the success of *Batman Begins* (2005) might have divorced Christopher Nolan completely from his origins in independent cinema. The critical acclaim and $370 million worldwide gross for the film might have set him down the road of sequels and other superhero films. But before his popular sequel to *Batman Begins*, Nolan returned to a smaller-scale project. While it is true that his follow-up film, *The Prestige* (2006), used major stars and had adequate financing, it is also the case that Nolan here returned to the look and feel of his films before *Insomnia* (2002). Though Nolan shot the film in color, it had a washed-out look appropriate to its depiction of working-class London at the end of the nineteenth century. But it was not just the look that was different. Nolan created a film that lacked the flash of the films he made just before and after it. *The Prestige* benefited from wide distribution and was the top earner on its opening weekend, but it would make less than a third of the money that *Batman Begins* brought in.

Regardless of its commercial success or where one might classify it among Nolan's films, I contend that *The Prestige* is the central Nolan film, the film that makes evident the ontological priority of the fiction—and the ramifications of this priority—in the starkest terms. Even though other films like *Following* (1998) or *Memento* (2000) might go further toward duping the spectator, none of them highlights the creative power of the fiction in the way that *The Prestige* does. In this film, we see that even though fictions create misunderstanding and violent conflict, without them there is nothing but brute and insignificant materiality. The celebration of the magician that occurs in the film is also a celebration of the artwork as such. Thanks to the magic of art and the fiction it produces, we have something rather than nothing.

As in Nolan's earlier films *Following* and *Memento*, time does not follow a linear chronology in *The Prestige*. Here, however, in contrast to *Memento*, the reason for this narrative structure is not immediately evident. Set in turn of the century London, the film recounts the story of two rival magicians—Alfred Borden (Christian Bale) and Robert Angier

THE VIOLENCE OF CREATION
IN *THE PRESTIGE*

(Hugh Jackman)—who seek each other's secrets and punish each other in what becomes an increasingly vicious feud that results in multiple deaths and much unnecessary suffering. Due to their simultaneous determination to be the better magician and to destroy the other, they each lose their wives to tragic deaths and finally die themselves as a direct result of their rivalry. One could easily imagine this story told in a straightforward fashion without significantly altering the experience of it. The film would begin with the young magicians meeting each other and recount their acts of vengeance successively, rather than beginning with Borden's apparent murder of Angier and concluding with the actual thing. As it stands, the spectator can, without too much trouble, figure out the story from the complex but not indecipherable filmic discourse, which leads one to believe that the nonlinear narrative exists simply for the sake of the gimmick itself. But the linear account of the story would have the effect of eliminating a major contribution to our understanding of creation that the film makes.

According to the logic set forth by *The Prestige*, the idea of time as linear forward motion is the effect of an illusion—or of illusion as such—and it serves to disguise the role that sacrifice or work plays in the process of creation. A genuinely new creation is possible, but the source of this creation is not, as we tend to think, the forward motion of time. Instead, *The Prestige* makes clear that the source of the new is the repetition of sacrifice. Rather than lifting us beyond sacrifice and loss, the genuinely new creation always has the ultimate effect of returning us to the experience of loss. As the film shows, the new exists as a means for finding our way back to the inevitability of loss. The connection between the newness born from artistic creation and the sacrifice that makes that newness possible is most often obscured in the work of art and especially in the cinema. The end product serves as a fetish allowing spectators to disavow loss and to experience a false sense of wholeness. The burden of *The Prestige* lies in exposing it, but this exposure is possible only through a fiction.[1]

Borden and Angier represent the two sides of the magician (and the artist in general). Borden's skill lies in creating the illusion—the magic act itself—and he relishes the life of sacrifice necessary to produce the illusion. Angier, on the other hand, is the showman who knows how to sell a trick to the audience. In contrast to Borden, he cherishes the audience's reaction to the illusion because he sees in this reaction the awareness that something transcendent has occurred, that the illusion has generated an experience of the genuinely new. At one point in the film, Angier considers the audience's lukewarm reception to Borden's "Transported Man" illusion and exclaims, "He's a dreadful magician." His mentor, Cutter (Michael Caine), corrects him, "No, he's a wonderful magician. He's a dreadful showman. He doesn't know how to dress it up, how to sell the trick." The relationship that develops between Borden and Angier is not the typical rivalry. It does not involve two competitors seeking the same object but instead two fundamentally different modes of conceiving magic.[2] Borden sees Angier's emphasis on spectacle as a betrayal of the art and as a refusal to embrace the sacrifice that the art demands. Angier, as Borden sees it, wants the spectacle without the cost. For his part, Angier views Borden's failure to sell his illusions as an inability to appreciate the creative power of their art. Borden doesn't understand the transcendence that occurs when the magician compels the audience to believe the fiction.

The film makes apparent the limitations inhering in both Borden's and Angier's position. In the case of Borden, we see both the direct suffering and the collateral damage that his devotion to artistic sacrifice engenders. The primary illusion of the film itself lies in the nature of Borden's identity, which represents the sacrifice of an individual existence. Borden is not one person but two, a pair of identical twins who alternate being Borden and his mysterious silent friend, Fallon. The twins sacrifice their lives as separate individuals just to perform a single magic trick—the Transported Man. Borden can appear to vanish on one side of the stage and reappear immediately on the other because he is not one person but two. This is a magic act that no one can easily duplicate because it requires a lifetime of sacrificing independent public identities—and an accident of birth. While it results in an effective and convincing illusion, the arrangement has a steep personal cost. Borden must share the experience of being a husband to his wife, Sarah (Rebecca Hall), a father to his daughter, Jess (Samantha Mahurin), and a lover to his assistant, Olivia Wenscombe (Scarlett Johansson). After Angier shoots off two fingers of one of the twins during a bullet-catch illusion, the other twin must submit to having his fingers cut off in order to sustain their identical look. The original sacrifice of separate lives for the sake of the Transported Man trick does not suffice, as the illusion continues to demand increasingly costly payments.

Others pay the price for Borden's sacrifice as well. Near the beginning of the film, Angier's wife, Julia McCullough (Piper Perabo), drowns during the Submerged Woman illusion, apparently because Borden insisted on tying a more complex knot (the Langford Double) that she could not slip while underwater. He values the art of slipping the more difficult knot more than he values McCullough's safety. Later, Borden's own wife kills herself out of the desperation that comes from unknowingly living with two men playing the part of one. Borden's necessarily divided personality renders any sustained relationship with him impossible.

It is not, however, the cost of Borden's devotion to sacrifice with which the film takes issue. Nolan suggests that such sacrifice is necessary for art and that art is worth the steep personal cost that it demands. The real limitation of Borden's position stems from his blindness to what his sacrifice enables. He is so intently focused on the act of sacrifice that he misses the transcendent experience that the magic act creates. He fails to link loss to productivity. His perverse attachment to sacrifice for its own sake limits his capacity for authentic art. He can't see the way that the repetition of sacrifice in art miraculously produces the new.[3]

Borden's inability to recognize the creative power inherent in the magic trick's deception—and in the deception perpetuated by all art—reveals itself initially in the diary that he constructs in order to deceive Angier. To revenge himself on Angier, Borden convinces the latter that he found the secret of the Transported Man illusion in the United States, where Nikola Tesla (David Bowie) invented a teleportation machine for him. The deception in the diary convinces Angier to travel to Colorado to see Tesla and to pay him to build a similar machine for him. When he finally reads to the end of the coded diary, he discovers the lie, but Tesla nonetheless does invent a teleportation machine for Angier, even though he had never made one for Borden. Borden's fiction, the artistic deception of the diary, leads to the miracle of teleportation. The lie is a productive one. But Borden himself could never have anticipated this because his concern remains single mindedly focused on the act of sacrifice as an end in itself.

As Angier is dying at the end of the film, the surviving Borden twin upbraids him for having done "terrible things . . . all for nothing." Angier responds by rebuking Borden for his great failure to understand. In what are the most important lines of the film, he says to his rival, "You never understood why we did this. The audience knows the truth. The world is simple, miserable, solid all the way through. But if you can fool them, even for a second, then you can make them wonder. Then you got to see something very special. You really don't know. It was the look on their faces."[4] Angier recognizes that there are no naturally occurring miracles, that there is no transcendence in the given world. The world is banal and mundane; it offers us nothing to believe in. But the work of art introduces a cut into this mundane world and suggests that something exists beyond it. Through the deception that they create, magic and art break through the solidity of the world and allow audiences to see a fissure where none naturally exists. Without the lie, without the magician's conjuring trick, we would remain stuck in the monotony of being.

Here, Angier sounds somewhat like Alain Badiou contrasting the mundane situation with the significance of the event. According to Badiou, "The event extracts from one time the possibility of another time. This other time, whose materiality envelops the consequences of the event, deserves the name of new present. The event is neither past nor future. It presents us with the present."[5] As Angier (and Nolan) conceive it, this is precisely what the deception of the magic act or the work of art does. It lifts us out of the situation in order to create a new present in which we transcend our natural being. Badiou links the event to truth procedures, but here Nolan formulates the event as possible only by succumbing to a deceit.[6] When the audience enters into an artistic fiction and believes in it, they enter into the possibilities of a genuine event.

Earlier in the film, Borden mocks the fact that in Angier's version of the Transported Man he must hear the applause of the audience under the stage while his double receives the ovation above. But as his dying statement reveals, Angier's desire to see the audience cannot be reduced only to vanity. He sees in the audience's reaction the very reason why one performs magic—its ability to generate a transcendent belief visible in the spectators' looks of awe. Even though what audiences see is completely illusory, the act of seeing itself is not, and this is what Angier celebrates in his statement.

The infinite lies not in the nature of being itself but in the power of the look capable of discerning it. This look, however, is not inherent in the makeup of the subject; it does not inhere in human rationality or in the essence of language. The look that embodies the infinite owes its emergence to the deceptive power of the artistic illusion. The sublimity of art elevates its audience out of their finitude, producing a transcendence that the artists themselves don't experience.[7] Hegel makes this clear in his philosophy of art, where he credits the work of art with the capacity for lifting the subject out of its immersion in the finite world of sensation. He says, "Art by means of its representations, while remaining within the sensuous sphere, liberates man at the same time from the power of sensuousness."[8] Art uses sensuousness to elevate the subject out of sensuousness; it employs a fiction in order to provide access to truth. Through the sublimity of the work of art, the infinite becomes available to the subject in a way that would otherwise remain impossible. This is why Angier is desperate to see the faces of those he has duped with his illusions. Only the spectators reveal what the magic act or work of art achieves.

But despite his insight into what magic creates, Angier is not the perfect magician. The film criticizes his position on art just as vehemently as that of Borden. Angier fails to appreciate the necessary role that sacrifice has in making the art possible. His pursuit of Borden's secret in the United States derives from his inability to recognize what is obvious to the expert Cutter: that the Transported Man relies on the existence of a twin. Angier can't accept this because he can't imagine the sacrifice that this version of the illusion would require, so he seeks a tidier explanation. He believes that magic is the result of a secret or a trick rather than hard labor and incredible sacrifice. He seeks magic on the cheap. This leads Angier to Tesla's teleportation machine, which does produce the genuine miracle for him, but at an incredible cost.

Ironically, Angier's refusal to accept the necessity of sacrifice in magic—his repression of sacrifice—ultimately results in an act that requires a much more horrific sacrifice than does Borden's.[9] Performing the "New Transported Man" demands that Angier drown a version of himself during each show in order to erase the evidence of the doubling that occurs during the teleportation. He willingly undergoes this drowning because he knows that a version of himself will survive and because, at his wife's funeral, he heard Cutter recount the story of a sailor who almost drowned and claimed that the experience felt like "going home."[10] Later, when Cutter realizes the role that drowning plays in the magic act, he confronts Angier, reminding him, "I once told you about a sailor who described drowning to me." Angier responds, "Yes, he said it was like going home." Cutter evinces disgust, proclaiming, "I was lying. He said it was agony." After he says this, the film shows Cutter turning and walking away in the dark, making clear his disapprobation. Angier's effort to find an easy path to magic transforms him into a murderer of different versions of himself.[11]

The film absolutely refuses to take a side in the rivalry between Borden and Angier. Nor does it suggest that both are wrong, that the problem lies in magic itself. It would be more correct to say that the implication of the film is that both are right: magic demands self-sacrifice, as Borden recognizes, but it also creates transcendence, as

Angier sees. The solution to the rivalry is not a compromise between the two positions—a little sacrifice and a little transcendence—but the difficult task of thinking the two together. *The Prestige* enjoins us to conceive of the emergence of the new as immanent within the act of sacrifice and the act of sacrifice as immanent within the emergence of the new. To do so is to reimagine the artistic fiction.

A CALL TO SACRIFICE

Nolan constructs the discourse of the film the way he does to emphasize the connection between the illusion that the magic act produces and the sacrifice that goes into creating that illusion. One of the chief effects of magic—and of cinema—is its tendency to focus audience attention on the result. If the illusionist (the magician or the film director) performs the art well, the audience pays attention to what appears either on the stage or the screen rather than to the work occurring outside of the audience's vision, the work that goes into constructing the illusion. Many Marxist theorists of the cinema have contended that the tendency to hide work bespeaks this art form's irrevocably ideological nature. Just like capitalism itself hides the fact that labor rather than exchange is the source of value (by realizing profit in the act of exchange), so the cinema obscures the work necessary to produce a film by its mode of presentation, which includes no actual human beings but only images of them. In the theater, at least the spectator can see the actors sweat and the stagehands move props around, but the cinema prevents even this minimal degree of attunement to the labor behind the illusion.[12]

Since the cinematic medium cannot directly convey the sacrifice that goes into creating the illusion, filmmakers who want to draw attention to it must find another route. In *The Prestige*, Nolan chooses to include an indication of the sacrifice within the filmic image—as a part of the illusion that hints at what the illusion obscures. That is, the film depicts sacrifice as a remainder that exceeds and stains the cinematic illusion, thereby skewing the spectator's relationship to it. The opening shot of *The Prestige* tracks along a clearing in a woods where multiple black top hats lie strewn across the ground. The penultimate shot of the film repeats this image, followed by a shot of the theater basement where Angier has stored his drowned doubles that Tesla's teleportation machine has produced. The final shot moves slowly to a stop on Angier's body upright in the water tank.

The repetition of the shot depicting the hats reveals the work and sacrifice that went into the construction of the magical teleportation device. While building the machine, Tesla experimented many times with Angier's top hat, and because he did not recognize that the machine produced a duplicate in addition to teleporting, he remained unaware of the growing pile of hats outside his laboratory. The excess hats are the waste product that creation necessarily produces, but most works of art—and especially films—try to draw the spectator's attention away from this waste, to obscure it through the fascinating power of the cinematic illusion. Nolan opts instead to emphasize it by using the image of the hats as the beginning and ending point of the narrative.

But the film doesn't stop with the image of the hat as the leftover of the production process. By depicting the drowned body of one of Angier's doubles in the final shot, Nolan reveals the human cost that creating illusions entails. Angier himself is a waste product of the artistic process, and this represents the cost of the fiction. By concluding with the image of Angier's body, the film partakes in Walter Benjamin's critique of the notion of progress and attempts to embody the position he extols as an alternative, that of the historical materialist. According to Benjamin, the historical materialist views great creations or "'cultural treasures' . . . with cautious detachment. For in every case these treasures have a lineage which he cannot contemplate without horror. They owe their existence not only to the efforts of the great geniuses who created them, but also to the anonymous toil of others who lived in the same period. There is no document of culture which is not at the same time a document of barbarism."[13] Benjamin rejects progress because he recognizes that it is a storm "which keeps piling wreckage upon wreckage."[14] The cost of the triumphs of history militates against the consideration of them as progressive. One must instead pay attention to what has been left behind or produced in excess—like the drowned body of Angier's double.

The Prestige does not conclude as it does in order to inveigh against magic or the artistic process in general. This would be completely hypocritical within the cinematic medium, and it would also indicate a failure to grasp the miraculous nature of the artistic fiction. Even as it points out the horrible sacrifice inherent in creating a fiction, *The Prestige* suggests that magic or art is worth the cost. Not only is the film a call for the recognition of sacrifice and loss as integral to the process of creating a fiction; it also enjoins the spectator to participate in this process through sacrifice.

The film's appreciation for the sacrifice that magic requires becomes apparent in an early sequence where Cutter sends Borden and Angier to watch Chung Ling Soo (Chao Li Si) perform and to learn from him. During his show, Chung Ling causes a large fishbowl to appear on a table in front of him. This trick stumps Angier, but Borden quickly figures it out. From a distance, Borden and Angier watch a decrepit Chung Ling hobble to a carriage with assistance from those around him. Seeing this display of near helplessness, Borden proclaims, "This is the trick. This is the performance. . . . This is why no one can detect his method. Total devotion to his art. A lot of self-sacrifice, you know?" By playing the part of a frail old man who can't walk properly, Chung Ling is able to hold a large fishbowl under his robe without anyone noticing. His shuffling walk appears as his normal gait rather than as the result of the fishbowl held between his legs. Only the sacrifice of a life of normal walking, something few would be willing to give up, allows Chung Ling to perpetuate the illusion during his show. But the film nonetheless nods its approval.

Through acts like Chung Ling's sacrifice, the magician creates a transcendence that otherwise would not exist. As Borden concludes his explanation of the trick to Angier, he says, "It's the only way to escape—all this." While he says this, the film shows him hit his fist against the dirty brick edifice next to him, thereby giving his statement a referent. Self-sacrifice allows Chung Ling and his spectators to escape the misery of existence in turn of the century London, to transcend the limitations of this world. *The Prestige* is a panegyric to Chung Ling and the other magicians who suffer in order to illuminate this transcendence.

One should always be wary in the face of calls for sacrifice, especially when one is in the vicinity of Christianity. Christian ideology has at its foundation the conceit of self-sacrifice performed to garner eternal life. What made Protestantism so conducive to the birth of capitalism were precisely the sacrificial demands that it placed on believers. As Max Weber notes in his classic analysis, "Labor came to be considered in itself the end of life, as ordained by God."[15] Though Protestantism disbelieved in the power of works for attaining salvation, it nonetheless championed work itself as the path to grace. One can take this critique of sacrifice even further: self-sacrifice is the central pillar of not just Christian ideology but all forms of ideology. Ideology as such justifies the sacrifice of enjoyment in order for the subject to invest itself in the social order and in the identity underwritten by that order. Far from

111

being an ethical or authentic act, this sacrifice represents the subject's first betrayal of itself—its original sin.

And yet, taking several recent films as his point of departure, Slavoj Žižek theorizes the act of self-sacrifice as the ultimate political gesture that allows the subject to break its libidinal attachment to the ruling order. He argues,

> When we are subjected to a power mechanism, this subjection is always and by definition sustained by some libidinal investment: the subjection itself generates a surplus-enjoyment of its own. This subjection is embodied in a network of "material" bodily practices, and, for this reason, we cannot get rid of our subjection through a merely intellectual reflection. Our liberation has to be *staged* in some kind of bodily performance, and, furthermore, this performance *has* to be of an apparently "masochistic" nature; it *has* to stage the painful process of hitting back at oneself.[16]

Rather than ensconcing one within the power of ideology, the act of self-sacrifice, as Žižek conceives it, frees one from that power insofar as it breaks the subject's fantasmatic investment in ideology.

Self-sacrifice functions ideologically when it is tied to the promise of a recovered wholeness for the subject. In the terms of Christian ideology, this wholeness can be found in the afterlife. For fascist ideology, it exists in the complete identification with the fatherland. An emancipatory self-sacrifice, in contrast, works to shatter the image of wholeness. It targets the source of the illusion of wholeness in order to indicate that there is an opening to a beyond within the seemingly closed whole. Self-sacrifice that shatters the image of wholeness provides the basis for what Eric Santner calls "the experience of miracle [that] persists into modernity."[17] The modern miracle allows us to suspend the "peculiar topological knot—the outlaw dimension internal to law—that serves to sustain the symbolic function of sovereignty."[18] The sacrifice of one's libidinal attachment to symbolic authority allows one to bypass that authority and reveal its limits.

Žižek sees the sacrificial act at work in films such as *Fight Club* (David Fincher, 1999), *Speed* (Jan de Bont, 1994), *Ransom* (Ron Howard, 1996), and *The Usual Suspects* (Bryan Singer, 1995), and one could imagine him extending this analysis to *The Prestige*. But the latter film explicitly links self-sacrifice to artistic creation in a way that the other films don't. Here, the magic act has a clear creative power. By causing an

112

object to disappear and then reappear, magic, like all art, attests to the existence of a hole in the world, a gap in the structure of signification. It momentarily renders visible a point of nonsense within the world of sense, and it allows the spectator to leave the world of sense behind. The magician's sacrifice is the key to an existence beyond the limits of the law.

THE TEMPORALITY OF CAPITALISM

Nolan's exploration of magic in *The Prestige* is also an exploration of cinema. The magic of Borden and Angier is the magic of cinema. Like the magic act, the film creates through sacrifice and then hides the sacrifice—the labor that goes into making the film—through its spectacle. While cinema hides the sacrifice of labor, it also creates transcendence through its fiction. But Nolan's film seeks to connect the moment of transcendence with the necessity of sacrifice.

The critical analysis that *The Prestige* provides is not confined to just magic or cinema. Though it focuses on the sacrifice that goes into the production of artistic illusion, the film actually intervenes on the larger question of creation itself. According to the film, a miracle occurs in every act of creation: something emerges out of nothing; an effect is produced that transcends its cause; we receive more value in the created object than we put into creating it. Creation in this sense is the lifeblood of capitalism. Though capitalism on the one hand creates a world without transcendent miracles in which "all that is solid melts into air, all that is holy is profaned, and man is at last compelled to face with sober senses, his real conditions of life, and his relations with his kind,"[19] on the other hand it depends on the miraculous creation of value for its daily sustenance. The appropriation of surplus labor produces more value in the commodity than the capitalist puts into it, and this miracle provides the basis for the capitalist's profit. But despite the central role that surplus labor plays in the creation of value, those who are exchanging commodities don't recognize this. *The Prestige* works to illuminate it.

In the third volume of *Capital*, Marx claims that it is not so much capitalist ideology as the very capitalist relations of production themselves that have the effect of obscuring how value is created. Because capitalists realize their profit at the moment of exchange, exchange seems to generate value. The act of exchange appears to be the site of a miracle

113

in which one receives more for one's product than one has invested in it. But Marx's radical discovery—and the essence of his thought—lies in seeing exchange as but the realization of a value created beforehand through labor. The miracle occurs through labor, not through exchange. The capitalist's profit is the realization of the surplus value that the worker, not the capitalist, creates. As Marx puts it, "Profit, as we are originally faced with it, is thus the same thing as surplus-value, save in a mystified form, though one that necessarily arises from the capitalist mode of production. . . . The excess value or surplus-value realized with the sale of the commodity thus appears to the capitalist as an excess of its sale price over its value, instead of an excess of its value over its cost price, so that the surplus-value concealed in the commodity is not simply realized by its sale, but actually derives from the sale itself."[20] The intrinsic priority placed on exchange for making a profit within capitalist relations of production necessarily blinds the individual capitalist to the real source of that profit, which is the surplus value created by the worker who produced the commodity.

The great contribution of Marx on this question stems from his ability to see the deception of capitalism as written into its very structure rather than as the product of conscious manipulation. One can escape conscious manipulation through the vigilance of consciousness-raising, but one cannot escape a structural deception so easily. As a result, Marx insists, "In a social order dominated by capitalist production, even the non-capitalist producer is dominated by capitalist ways of thinking."[21] The act of participating in capitalist exchange—what no one within capitalist society can avoid—creates a blindness to surplus labor as the source of value. When he involves himself in exchange, even Marx himself, despite his theoretical insights into the process, succumbs to this illusion.

But *The Prestige* pushes Marx's structural critique one step further. The problem of the erasure of labor does not derive solely from the priority of the act of exchange within capitalist relations of production. It has a more fundamental basis in a conception of time as a linear movement forward that Marx himself shares. Our collective blindness to labor as the source of value owes its intransigence to the predominance of this conception of time. Even though many twentieth-century thinkers reject the idea of progress, they nonetheless accept the concept of time as linear forward movement. Though they each critique the mechanical chronology of the clock, thinkers as different as Bergson, Heidegger, and Deleuze all theorize time as a forward motion, which they see as the source of its fecundity. Temporality, as opposed to stasis, allows for the new to arise. But when we seek the new in the possibilities of the unforeseen future, as these theorists do, we end up succumbing to the structure that blinds us to labor as the source of value.

Time is not moving toward a different future that might free us from loss but returning us back to the experience of loss. Rather than being a movement forward, it is a movement of return. The temporality of the subject is the temporality of the repetition of a fiction, which circulates around a traumatic kernel rather than proceeding in a linear fashion toward the future or toward an ultimate truth. Time provides a venue for this repetition, from which there is no possible respite.

Only those attuned to this conception of time will be able to see the commodity for what it is: a signifier of the worker's sacrifice. The exchange of commodities is the exchange of different degrees of sacrifice, and one can recognize this only after having shed the promise of a different future, which constitutes the essence of the commodity's appeal for both the capitalist and the consumer. Capitalist society functions only insofar as we collectively believe in the idea of temporality that provides the basis for the commodity. To exist in the temporality of repetition and loss is to leave the commodity's appeal behind, but it is only through the temporality of repetition that we can access the artistic fiction.

THE LYING DIARY

Though art has the power to reveal the truth of sacrifice and loss to us, to break the hold of the commodity over us, it can reveal this truth only through a fiction. The sacrifice at the base of magic and art is made for the purposes of creating an illusion that deceives spectators. Deception thus acts as the basis for an authentic conception of temporality as repetition. This is the case not just for the magic performed within the film's narrative but also for the film's narrative structure itself. Artistic deception is the vehicle through which Christopher Nolan establishes an alternative temporality in the film.

The device through which Nolan shifts the time period in the film is often (though not exclusively) the diaries of Borden and Angier. The narrative moves as either Borden or Angier reads the other's diary. The use of the diary as a vehicle for temporal shifts has the effect of emphasizing the mediated—and thus deceptive—nature of the events depicted in the film. The film never simply lays its cards on the table: even when it appears to do so, it does so for the sake of furthering its deception. This is especially true in the use of the diary as means for moving in time within the narrative.

Diaries often appear in novels and films as representations of the inner consciousness of a character. When we read someone else's diary, we have the sense that we are accessing a private arena of this person's life, one not visible to the public at large, just as Bill (Jeremy Theobald) does when he looks in the secret box in *Following*. What makes reading a diary compelling—and leads people to sneak a look at the diaries of those close to them—is that the diary form seems to be a repository of truth. In contrast to speaking in public or even writing a letter, there is no motivation to lie in one's diary since the only audience is oneself. By using the diary as a narrative device, a fictional work like a film or a novel can insinuate its truthfulness and, to some extent, obscure its fictionality.[22] The use of the diary in *The Prestige*, however, operates in the other direction.

Rather than permitting the diary to validate the veracity of the filmic illusion, *The Prestige* as a fiction works to impugn the truthfulness of the diary as such. The only type of diary that the film envisions is one written for the purpose of deception or frustration. Borden composes his encoded diary in order to send Angier on a fruitless voyage to the United States in search of a nonexistent teleportation machine, which the diary—until its final page—claims Tesla has made for Borden. In a similar vein, Angier creates his diary with Borden in mind, leading up to the final secret of the device that Tesla actually made for him and then not revealing it. The diary form, as the film conceives it, is nothing but a mode of seducing the Other with the allure of a private moment of nonfiction. The nonfiction form of the diary simply makes it a more effective fiction in relation to the audience.[23]

The prominent position given to the deceptive diary in controlling the movement of the narrative in *The Prestige* underlines the spectator's sentiment that one is never outside the illusion. Even when it discloses its own fictionality, the film never speaks directly to the spectator. Every shot is mediated through a fictionalized diary or some other fiction-producing device, even the shot that depicts someone reading a diary. When we see Angier reading Borden's diary, for instance, it occurs within a story being related by someone else. The truth of the film occurs through its fictionality, not in spite of it.[24]

The problem with making a film like *The Prestige* that reveals the

116

nature of cinematic deception is that the film itself necessarily partakes in this same deception. It cannot simply remain a commentary on cinematic deception. As Orson Welles demonstrates in his late masterpiece *F for Fake* (1974), there is no external position from which a filmmaker could expose the cinematic illusion. Welles's film tells the story of famous incidents of forgery and deception, but in turn it deceives the spectator, even using claims about its truthfulness to do so. Even though *F for Fake* reveals its artifice on different occasions, it ultimately can't avoid being a part of the process of forgery that it documents. Every film—perhaps especially the documentary film—dupes its audience with an illusion. The absence of a position from which to speak the truth about illusion becomes apparent in *The Prestige*. Nolan's film about the magician's deception utilizes the deception of filmmaking to relate this story. Just as Lacan insists that "there is no meta-language," the film insists that there is no meta-cinema.[25]

As a result, the film must deceive the spectator in a way that draws attention to the deception—not to deconstruct or debunk it, but rather to reveal what it produces. Through editing, the chief tool of deception that the cinema offers, Nolan creates the illusion that a truth exists beyond what appears on the screen. He does this most often by cutting from a scene before the action concludes. The cut allows the spectator to think that the conclusion follows evidently from what has already transpired—that the elided events would not significantly change our impression of the scene—but this is entirely deceptive. In each case, further revelations (which become visible only later) occur as the scene plays out, and these events completely change its significance. When the truth of the scenes finally becomes apparent, the deception inherent in the editing process becomes apparent as well.

The first great deception of the film occurs very early (though very late in the actual chronology of events), when Borden goes beneath the stage during Angier's New Transported Man show and watches Angier appear to drown. Nolan shows interspersed shots of Borden watching the trick from the audience and going below the stage with shots of Cutter demonstrating a magic trick to Jess, while on the audio track Cutter is explaining the three parts of a magic trick to a court, which is trying Borden for Angier's murder. The film reveals one deception in this sequence right away: Cutter appears to be describing the magic act to Jess while performing a trick for her, but in fact he is speaking to the court, which is not visible until the end of his description. But the more important deception occurs as a result of the cut from Borden standing outside the tank where Angier is drowning. We don't see Borden struggle to free Angier from the tank, which would have had the effect of bringing his guilt into doubt. And at the same time, we don't see the double of Angier appear, which furthers the belief that Borden is guilty of Angier's murder. Toward the end of the film, Nolan shows the same scene in its entirety, which allows us to recognize the earlier deception.

Two subsequent deceptions in the film also rely on the misleading cut. When Angier sends Olivia to spy on Borden, Borden asks her if she is being truthful with him. After he asks, an extended shot of Olivia shows her saying nothing, indicating a tacit affirmation. But we later see what occurs in the next seconds and learn that the cut occurred before she reveals the truth of her mission to Borden, expresses her disdain for Angier for sending her to Borden, and pledges her loyalty to Borden. The withholding of this information allows the spectator to believe in the integrity of Borden's diary, which Olivia claims to have stolen for Angier but which Borden told her to give to him. The film also cuts away after Angier tests the teleportation machine for the first time, so that we don't see him shoot the double that it creates (as a later repetition of the scene reveals). In all these cases, the misleading cut prompts the spectator to make an assumption that ultimately turns out to be false. By using editing to create wrong assumptions, Nolan performs his version of magic, revealing that the relationship between the magicians and the spectators within the film corresponds to that between the director and the spectators of the film itself.

The primary deception of the film involves the secret behind Borden's Transported Man illusion. Until the montage sequence at the end of the film, the spectator never sees the secret revealed, though there are numerous hints at the solution throughout.[26] During a final montage sequence at the end of the film, Nolan lays the secret bare. As Borden explains the trick to the dying Angier, the spectator sees a flashback depicting the twins together, changing identities between Borden and Fallon. We also see the one twin cut off the other's fingers in order to sustain their identical appearance. These revelations would appear to distance the film from the magic trick, which loses all its power at the moment of the revelation.[27] But even though the secret of Borden's illusion is the primary deception within the film's narrative, it does not represent the film's magic.

The fundamental deception of the cinema as such—the magic or art of the medium—consists not in the deception that spectators might figure out or not, like the existence of twins in *The Prestige*. This is the kind of deception operative in films like M. Night Shyamalan's *Unbreakable* (2000) or *The Village* (2004). A Shyamalan film relies on a deception about the nature of the world that it presents and challenges the spectator to figure out the puzzle. The key to *Unbreakable* is that the frail and seemingly harmless Elijah Price (Samuel L. Jackson) is actually a murderous super-villain, and the key to *The Village* is that the seemingly eighteenth-century village is actually an isolated world located within the contemporary one.[28] In these cases, the deception is internal to the filmic narrative, but there is also a deception inherent in the cinematic form itself, which is what *The Prestige* emphasizes.[29]

Cinema deceives its spectators by inducing them to invest themselves in the significance of what they see on the screen. The point is not that spectators take the screen events for real events, but that they believe in the depth and coherence of the world they see. This belief leads spectators to assume that there is something to figure out in the film, that each film—especially the puzzle film—has a secret truth that the spectator can access. According to this belief, there are events happening in the filmic world beyond what we see on the screen. Borden really is a pair of twins; Angier really drowned his doubles produced by the teleportation machine; and so on. The cinematic deception produces spectator fascination, which is nothing but the spectator's investment in the significance and worldliness of the images on the screen.

Because the film ends with Cutter's dramatic voiceover proclaiming that the spectator will not discover the real secret of the film, many spectators and critics have speculated about another hidden layer to the film. Cutter says, "Now you're looking for the secret, but you won't find it because, of course, you're not really looking. You don't really want to work it out. You want to be fooled." To work out the solution to the cinematic deception is to break the illusion that it creates, and this would destroy the enjoyment that cinema provides—which is why spectators "want to be fooled," as Cutter puts it. The very act of searching for the film's real secret betrays the extent to which one has already been duped by the fundamental cinematic illusion.

But the alternative does not consist in not allowing oneself to be duped. To be cynical about all artistic creations is to remain wholly ensconced within a deeper deception. This is why Lacan devotes an entire year of his seminar to the idea that "the non-duped err." By refusing to allow oneself to be duped by the fiction, one errs and misses any possibility of discovering truth. The artistic illusion carries the spectator to a truth that would otherwise be inaccessible, and those who see through this illusion never recognize the truth that it opens up. It is the truth of the infinite nature of the subject's power: the subject has the ability to transcend the world that conditions it, but it can only achieve this transcendence with the help of the magic contained in an artistic illusion, a magic produced through profound sacrifice.

Toward the end of the *Science of Logic*, at the moment when he prepares to celebrate philosophy reaching its end point, Hegel engages in an unexpected panegyric to pain. This seemingly incongruent turn in Hegel's thought testifies to his profound kinship with the filmmaking of Christopher Nolan. Just as Nolan illustrates the relationship between sacrifice and transcendence, Hegel grasps the bond between pain and arriving at the infinite. He says, "From pain begin the *need* and the *urge* that constitute the transition by which the individual, which is explicitly the negation of itself, becomes also explicitly its own identity—an identity that exists only as the negation of the former negation."[30] As Hegel sees it, pain is a privilege granted to living beings, and it enables them to become what they are not and escape the confines of self-identical being. Overcoming is always painful because it demands sacrifice, but the alternative is the monotony of pure being or nothingness.

THE END MATTERS

Many directors create narratives that deflect attention from the end result and onto the process that produces that result. This occurs most obviously in films that break from a chronological narration, such as Quentin Tarantino's *Reservoir Dogs* (1992) or *Pulp Fiction* (1994), both of which emphasize the decisions that lead to the narrative's denouement rather than that denouement itself. But it also takes place in films that adhere to traditional chronology, like Agnès Varda's *Cléo de 5 à 7* (1961) or Spike Lee's *25th Hour* (2002), in which the ending—the medical diagnosis in the former and the fantasy of a future life in the latter—serves almost as an afterthought.

According to the logic elaborated in *The Prestige*, the end remains crucial. Near the end of the film, Cutter makes this clear as he is explaining the process of magic to Jess. He tells her (in a way that echoes the film's opening), "Every magic trick consists of three parts or acts. The first part is called the pledge. The magician shows you something ordinary. The second act is called the turn. The magician takes the ordinary something and makes it into something extraordinary. But you wouldn't clap yet, because making something disappear isn't enough. You have to bring it back." By emphasizing the necessity of the object's return, Cutter gives voice to the film's central idea: neither magic nor cinema is reducible to its end product, but this end product is nonetheless essential. In other words, the film does not ask us to dismiss the significance of the illusion in the name of the sacrifice that goes into creating it.

This is the path taken by many avant-garde films. Jean-Luc Godard's *Prénom: Carmen* (1983), for instance, relentlessly exposes the artifice of cinematic illusionism as it takes the spectator behind the scenes of the making of a film. *The Prestige*, in contrast, allows us to see the dialectical relation between the work and the illusion in both magic and the cinema. The film creates an illusion that returns us to the sacrifice rather than repressing it. What the film thereby shows is that the spectacle of the illusion does not just require past sacrifice; it also leads one back down the path of sacrifice and loss.

The narrative structure of *The Prestige* challenges the obfuscatory power of the cinematic medium by juxtaposing sacrifice and spectacle, but it does so in order to celebrate both rather than to condemn either one. At the same time, it calls for a change in our relation to both sacrifice and artistic fiction. Rather than seeing sacrifice as a burden to be avoided, we might instead recognize within it the beauty of the work of art, and rather than viewing art as an escape from suffering, we might recognize it as the path to a more profound experience of sacrifice. Moving in this direction requires abandoning the hope that one day one could move beyond the necessity of sacrifice. It involves a new way of looking at the suffering involved in labor.

Marx, who was the first to fully understand the connection between sacrifice and creation, offers a hint at what this changed perception might look like in his famous discussion distinguishing the realm of freedom from the realm of necessity. He first insists on the absolute distinction between these two realms, and then he goes on to say that "the true realm of freedom" allows for "the development of human powers as an end in itself."[31] In this realm, rather than working for the sake of survival or external necessity, one would sacrifice purely for the sake of creation. This act of sacrifice would no longer point toward the future but would instead provide its own internal justification. In this sense, it would represent the realization of the nature of all sacrifice.

Nolan's exploration of artistic fiction in *The Prestige* refuses to decouple the act of creation from the act of sacrifice. The film demonstrates that the sacrifice involved in creating a fiction inaugurates a transcendent space otherwise inaccessible. This transcendence depends on deception—and on the audience's willingness to allow itself to be deceived. Nolan feels at home in Hollywood because he believes in the transcendent power of deception, and deception is the sine qua non of Hollywood filmmaking. But Nolan always shows the cost of this transcendence, a cost that Hollywood most often takes great pains to hide. By submitting to the artistic fiction, we enter into a beyond, but it is a beyond that always brings us back to the repetition of sacrifice. The new that emerges through the deception is not what we have lost but our loss itself.

The critical and popular success of *Batman Begins* (2005) ensured that Christopher Nolan would have the opportunity to direct a sequel. The three years that he took between the original and the sequel created great anticipation among fans of both Nolan and Batman. The anticipation that awaited the film brought with it tremendous pressure to outdo the original. Thanks in part to the singular performance by Heath Ledger as the Joker, *The Dark Knight* (2008) far surpassed the critical and popular success of *Batman Begins*. In addition to becoming the second-highest grossing film of all time, it indirectly engaged contemporary political questions.

Nolan worked on the sequel during the middle of George Bush's war on terror, which led to an expansion of figures of authority functioning outside the law in a position similar to that of Batman. *The Dark Knight* responds directly to this development, though it never mentions the war on terror or any political struggle. In the film, Nolan addresses the criminality of the exception to the law, even if this exception is Batman rather than Scooter Libby. But he also begins by acknowledging the necessity of the exception.

The fundamental contention of the superhero film (and its comic book source) is that the law alone is not a sufficient condition for justice. Under even the most benign historical circumstances, injustice is more powerful than justice, and as a result, justice requires an exceptional figure who operates outside or on the periphery of the law. This figure, the superhero, goes where the law can't and accomplishes what it can't. According to the logic of the superhero film, superheroes earn their exceptional status by dint of some extra-human ability or special skill that others lack. Endowed by this ability or skill, the superhero acquires an exceptional relation to the law. By skirting or even violating particular laws to sustain the order of law, the superhero provides the extralegal supplement that the law requires to deliver justice. The superhero is the lie on which the truth of the law relies.

THE HERO'S FORM OF APPEARANCE
THE NECESSARY DARKNESS OF *THE DARK KNIGHT*

The mask that superheroes wear—their investment in creating a fiction about themselves—indicates their complex relationship to the law. Ordinary police officers can avow their identity publicly, and this is what separates them from criminals, who would be in jail if they publicly avowed their criminality. Even undercover police officers cease hiding their identity after each assignment, and those who can't effectively become criminals themselves. Being a figure of the law includes implicitly the public avowal of one's status.[1] The superhero is a different animal. While they struggle against criminals who break the law, superheroes cannot openly identify themselves with the public nature of law. They represent instead the underside of public law, the dimension of private support that it requires to function effectively as a public institution.[2]

Even the most ethical superheroes occupy a position outside the order of law simply by virtue of their heightened power. Critics usually see Superman as one of the least engaging superheroes precisely because of his probity, the absence of any dark side to his character.[3] Unlike other superheroes, Superman almost never violates the law—except perhaps due to his indecent exposure in phone booths—in order to uphold the legal order. But he does, in Richard Donner's original *Superman* (1978), violate the laws of the universe (causing the earth to spin backward and time to reverse itself) in order to save Lois Lane (Margot Kidder). The film presents this act as a moment of ethical crisis because it reveals Superman's exceptional relationship to law and the way that his superpower places him at odds with the limited and limiting nature of law. On a more mundane level, Superman operates outside the law by never obtaining a search warrant, reading criminals their rights, or going through any of the other bureaucratic procedures that the law requires of the police. The uneasiness of the superhero's coexistence—and, in fact, that of the hero as such—with the law prompts Hegel to see them as antithetical.

Though he was unacquainted with Superman, Hegel thought a great deal about the phenomenon that Superman represents. In his aesthetic philosophy, he distinguishes between a heroic age and the era of the legal order. In the latter, ethical activity is realized in the laws of the state rather than in individual action. Though laws can be unjust and we may have to change them, our ethical activity occurs through the law rather than outside it. The legal order thus leaves no room for the hero, the figure who acts outside of the law's constraints. Heroism is antithetical to law because it always serves to constitute its own law even if it doesn't mean to do so. For the hero, as Hegel puts it, "individuality is a law unto itself, without being subjected to an independently subsisting law, judgement, and tribunal."[4] In the context of a legal order, the hero's activity would become criminality, and there would be no way to differentiate it from evil. This is why Hegel rejects the idea of the modern hero. Such a figure fails to see how the private morality that it proffers as an alternative or a supplement to the legal order is already included within that order. As a result of its structural incompatibility, the hero's activity will have the effect of undermining the law even if it is done to supplement the law. But the problem is that left to itself, the law cannot arrive at justice, and the persistence of injustice within the legal order leads to the demand for the hero and for the heroic exception to the law.[5]

Christopher Nolan's *Dark Knight* takes as its overriding concern the problem posed by the hero and the hero's exceptional status in relation to the law. But the film is not simply a critique of heroic exceptionality. In the universe of the film, the need for an exception to the law is evident. Without Batman (Christian Bale) providing extralegal assistance to Police Lieutenant James Gordon (Gary Oldman), the crime lords that menace Gotham would render the city uninhabitable. Even with Batman's help, the film's ominous and brooding mise-en-scène reveals the extent to which criminality sets the tone for life in the city. Unlike Nolan's earlier film *Batman Begins*, in which Gotham appears futuristic despite its crime problem, here crime shapes the look and feel of the city. Buildings are in disrepair; people's dress is generally disheveled; and even daytime scenes occur under dark skies.

Given the film's appreciation of the need for the heroic exception to the legal order, it is easy to understand why a right-wing political commentator, after viewing the film, might regard it as a tribute to George W. Bush and his prosecution of the Iraq War. In his *Wall Street Journal* article titled "What Bush and Batman Have in Common," Andrew Klavan contends, "There seems to me no question that the Batman film *The Dark Knight*, currently breaking every box office record in history, is at some level a paean of praise to the fortitude and moral courage that has been shown by George W. Bush in this time of terror and war. Like W, Batman is vilified and despised for confronting terrorists in the only terms they understand. Like W, Batman sometimes has to push the boundaries of civil rights to deal with an emergency, certain that he will re-establish those boundaries when the emergency is past."[6] The similarity between Bush and Batman consists in their joint recognition that an exceptional threat to the legal order requires an extralegal exception in order to quell the threat. Though Klavan has to read the film creatively to arrive at the thesis that it constitutes "a conservative movie about the war on terror," he does rightly grasp the film's fundamental contention that we need a figure of exception.[7]

The problem with the acceptance and celebration of the hero's exceptionality is not simply that it produces conservative misreadings but that this exceptionality has an inherent tendency to multiply itself exponentially. In *Dark Knight*, this proliferation occurs early in the film when copycat vigilantes place both themselves and others at risk. In the United States during the war on terror, it takes the form of an ever-increasing extension of surveillance and security. Once we grant the necessity of the position of the exception, the law can no longer define those who will occupy this position or restrain their activity. Once we violate the rights of noncitizens, we will soon be violating the rights of citizens as well, and finally we will end up with a society in which rights as such cease to exist. The exception necessarily exists beyond the limits of the law, and if the law could contain its magnitude, it would cease to be exceptional. The exception is a fiction or violation of the truth of the law that threatens to overrun law altogether, and yet the law requires it. This is the dilemma that shapes *The Dark Knight*. The film's incredible popularity attests not simply to Nolan's skill as a filmmaker or to a successful marketing campaign by Warner Bros., but also to the contemporary urgency of the question it addresses.

In one sense, Nolan is responding here to a problem of his own creation. The idea of *Batman Begins* is that subjects should identify themselves with the superhero qua gap in the social order. *The Dark Knight* begins with the problem of several citizens of Gotham taking this injunction literally by copying Batman's attire and methods. One could say that they misunderstand the nature of identifying with the gap, but they nonetheless expose the problem of the exception.

The film begins with Batman's grasp of the problem, as it depicts his attempt to relinquish his exceptional status and to allow the legal order to operate on its own. In order to do this, a different form of heroism is required, and the quest that constitutes *The Dark Knight* is Batman's attempt to find the proper public face for heroism. He is drawn to Harvey Dent (Aaron Eckhart) because Dent seems to embody the possibility of a heroism that would be consistent with the public law and that could consequently function without the need for disguise. After the death of Rachel Dawes (Maggie Gyllenhaal) and Dent's own serious facial burn transforms him from a defender of the law into the criminal figure Two-

126

Face, Batman sees the impossibility of doing away with the hero's mask. Dent, the would-be hero without a mask, quickly becomes a criminal himself when he experiences traumatic loss. This turn of events reveals that the hero must remain an exception, but it also shows that the heroism of the hero must pass itself off as its opposite. Nolan's film shows that the hero must lie.

Just as the truth that Leonard (Guy Pearce) discovers at the end of *Memento* (2000) is a constitutive lie, the conclusion of *The Dark Knight* illustrates that the true appearance of heroism is evil. The film concludes with Batman voluntarily taking responsibility for the murders that Dent/Two-Face committed. By doing so, he allows Dent to die as a hero in the public mind, but he also—and more importantly—changes the public perception of his own exceptional status. When he agrees to appear as a criminal at the end of the film, Batman avows simultaneously the need for the heroic exception and the need for this exception to appear as criminality. If the heroic exception is not to multiply itself in a way that threatens any possibility for justice, then its appearance must become indistinguishable from criminality.

Taking on the appearance of criminality does involve becoming a criminal. This is the difference between Batman in *The Dark Knight* and Ra's Al Ghul (Liam Neeson) in *Batman Begins*, and this is how one should interpret Batman's absolute reluctance to kill. Ra's willingly turns to criminal acts for the greater good because he believes in his own purity and in the potential purity of society. Batman takes on the appearance of criminality as an acknowledgment of his own impurity, and he maintains a prohibition on killing not in order to avoid descending into criminality but, ironically, in order to sustain his own impurity.

The heroic gesture, as *The Dark Knight* conceives it, does not consist in any of the particular crime-fighting or life-saving activities that Batman performs throughout the film. It lies rather in his embrace of the appearance of criminality that concludes the film. Gordon's voiceover panegyric to Batman that punctuates the film affirms that this is the truly heroic act. This act privileges and necessitates its own misrecognition: it is only through misrecognition that one sees it correctly. If the people of Gotham were to see through Batman's form of appearance and recognize his real heroism, the heroism would be instantly lost because this would multiply its exceptionality. As the film portrays it, the form of appearance of authentic heroism must be that of evil. Only in this way does the heroic exceptionality that the superhero embodies avoid placing us on the road to fascist rule.

127

The nearest cousin to the superhero film is the western. Both genres address the problem of exceptional violence that resides outside the legal order and yet is necessary for the existence of that order, but the western concerns the initial violence that founds the law, what Walter Benjamin labels "lawmaking violence."[8] In George Stevens's *Shane* (1953), for instance, the violence of Shane (Alan Ladd) helps to establish a democratic and agrarian society that will replace the lawless reign of the ranchers. Shane acts violently in defense of the Starrett family and their farm, but his violence has no legal authorization because it occurs before the law has been firmly constituted. In order for the social order that his violence founds to function as a legal entity, Shane must leave at the end of the film. His violence has a purely exceptional status, and his departure confirms that the exception can disappear after the new social order comes into existence.

There is no such recourse for exceptionality in the superhero film. This type of film confronts not the necessity of lawmaking violence but that of a certain necessary violence that exists outside the law.[9] The law evokes this violence in extreme situations that merely legal violence cannot properly address. In *The Dark Knight*, the extreme situation is the rampant criminality of the various gangs that control Gotham. Responding to each outburst of excessive criminal activity that the police themselves cannot handle, Lieutenant Gordon shines the Bat-Signal in the night sky and thus announces the decree of a temporary state of exception in which Batman will employ violence to supplement the police.

Unlike Shane, Batman does not ultimately leave the society that he sustains with his violence. Batman remains as a persistent exception that the law cannot do without, and as a result, the superhero film confronts a more imposing dilemma than the western does. A western can simply end with the departure of the hero (or his domestication, as in the conclusion of Howard Hawks's *Red River*, 1948), but the superhero film has no such recourse. For the sake of the possibility of justice, the superhero must remain. But his presence as an exception is problematic, calling into question the legality of the law. By their very presence, superheroes expose the law's inherent insufficiency and inspire everyone to doubt its efficacy. The heroic exception constantly works to undermine the law that it supplements.

Giorgio Agamben sees the great danger inherent in the exception. Exceptionality, for Agamben, launches a legal civil war and thereby plays the key role in the transition from democracy to fascist authoritarianism. The declaration of the state of exception attempts "to produce a situation in which the emergency becomes the rule, and the very distinction between peace and war (and between foreign and civil war) becomes impossible."[10] The problem is that the exceptional time never ends, and the disappearance of the distinction between an emergency and everyday life pushes the society toward a state of civil war that the very exception itself was supposed to quell. Rather than acting as a temporary stopgap for a society on the brink of self-annihilation, the state of exception actually pushes the society further down the path to this annihilation. By undermining the distinction between law and criminality and thereby helping to foster a Hobbesian war of all against all, every act of sovereign power is justified in the name of order.

The Dark Knight begins with a focus on the problem engendered by the state of exception embodied by Batman. He is a figure outside the law on whom the law relies to respond to the most recalcitrant criminal elements in Gotham. But Batman's very success at fighting crime outside the law has, when the film opens, spawned numerous imitators—vigilantes who dress like Batman and spend their nights fighting crime. The result is an increased degree of lawlessness and insecurity in the city. Through these copycat vigilantes, the film begins by making clear the danger of the sanctioned exception that exists outside the law. Once one embraces the exception, the need for exceptionality will constantly expand insofar as the exception augments the very problem that it is created to fight against.

The fake Batmen question Batman directly on the monopoly he attempts to hold on exceptionality. After Batman rescues them from their botched effort to interrupt a drug deal, he warns them against this type of activity. One says, "What gives you the right? What's the difference between you and me?" Batman responds, "I'm not wearing hockey pads." While amusing, this quip is actually wholly inadequate as an argument. Batman has no inherent right to guard exceptionality for himself, and as long as he occupies this position, others will be drawn to it—and a self-multiplying exceptionality portends the destruction of the social order.[11]

The state of exception justifies any type of action—any encroachment on civil liberties—in order to realize the justice that ordinary law is incapable of realizing. *The Dark Knight* explicitly links the heroic exception embodied by Batman with the violation of civil liberties associated with the official declaration of a state of emergency (in the war on terror, for instance). Batman acts exceptionally not just by wearing a mask and breaking a few traffic laws but also by creating a system of surveillance that completely erases the idea of private space within Gotham. When Batman commissions his technical designer Lucius Fox (Morgan Freeman) to create a device that will allow him to map the location of everyone within the entire city of Gotham, Fox balks at the violation of civil liberties that this entails. He agrees to help to catch the Joker (Heath Ledger) but promises to resign immediately afterward. From an erstwhile supporter of Batman and his exceptionality, Fox's outrage signifies that Batman has crossed a line beyond heroic exceptionality where one can no longer differentiate him from the criminals he pursues. But in order to apprehend the Joker and disrupt his criminal plans, the film makes clear that Batman must cross this line. It places him fully on the terrain of contemporary politics and in the company of conservative political figures.

The logic of the war on terror initially waged by President George W. Bush and Vice President Dick Cheney (and continued after their departure) derives entirely from the idea that they rule in a state of emergency, where the normal rule of law will be insufficient for safeguarding the American populace. One must thus carve out an exceptional position outside the law. One of the ramifications of this idea is the legitimization of torture as a normal practice during the interrogation of anyone suspected of having a link with a terrorist organization. But the other ramification touches directly on the actions of Batman in *The Dark Knight*: the war on terror, as conceived by Bush and Cheney, is being fought with increased surveillance more than with additional weapons. The nature of the emergency calls for exceptional measures of surveillance—including eavesdropping on telephone calls, spying on e-mails, and using satellites to track movements, all without court authorization. When he uses the device that Fox builds for him, Batman elevates himself to an exception in the Bush and Cheney sense of the term. This is one of the points of resonance that led Klavan to link Batman and Bush. But there is nonetheless a fundamental distinction between the two and between Batman's relationship to exceptionality and that displayed by Bush.

One might assume that the difference lies in Batman's readiness to abandon the system of total surveillance after he catches the Joker and the emergency ends. Batman arranges for the system to self-destruct after Lucius Fox has finished using it, and as he walks away from the exploding apparatus, Fox smiles to himself, cheered by Batman's ethical commitment to abandoning the power he has amassed for himself. This image does certainly seem to contrast with the image of the system of surveillance established during the war on terror, which increases rather than self-destructs as the September 11 attacks move further and further into history. Neither President Bush nor President Obama will call an end to the war on terror or revoke all aspects of the Patriot Act. But Klavan can nonetheless see a parallel between Batman's restoration of full civil rights and Bush's intention to do so after the emergency ends. The difference between Bush's version of the state of exception and Batman's—between the conservative and the leftist—does not ultimately reside in the fact that it is temporary for Batman and permanent for Bush. Both figures view it as temporary, but what separates Batman is the attitude he takes toward this violation of the law: he accepts that his willingness to embrace this type of exceptionality constitutes him as a criminal. Because he views it as a criminal act, Batman is quick to eliminate it. But this is precisely what Bush would be loath to accept and why he views the war on terror as a quasi-eternal struggle.

The superhero film has emerged as a popular genre when the problem of the state of exception has moved to the foreground historically. That is not to say, of course, that superhero films owe their popularity to George W. Bush but that they attract an audience when the relationship between exceptionality and the law has increasingly come into question. As Agamben notes, "The state of exception tends increasingly to appear as the dominant paradigm of government in contemporary politics. This transformation of a provisional and exceptional measure into a technique of government threatens radically to alter—in fact, has already palpably altered—the structure and meaning of the traditional distinction between constitutional forms."[12] The state of exception, for Agamben, is the path by which democracy falls into fascism. The exception becomes confounded with the rule and soon takes its place. From that point forward, a total authority emerges that exercises authority over the people with their own security as its justification. Because the heroic exception is written into the generic requirements, the superhero film exists within this political context.

Most superhero films simply affirm our need for the heroic exception and don't call the status of this exception into question. This is true for Jon Favreau's *Iron Man* (2008) and Louis Leterrier's *The Incredible Hulk* (2008), to name just two released around the same time as *The Dark Knight*. As a result, even when they have some critical content about the ruling ideology—as with the (albeit limited) critique of the military-industrial complex in *Iron Man*—their form employing the heroic exception vitiates this content and ends up justifying the conservative direction of contemporary politics. In these films, even if the heroic exception causes certain problems, it is fundamentally necessary for the cause of justice, which would simply be overpowered without it.

The hero's relationship to heroic exceptionality forms the basis of authentic heroism. If the hero adopts the position of the exception as the difficult duty that one must perform for the sake of a greater good (the position of Iron Man, President Bush, Superman, and most exceptional heroes), then exceptionality becomes an unlimited end in itself that will never cease to be required. If, however, the hero adopts the position of the exception as a criminal duty, as a necessity that removes him from the realm of heroism altogether, then exceptionality can realize itself in justice rather than in the production of an increasing amount of injustice. Nolan's film shows us that authentic heroism necessarily appears in the form of evil.

JOCULAR ETHICS

Justice requires an exception because our adherence to the law is always compromised from the outset. Many theorists who have tackled the question of the subject's relationship to the law have run up against the same problem. Freud, for one, contends that the basis of our acquiescence to the law lies in envy—the envy of the other's satisfaction—and that this inevitably distorts all social arrangements. Similarly, Kant sees that our devotion to the law is never devotion to the law for its own sake but for some attendant pathological motivation. Even if we initially and instinctively obey the law, we do not do so for the right reasons.

When we emerge as subjects, we do so as beings of radical evil—that is, beings who do good for evil reasons. We help our neighbor for the recognition that it will gain us; we volunteer at the school in order to seem like a committed parent; we give money for disaster relief in order to feel comfortable about our level of material comfort; and so on. For Kant, this is the fundamental problem that morality confronts and the most difficult type of evil to extirpate. He explains,

> The human being (even the best) is evil only because he reverses the moral order of his incentives in incorporating them into his maxims. He indeed incorporates the moral law into those maxims, together

with the law of self-love; since, however, he realizes that the two cannot stand on an equal footing, but one must be subordinated to the other as its supreme condition, he makes the incentives of self-love and their inclinations the condition of compliance with the moral law—whereas it is this latter that, as *the supreme condition* of the satisfaction of the former, should have been incorporated into the universal maxim of the power of choice as the sole incentive.[13]

Though Kant believes that we have the capacity to turn from beings of radical evil to moral beings, we cannot escape a certain originary radical evil that leads us to place our incentives of self-love above the law and that prevents us from adhering to the law for its own sake.[14]

The presence of radical evil at the heart of the obedience to the law reveals the law's fundamental inadequacy. The problem is not, as Kant correctly grasps, that the law cannot overcome some natural proclivity for self-love but that it can emerge only against the background of radical evil. Without this background, there would be no law as such, nor any freedom, because the recognition of the law would entail de facto obedience. The law thus relies on the very evil that it would eliminate. Most obedience to the moral law, as Kant sees it, is in fact radical evil—obedience for the wrong reasons.

There is always a fundamental imbalance between law and criminality. Criminality is inscribed into the law itself in the form of misdirected obedience, and no law can free itself from reliance on the evil of such obedience. A consequentialist ethics develops as a compromise with this radical evil at the heart of the law. For this ethical position, what matters is the end—obedience—and not the evil means that the subject uses to arrive at that obedience. Those who take up the compromise with radical evil predominate within society, and they constitute the behavioral norm. They obey the law when necessary, but they do so in order to satisfy some incentive of self-love. Theirs is a morality of calculation in which acts have value in terms of the ultimate good they produce or the interest they serve. Anyone who obeys the law for its own sake becomes exceptional.

Both Batman and the Joker exist outside the calculating morality that predominates among the police, the law-abiding citizens, and the criminal underworld in Gotham. Both have the status of an exception because they adhere to a code that cuts against their incentives for self-love and violates any consequentialist morality. Though Batman tries to save Gotham and the Joker tries to destroy it, though Batman commits

133

himself to justice and the Joker commits himself to injustice, they share a position that transcends the inadequate and calculated ethics authorized by the law itself. Their differences mask a similar relationship to Kantian morality. Through the parallel between them, Christopher Nolan makes clear the role that evil must play in authentic heroism.

The Joker is Nolan's great contribution to the story of Batman. Of course, this character existed long before Nolan's film and even appeared in Tim Burton's first *Batman* film in 1989, to say nothing of the comic books or the television series. He is the primary enemy of Batman. But Nolan gives a new form to the Joker in *The Dark Knight*. Rather than remaining a figure of comic villainy, the Joker becomes the ethical center of the film, and he does so because he is a pure fiction without any underlying truth, an appearance without any reality. The creation of this character represents a pivotal moment in Nolan's cinematic exploration of deception.

It is the Joker, not Batman, who gives the most eloquent account of the ethical position that they occupy together. He sets himself up against the consequentialist and utilitarian ethic that rules Gotham, and he tries to analyze this ethic in order to understand what motivates it. As the Joker sees it, despite their apparent differences, all the different groups in Gotham indulge in an ethics of what he calls "scheming." That is to say, they act not on the basis of the rightness or wrongness of the act itself but in order to achieve some ultimate object. In doing so, they inherently degrade their acts and deprive them of their basis in freedom. Scheming enslaves one to the object of one's scheme.

For the Joker, the problem with scheming is not so much moral as it is aesthetic.[15] When one thinks of an action in terms of the end it will produce, one robs the action of its independence. When he talks to Dent after the latter's disfigurement, he explains, "I don't have a plan. The mob has plans, the cops have plans. You know what I am, Harvey? I'm a dog chasing cars. I wouldn't know what to do if I caught one. I just do things. I'm a wrench in the gears. I hate plans. Yours, theirs, everyone's. Maroni has plans. Gordon has plans. Schemers trying to control their worlds. I am not a schemer. I show schemers how pathetic their attempts to control things really are. So when I say that what happened to you and your girlfriend wasn't personal, you know I'm telling the truth." The Joker explicitly denies seeking any object in his criminal activity, which separates him decisively from the other criminals in the film. This provides him a freedom that no one else, save Batman, can enjoy. He can burn piles of money or put his life at risk because he doesn't think of his acts in terms of the ends they will accomplish for him. He breaks out of what Kant calls heteronomy in order to achieve autonomy.[16]

For Kant, adherence to the law designed to procure some object or some ultimate good leaves one inevitably bereft of freedom. As he points out in the *Groundwork of the Metaphysics of Morals*, "If the will seeks the law that is to determine it *anywhere else* than in the fitness of its maxims for its own giving of universal law—consequently if, in going beyond itself, it seeks this law in a property of any of its objects—*heteronomy* always results. The will in that case does not give itself the law; instead the object, by means of its relation to the will, gives the law to it."[17] Though Kant would not hold up the Joker as an exemplar of his morality, the latter does avoid elevating an object above the law, unlike, say, the law-abiding citizens in the film. The Joker's law, however, is one that Kant would not recognize. He values doing evil for its own sake, being "a wrench in the gears," which marks out an ethical position that Kant believes cannot exist—that of the diabolically evil subject.[18]

The Joker and Batman have an exceptional status in the film because they refuse the heteronomy that results from acting according to a calculus of ends. Both are figures who devote themselves to an ethical principle and follow it to its end point. For Batman, this is fighting injustice, and for the Joker, it is creating chaos. Even when this principle causes them harm or threatens their happiness, they nonetheless adhere to it. On several occasions in the film, the Joker welcomes his own death as part of his effort to unleash chaos, and Batman endures not only the physical pain that stems from his fight against injustice but also the absence of any recognition for what he does. Not only must he avoid revealing that Batman is really Bruce Wayne, but at the end of the film, he must also accept being an outcast and criminal figure as Batman himself. Even the one outsider who knows his true identity, Rachel, cannot properly love him because the singularity of his devotion to fighting injustice renders him incapable of existing in a love relationship. Both Batman and the Joker are completely isolated because they exist on a different ethical plane from everyone else in the film.[19]

Though the Joker and Batman occupy the same terrain of the exception, Nolan shows the ethical priority of the figure of evil. The Joker goes further than Batman in his pursuit of an ethical position that privileges the act over its consequences. Unlike Batman, the Joker does not hold onto a symbolic identity that he hides beneath his makeup. In this sense, the film creates a clear contrast between makeup and a mask. If one removed Batman's mask, one would discover his true identity. The Joker's makeup does not hide his true identity, but instead attests to the absence of one. All he is in the world is located in his appearance. He is the pure fiction without any truth hiding underneath.

The status of the Joker's makeup throughout the film reveals that its function is not to hide his true identity. Even when we first see him, robbing a bank, the white makeup that covers his face is not complete. The wrinkles on his forehead mark gaps through which his bare skin becomes visible. Later, during his interrogation at the police station, more gaps appear in the white makeup, and the black color around his eyes is smeared over his forehead. Though it distorts his appearance, the gradual disintegration of the Joker's makeup never bothers him or threatens to reveal his identity.

The Joker's lack of attention to his makeup raises the question of why he puts it on in the first place. He does not attempt to deceive in the traditional way, but instead his makeup hides the fact that he has nothing to hide. He deceives characters in the film because they attribute motives behind his actions when these actions actually serve as their own motivation. That is, the Joker acts for the sake of acting, not in response to some grievance or in order to gain some object. This complete investment in the act itself creates a freedom for him that no other characters in the film—not even Batman—are able to share. As Batman interrogates him, he can say with complete believability, "You have nothing to threaten me with." The Joker acts without concern for some object and without a basis in an identity that someone might exploit.

The identity (or lack of identity) of the Joker bespeaks his commitment to the act itself. Unlike the other characters in the film (including Batman), he has no identity that the film reveals. Nolan leaves the character of the Joker—his origins, his motivations, his real name—a complete mystery for the spectator, and not the kind of mystery one might figure out. The mystery is its own solution. Even after the police take him into custody, they can discover no information about him. Responding to the mayor's question concerning what they know about the Joker, Gordon says, "Nothing. No DNA, no fingerprints. Clothing is custom, no tags or brand labels. Nothing in his pockets but knives and lint. No name, no other alias." This complete absence of identifying information is not an indication that the Joker has successfully hidden who he really is but that he has no identity to hide. There is no real person beneath the illusion.

The film further shows that even biographical information about the Joker has the status of pure appearance. On two occasions, he provides an account of how his face became disfigured. When we hear the first account, it appears to be a plausible description of a childhood trauma. As he prepares to kill the gangster Gambol (Michael Jai White), he explains, "Want to know how I got these scars? My father was a drinker. And a fiend. And one night he goes off crazier than usual. Mommy gets the kitchen knife to defend herself. He doesn't like that. Not . . . one . . . bit. So, me watching, he takes the knife to her, laughing while he does it, turns to me, and he says, 'Why so serious?' Comes at me with the knife. 'Why so serious?' He sticks the blade in my mouth. 'Let's put a smile on that face.'" Nolan films this explanation in a series of close-ups alternating between the Joker and Gambol, and the intensity visible on the Joker's face gives a sense of authenticity to this story. When he kills Gambol immediately afterward by slicing his face, the act appears to have its ultimate motivation in the violence done to the Joker when he was a child.

But later, the Joker provides a conflicting account, and this second version reveals to the film's spectators that they know nothing about the Joker's past or about the trauma that disfigured his face. When he invades the fundraiser for Dent, he seizes Rachel and tells her the following story:

> So I had a wife, beautiful, like you, who tells me I worry too much.
> Who tells me I ought to smile more. Who gambles and gets in deep
> with the sharks. Look at me! One day, they carve her face. And we
> have no money for surgeries. She can't take it. I just want to see her
> smile again. I just want her to know that I don't care about the scars.
> So I stick a razor in my mouth and do this to myself. And you know
> what? She can't stand the sight of me. She leaves. Now I see the funny
> side. Now I'm always smiling.

In contrast to the first scene, where the Joker relates the origins of his scars in a series of close-ups, in this one the explanation occurs while a 360 degree tracking shot circles the Joker and Rachel. The formal shift in the depiction of the Joker's explanation helps to transform the spectator's response to him.

The Joker's first account of extreme child abuse at the hands of his father plays into contemporary explanations for violent criminality and thus provides a plausible, though perhaps not entirely justifiable, rea-

137

son for the Joker's activity. The form of the film during this first account further authenticates it. The close-ups of the Joker and his victim register the seriousness of what he says. But when he repeats the history of his scars with new content, the lack of seriousness of the history becomes apparent. The 360 degree tracking shot creates disequilibrium in the spectator appropriate to the revelation that the Joker is not really telling the history of his scars. We move from the close-ups, which provide a direct and seemingly veridical account of his history, to the 360 degree tracking shot, which enacts the circumlocution evident as we hear a new version of the story. The film offers us no way of adjudicating between the conflicting accounts but instead suggests that the truth of the origin of the scars is unimportant. The Joker uses the story of their origin to shock and to create terror rather than to offer an explanation for his criminal acts.[20] His acts cannot be reduced to what motivates them, and he attempts to promulgate the proper respect for these acts throughout the film.

Because the Joker detests and wants to destroy the morality of scheming or consequentialism, he sets up a series of tests that challenge the capacity of this morality. He forces Batman to choose between saving Harvey Dent and Rachel Dawes; he threatens to blow up a hospital if no one murders within an hour the man who threatens to reveal Batman's identity; and he gives two boats fleeing Gotham Island a detonator for explosives on the other boat, promising to blow up both boats unless one blows up the other before midnight. This last test actually paves the way for the citizens of Gotham to transcend the morality of calculation in the way that the Joker himself does. The problem of the two boats seems to provide a simple moral dilemma. If one thinks in terms of the greatest good for the greatest number—if one adopts the position of the schemer—it is clear that one boat must blow up the other so that the people on both boats don't perish. And since one boat is filled with criminals being transferred and the other is filled with ordinary citizens, the ethical dilemma that the Joker offers seems easy to solve.[21] But Nolan depicts an abandonment of the morality of the schemer that at first appears to represent the typical narrative cheating that one finds in Hollywood films.

The two ethical acts that culminate the film seem to mark a turn away from the critical edge that the film displays earlier and a capitulation to sentimental morality that sees the underlying goodness of humanity. One could view the end of *The Dark Knight* as a new version of the conclusion of Frank Capra's *It's a Wonderful Life* (1946), where

138

a mass eruption of compassion comes to rescue George Bailey (Jimmy Stewart) from financial ruin. In *The Dark Knight*, the people on both boats decide to accept their own deaths rather than take responsibility for killing the people on the other boat. But in contrast to Capra, Nolan complicates the ethical dimension of these acts. He begins by showing the utter immorality of traditional consequentialist or utilitarian moral claims. The civilians on the first boat begin by insisting on their moral right to destroy the group of criminals on the second boat. One argues for blowing up the other boat by claiming, "They had their chance." According to this line of thought, the commission of a crime leaves one less worthy of survival. If one group must die to save the other—this is the ground rule that the Joker establishes—then it is clear, for the law-abiding civilians, which group should live and which should perish. No one on the civilian boat argues for not blowing up the other boat, and it is clear that their arguments have nothing to do with morality and everything to do with their own survival.

What's more, the film reveals the completely antithetical relationship between ethical action and the institutions of democracy. The authorities on the civilian boat decide—prompted by an outspoken passenger and due presumably to their devotion to the ideology of democracy—to vote on whether to destroy the other boat. As the film shows it, the simple act of voting on a question such as this underscores the inappropriateness of this type of response. But when the authorities count the votes and a large majority (396–140) opts to blow up the criminal boat, we see baldly that democratic procedures (such as the popular vote) have no ethical status at all. In fact, the secret ballot allows each subject to retreat from the trauma of the ethical decision rather than confronting it directly. The film shows one passenger writing out his vote and handing it in with great determination, while a shot of another reveals his emotional struggle with the difficulties of the moral issue. But the way that Nolan films these two passengers—and his entire treatment of the vote—is replete with irony. Both of these attitudes toward the vote serve only to illustrate the absurdity of voting on the decision to blow up another boat full of people. The vote is an inadequate mechanism for approaching a decision of this magnitude.

The ethical act occurs not through the hastily put-together franchise on the civilian boat but through the revolutionary seizure of power on the prisoners' boat. During the crisis, Nolan focuses several shots on a group of large prisoners huddled together, appearing to conspire to take the detonator from the authorities on the boat. The way that the prisoners are depicted accentuates their menace: they stare ominously at the authorities; they whisper to one another; and they maintain a determined, grimacing expression. These visual clues, added to the fact that the film establishes them as dangerous criminals, suggest that they are planning to seize the detonator and blow up the civilian ship in order to save their own lives. But the film turns the tables on the spectator's expectation.

The leader of this group of prisoners approaches the authority holding the detonator and confronts him. A shot of the frightened look on the guard's face shows how the prisoner intimidates him, not because the guard fears being overpowered but because he believes that the prisoner will force him to do what he wants to do anyway—that is, blow up the other boat. The prisoner upbraids the guard, saying, "You don't want to die, but you don't know how to take a life." After the prisoner says this, Nolan cuts back to the other boat, where a civilian proclaims, "Those men on that boat, they made their choices." This crosscutting sequence appears to establish a kind of moral equivalency: though the prisoner is more straightforward about his willingness to kill in order to survive, the civilian partakes in exactly the same attitude. When the film cuts back to the prisoner's boat, the prisoner makes his final argument before taking the detonator. He says, "Give it to me. You can tell them I took it by force. Give it to me, and I'll do what you should have done ten minutes ago." These words put the final touch on the conviction that the prisoner plans to blow up the other boat, but instead we see him take the detonator and throw it out the window into the water, apparently destroying his own chance at survival. In a subsequent close-up, the civilian who had volunteered to press the detonator softly lays it back in its box.

Both the prisoners and the civilians act in a way that violates not only their self-interest (risking death by refusing to kill someone else) but in a way that defies all rational calculation. According to the rules of the game that the Joker established, if neither boat uses the detonator, both boats will be destroyed. Rejecting this wager requires rejecting the morality of calculation because according to any calculation of good ends, it will be preferable that one boat survives rather than both being destroyed. Here, Nolan reveals that a group of anonymous people are capable of a great ethical act, but what saves this depiction from becoming Capraesque—and thus perpetuating an ideological fantasy, allowing the spectator to leave the film assured of intrinsic human goodness—is

140

where he locates the source of the ethical act and what factors militate against it.

The source of the ethical act is not the popular vote (which goes decidedly against acting ethically), nor is it the good mother trying to protect her child (who argues for blowing up the prisoners), nor is it the figures of authority (who come across as feckless, unable to decide one way or the other). Instead, it is the prisoner, the figure of criminality, who is able to make the ethical gesture. And ultimately the Joker himself acts as the source for the display of ethics that we see at the end of the film. By setting up an abhorrent ethical situation where he expects people to act in a calculating fashion, the Joker provides an opportunity for them to break out of calculation. He confronts them with the logic of their scheming taken to its end point, and this creates the possibility for a recoil from scheming, which is what occurs.

The Joker is the ethical center of *The Dark Knight* because he manages to challenge the hegemony of calculation that controls Gotham, and to show that another world, one where ethical acts are not part of a scheming calculation, is possible. Of course, the Joker does horrible things: he stabs a pencil through a man's eye; he blows up a hospital; he kills countless people; and so on. By placing the Joker at the ethical center of the film, Nolan does not exculpate him for these deeds or celebrate them. He shows rather that there is a certain necessary violence behind all ethical acts. They must violently wipe away the predominating world of calculation that underlies and pathologizes all obedience to the law. Though he is himself a figure of evil in the film, the violence of the Joker takes aim at the radical evil present in typical obedience to the law—the fact that we obey the law, as Kant notes, for reasons other than the law itself. The Joker's evil provides the basis for any ethical heroism because it highlights and strives to eliminate the evil of calculation that defines the subject's original relation to the law. He thereby constitutes the ground on which the ethical act can emerge.

THE PUBLIC FACE OF THE HERO

Just as *The Dark Knight* illustrates the inextricable relationship between heroism and evil, it undermines the idea of the hero who can appear as heroic. From early in the film, Batman proclaims his desire to step aside in order to cede his position to someone who can be heroic without wearing a mask. He sees this possibility in the figure of Harvey Dent. But the film shows that there is no hero without a mask—and, more specifically, without a mask of evil. As Slavoj Žižek puts it, "The properly human good, the good elevated above the natural good, the infinite spiritual good, is ultimately *the mask of evil*."[22] Without the mask of evil, good cannot emerge and remains stuck in the calculation of interest; without the mask of evil, good remains scheming. This is precisely what Harvey Dent evinces, despite the promise that Batman sees in him for the perfect form of heroism.

Throughout the beginning part of the film, Harvey Dent seems like a figure of pure good. This goodness allows him to never be at a loss for what to do or say. Even when a mobster tries to shoot him in open court, he calmly grabs the gun from the mobster's hand and punches him in the face. After the punch, we see Dent's expression of total equanimity, even amid an attempted assassination. This coolness stems from his absolute certainty that events will follow according to his plans. The rapidity with which Nolan edits together the threat from the mobster and Dent's response minimizes the spectator's sense of danger. The threat against Dent's life disappears almost before we can experience it as such, which suggests that it lacks a quality of realness, both for Dent and for the spectator. The court scene establishes him as a hero whom one cannot harm. Ironically, the superhero in the film, Batman, shows himself to be vulnerable when he first appears in the film, as dogs bite him through his protective armor. This distinction between the vulnerability of Dent and Batman explains why the former cannot be an authentic hero.

In contrast to Batman, Dent's heroism does not involve the experience of loss; in fact, it is based on a repudiation of the very possibility of losing. Bruce Wayne adopted the identity of Batman after the trauma of being dropped in a cave full of bats and losing his parents, but no such traumatic loss animates the heroism of Dent. He is heroic through an immediate identification with the good, which enables him to have a purity that Batman doesn't have. No rupture and subsequent return animates his commitment to justice. He can publicly avow his heroic actions because he performs them in a pure way, without resorting to the guise of evil. But the falsity of this immediate identification with the good becomes apparent in Dent's disavowal of loss, which Nolan locates in the tic that marks Dent's character—his proclivity for flipping a coin to resolve dilemmas.

On several occasions, he flips the coin (a gift from his father) to introduce the possibility of loss into his activities. By flipping a coin, one admits that events might not go according to plan, that the other might win, and that loss is an ever-present possibility. Though the coin flip represents an attempt to master loss by rendering it random rather than necessary or constitutive, it nonetheless accedes to the fact that one might lose. Dent first flips the coin when he is late to examine a key witness in court, and the coin flip will determine whether he or his assistant Rachel will do the questioning. When Rachel wonders how he could leave something so important to chance, Dent replies, "I make my own luck." It is just after this that the mobster tries and fails to shoot Dent, further suggesting his invulnerability.

Dent wins this and subsequent coin flips in the first part of the film because he uses a loaded coin, a coin with two heads. When it comes to the coin flip, Dent does make his own luck by eliminating the element of chance. The coin that he uses ensures that he will avoid the possibility of losing. The coin with two heads is certainly a clever device, but it also stands as the objective correlative for Dent's lack of authentic heroism. The immediacy of his heroism cannot survive any mediation. Once loss is introduced into Dent's world, his heroism disappears and he becomes a figure of criminality.

The transformation of Harvey Dent after his disfigurement is so precipitous that it strains credulity. One day he is the pure defender of absolute justice, and the next he is on a homicidal warpath, willing to shoot innocent children. One could chalk up this rapid change to sloppy filmmaking on Christopher Nolan's part, to an eagerness to move too quickly to the film's concluding moments of tension. But the rapidity of the transformation signifies all the more because it seems so forced and jarring. It allows us to retroactively examine Harvey Dent's relationship to the law earlier in the film.

Dent becomes the villain Two-Face after his injury, but in doing so he merely takes up the identity that the police department had adopted for him when he was working for the internal affairs division. As an investigator of other officers, Dent earned the nickname "Two-Face" by insisting on absolute purity and by targeting any sign of police corruption. Even Gordon, an officer who is not corrupt, complains to Dent of the paralyzing effects of these tactics on the department. On the one hand, an insistence on purity seems to be a consistently non-calculating ethical position. One can imagine this insistence obstructing the long-term goal of better law enforcement (which is why Gordon objects to it). On the other hand, however, the demand for purity always anticipates its

143

own failure. The pure hero quickly becomes the criminal when an experience of loss disrupts this purity.

This first occurs when Gordon is apparently killed at the police commissioner's funeral. In response to this blatant display of public criminality, Dent abuses a suspect from the shooting and even threatens to kill him, using his trick coin as a device for mental torture. Even though Dent has no intention of actually shooting the suspect, Batman nonetheless scolds Dent for his methods when he interrupts the private interrogation. This scene offers the first insight into what Dent will become later in the film, but it also shows the implications of his form of heroism. Dent resorts to torture because he has no ontological space for loss. When it occurs, his heroism becomes completely derailed.

The death of Rachel and his own disfigurement introduce traumatic loss into Dent's existence. Nolan shows the ramifications of this change through the transformation that his coin undergoes during the explosion that kills Rachel. The explosion chars one side of Dent's two-headed coin (which he had earlier flipped to Rachel as he was taken away to jail), so that it becomes, through traumatic force, a coin with two different sides. The film indicates here how trauma introduces loss into the world and how this removes all subjective certainty.

When Dent as Two-Face flips the newly marked coin, the act takes on an entirely new significance. Unlike earlier, he is no longer certain about the result of the flip. He flips to decide whether he will kill the Joker in the hospital room, whether he will kill Detective Wuertz (Ron Dean) in a bar, and whether he will kill Detective Ramirez (Monique Curnen) in an alley. Of the three, only Wuertz ends up dead, but Dent also kills another officer and the criminal boss Maroni along with some of his men. This rampage ends with Dent holding Gordon's family hostage and threatening to kill the one Gordon holds most dear. Dent becomes a killer to inflict his own experience of loss on others: he tells Gordon that he wants to kill what is most precious to him so that Gordon will feel what he felt.

After Dent's death, the film ends with Batman accepting responsibility for Dent's killings to salvage Dent's public reputation and thereby sustain the image of the public hero. Gordon and Batman believe that this gesture is necessary for saving the city and keeping alive its hope for justice. When Gordon says, "Gotham needs its true hero," we see a shot of him turning Dent's face over, obscuring the burned side and exposing the human side. In death, Dent will begin to wear the mask that he would never wear in life: a mask of heroism will cover his criminality.

144

As the film conceives it, this lie—that purity is possible—represents the sine qua non of social being. Without the idea that one can sustain an ethical position, calculation of interest would have nothing to offset it, and the city would become identified with criminality.[23]

But the real interest of the film's conclusion lies with Batman and the form of appearance that his heroism takes. It is as if Batman takes responsibility for Dent's act not to save Dent's face but to stain his own image irrevocably with evil. He must lie. He remains the heroic exception, but his status changes radically. To guarantee that Dent dies as a hero, Batman must take responsibility for the murders that Dent committed. With this gesture, he truly adopts the mask of evil. In the closing montage sequence, we see the police hunting him down, Gordon smashing the Bat-Signal, and finally Batman driving away into the night on his motorcycle. As this sequence concludes, we hear Gordon's say in a voiceover, "He's the hero Gotham deserves, but not the one it needs right now. And so we'll hunt him, because he can take it. Because he's not a hero. He's a silent guardian, a watchful protector . . . a dark knight." As Gordon pronounces the final word, the film cuts to black from the image of Batman on his motorcycle. The melodrama of this voiceover elevates the heroism of Batman, but it does so precisely because he agrees to appear as evil. This gesture, even more than any of his physical acts of courage, is the gesture of the true hero because it leaves him without any recognition for his heroism. For the hero who appears in the form of evil, heroic exceptionality must be an end in itself without any hope for a greater reward. When the exception takes this form, it loses the danger that adheres to the typical hero. The mask of evil allows the exception to persist without multiplying itself. By adopting this position at the end of the film, Batman reveals that he has taken up the lesson of the Joker and grasped the importance of the break from calculation. Dent, the hero who wants to appear heroic, descends into murderous evil, but Batman, the hero who accepts evil as his form of appearance, sustains the only possible path for heroic exceptionality.

In an epoch when the inadequacy of the law is evident, the need for the heroic exception becomes ever more pronounced, but the danger of the exception has also never been more apparent. Declarations of exceptionality abound in the contemporary world, and they allow us to see the negative ramifications that follow from the exception, no matter how heroic its intent. Audiences flock to superhero movies in search of a heroic exception that they can embrace, an exception that would work

145

toward justice without simultaneously adding to injustice in the manner of today's real-world exceptions. In *The Dark Knight*, Christopher Nolan offers a viable image of heroic exceptionality. The heroic form of appearance must be its opposite if it is to avoid being implicated in the injustice it fights. The only genuine hero lies about his or her heroism. The lesson for our real-world exceptions is thus a difficult one. Rather than being celebrated as the liberator of Iraq and the savior of American freedom, George W. Bush would have to act behind the scenes to encourage charges being brought against him as a war criminal at the World Court, and then he would have to flee to the streets of The Hague as the authorities pursue him there. In the eyes of the public, true heroes must identify themselves with the evil that we fight.

To do so, they must commit themselves as much to deception and disguise as to truth. Without the lie, there may be purity, but there is no heroism. *The Dark Knight* concludes with Batman appearing as a criminal because Nolan grasps the liberating power of the fiction. Through the fiction of the filmic medium, he creates moments of exception in which spectators can escape the domain of law, but he also guards against the identification of exception with law itself, which is what occurs whenever one proclaims a "state of emergency."

Of all Christopher Nolan's films, *Inception* (2010) took the longest time to appear. He had the idea for the film approximately nine years, as he himself notes, before he finally made the film in 2010.[1] It required the incredible success of *The Dark Knight* (2008) for a studio to give Nolan the opportunity to make a big-budget film on dreams, a film about which Nolan claims, "There are bits of *Inception* that people are going to think I ripped that straight out of *Last Year at Marienbad*."[2] Though Nolan explains that he hadn't even seen Alain Resnais's 1961 film prior to making *Inception*, the very association of a big-budget film—a summer blockbuster—with one of the most celebrated European art films in cinema history would afford any director, even the most accomplished, a chilly reception from a Hollywood studio. But *The Dark Knight* earned Nolan the faith that he could make a *Last Year at Marienbad* for the masses.

But *Inception* is not a popular version of *Last Year at Marienbad*. In fact, despite its superiority to the typical summer blockbuster and despite its popularity among both filmgoers and the vast majority of film critics, there were those who took the film to task for its mediocrity in comparison with the rest of Nolan's output. The fact that it is the first of Nolan's films to receive an Oscar nomination for Best Picture seems to confirm its status as Nolan's film for the masses, even more than *The Dark Knight*. Critic Christopher Orr complains that *Inception*, unlike a film such as *Memento* (2000), allows technical virtuosity to overwhelm everything else. He notes, "For all its elegant construction, *Inception* is a film in which nothing feels comparably at stake."[3] While Orr finds an absence of thought in the film, Robert Samuels objects to the film on political grounds. He sees the film as symptomatic of our increasing inability to differentiate between fantasy and reality. As he puts it, "With *Inception* we are told that we are in a dream that is in a dream that is in another dream, and the result is that by the end of the film, no one knows if we are in reality or still in a dream, but perhaps this is a very truthful way of seeing our contemporary world."[4] Nolan's film, accord-

A PLEA FOR THE ABANDONMENT OF
REALITY IN *INCEPTION*

SEVEN

ing to Samuels, simply mystifies the way that contemporary culture works: it inundates us with ideas so that we can't discern the difference between our own thoughts and the dictates of the capitalist culture.

Both Orr and Samuels view *Inception* as a symptom of Hollywood gone awry. In Orr's case, the demand to produce a seamless blockbuster has dissipated the "messiness" of the more insightful lower-budget films of Nolan's early career. For Samuels, the film's status as a blockbuster reduces it to nothing more than a symptom of larger cultural trends. To the extent that they exist at all, the ideas in *Inception* necessarily play second fiddle to its technical efficacy and expansive production. As much as any failure in writing or directing, it is the sheer size of the film that damns it. And yet, it does not really resemble Nolan's prior blockbuster, *The Dark Knight*.

Though it has a large budget and a clear status as a summer blockbuster, *Inception* resembles Nolan's small-budget film *Memento* much more than it does *The Dark Knight*. It is a return to the structure of his earlier films, even if it lacks the temporal distortions that occur in *Memento* and *Following* (1998).⁵ One of the key features in Nolan's largest productions—*The Dark Knight* and *Batman Begins* (2005)—is the trustworthiness of the protagonist. Even if the former film ends with Batman (Christian Bale) taking up the guise of a criminal to suggest that his type of activity must remain purely exceptional, the spectator retains complete confidence in him. One watches the film knowing that Batman is not really a criminal. The film depicts the lie without enacting it on the spectator. A similar process is at work in *Batman Begins*, where Bruce Wayne (Christian Bale) plays the part of a millionaire playboy to hide his real identity as Batman. In contrast, Nolan's comparatively low-budget films, like *Following* and *Memento*, deceive the spectator in addition to depicting the role that deception plays within the diegetic reality of the film. In this sense, the fact that Nolan had the idea for *Inception* before he made either *Batman Begins* or *The Dark Knight* is revelatory. It has much more in common with *Memento* than with these later films, despite its budget.⁶

As in *Memento*, *Inception* privileges its central character, Cobb (Leonardo DiCaprio), and encourages us to trust him. At the end of the former film, the spectator learns that Leonard (Guy Pearce) has intentionally deceived himself in order to sustain his quest for the murderer of his wife. This implies that everything the film shows up to this point has resulted from Leonard's desire for self-deception rather than, as the film leads the spectator to believe, a quest for the truth of his wife's death. Leonard's self-deception is simultaneously Nolan's way of deceiving the spectator. He establishes Leonard as a character seemingly in pursuit of knowledge and then reveals that pursuit disingenuous. The case is less clear with Cobb in *Inception*, but the procedure parallels that of *Memento*. Cobb's agenda involves not a quest to avenge his murdered wife but an effort to clear his name for the death of his wife, Mal (Marion Cotillard), and return home to see his children again. Cobb must enter into the dream world to regain his real life.

As the film opens, Cobb works as a corporate mind thief, stealing secrets from executives by invading their dreams. After trying to steal secrets from Saito (Ken Watanabe), Cobb organizes a gang of thieves—Arthur (Joseph Gordon-Levitt), Eames (Tom Hardy), Yusef (Dileep Rao), and Ariadne (Ellen Page)—to invade the unconscious of Robert Fischer (Cillian Murphy) and plant the idea in his mind to break up the multibillion-dollar company he inherited upon the death of his father, Maurice (Pete Postlethwaite).

As in the typical heist film, each member of the team has a specific function: Arthur handles their extraction from the dream world; Eames helps to plan and provides the weaponry; Yusef is the druggist who gets them into the dream state; and Ariadne is the architect who designs the various dreamscapes they will enter. Cobb and his gang perform the inception at the bequest of Saito, who accompanies the others into the dream world. Saito offers money, but he also promises to wipe Cobb's record clean in exchange for a successful inception.[7]

Though the film presents him as a thief, Cobb's criminality, like Leonard's in *Memento*, seems to be in service of a good cause—the reunion with his children that concludes the film. Just as *Memento* concludes with Leonard's lie to himself that reveals the spuriousness of the inquiry that dominates the film up to its conclusion, toward the end of *Inception* Cobb reveals to Ariadne that he bears a degree of responsibility for Mal's death and thus is not the innocent victim of her attempt to frame him when she committed suicide.

Memento leads the spectator to believe that the primary issue to resolve is the identity of the person who murdered Leonard's spouse. The narrative appears to be structured around this question and to be leading toward its resolution. The deception of *Memento* surrounds the subject of desire appearing as a subject of knowledge. *Inception* misleads the spectator by appearing to emphasize the importance of the difference between the dream world and reality when its real focus is the subject's relationship to trauma, a relationship that the dream often facilitates and reality enables us to avoid. The real flight, as *Inception* shows it, is not Mal's retreat into the dream world from which Cobb tries to rescue her but Cobb's own attempt to escape the trauma he finds in the dream world by returning to reality. *Inception* represents a further move in Nolan's filmmaking through its association of trauma with fiction and flight from trauma with reality.

There is a truth in *Inception*, but one discovers it not in reality but in the dream. Like all of Nolan's films, *Inception* reveals the fiction—or here, the dream—as the path to this truth rather than as a barrier to it. The insistence on the real world as a separate realm from that of the dream is the film's primary deception, and one must work through this deception to grasp its privileging of the dream world. Nolan demonstrates that waking up serves as a path for escaping the truth, not finding it.[8]

In his *Seminar XVII*, subtitled *The Other Side of Psychoanalysis*, Jacques Lacan makes precisely this point about the role that waking up has in relation to truth. He notes, "A dream wakes you up just when it might let the truth drop, so that the only reason one wakes up is so as to continue dreaming—dreaming in the real or, to be more exact, in reality."[9] In order to explain this idea, Lacan turns in an earlier seminar to an example from Freud, who recounts a father waking from a dream about his son burning to find the coffin of his recently deceased son having caught fire from nearby candles. Freud uses this dream to make a simple point about the dreamer's awareness of external reality while dreaming, but for Lacan, the interest of the dream is much more intricate. The father wakes up at the moment when the dream would reveal to him the horror of his own desire, a desire for the death of his son. The reality of the burning coffin to which the father awakens functions as a respite from the truth of the father's desire that the dream is on the verge of making evident.[10] Reality provides solace because it has the effect of insulating us from our desire, while the dream demands that we follow the logic of this desire, no matter how traumatic its revelations might be. One wakes in order to avoid encountering the truth of one's desire manifested in the dream.

As psychoanalysis (and *Inception*) shows, the distortion of the dream work does not only hide the truth, it also allows one to find it. Without this distortion, in the awakened world of everyday reality, truth ceases to be accessible because one's desire becomes hidden. *Memento* reveals how the pursuit of desire underwrites every quest for knowledge, and

150

Inception takes us into the dream world to illustrate the access to truth that exists there.

Inception deceives the spectator, not as Robert Samuels suggests—by confusing the difference between fantasy and reality—but by making it seem that reality has a privileged status relative to fantasy or the dream. This deception is necessary for the film because Nolan realizes that one cannot simply tell the truth about the primacy of the lie. Doing so violates the very concept that one attempts to illustrate. One must discover this primacy through the mechanism of the lie or the fiction itself, which is what *Inception* accomplishes. The deception that the spectators undergo enables them to arrive at an otherwise impossible truth.

Almost all the competing theories proffered about *Inception* focus on the status of Cobb at various moments in the film—and in particular at the end. Does he remain within the dream world (and whose dream world?), or has he returned to reality? The totem, an object important for psychoanalysis, appears to serve as the index for distinguishing the dream from reality. The film's final shot focuses on Cobb's totem (a top) that continues to spin on a table. At this point, the spectator knows that the top indicates a dream world if it doesn't fall or reality if it does, but the film leaves the status of world ambiguous by cutting to black before one sees what happens to the top. More than any other point in the film, this final shot has occasioned endless discussions about the status of Cobb relative to reality.

Nolan concludes the film with the ambiguity of the spinning top precisely in order to mislead the spectator about where the truth of the film resides. This ending gives birth to theorizing that misses the point, but this misstep is necessary for the spectator to grasp the desire that animates the film. One must allow oneself to be duped by the question of reality in order to see that this question is not the film's central concern.[11] The point is not so much that the various theories about the reality within the film are incorrect but that they begin with a misleading assumption. They presume that the question of the reality of our experience is the fundamental concern that confronts us as subjects. But the entirety of *Inception* marginalizes this question. It is only Cobb, a hero who shares Leonard Shelby's reliability, who leads us down this misleading path. To ask the proper question about *Inception* we must begin by calling Cobb himself, despite all his attractiveness as a character, into question.[12]

151

THE PRIVILEGE OF THE WIFE

In both *Memento* and *Inception*, we see the wives of Leonard and Cobb only through the lens of the two protagonists' fantasies. When the time depicted in each film begins, both women are, as far as the spectator knows, dead. By starting each film after the deaths of the spouses of the protagonists, Nolan would seem to exclude both women from the films. In fact, *Memento* depicts only a few scenes of Leonard's wife (Jorja Fox), and though Mal plays a much more prominent role in *Inception*, she functions primarily as an obstacle that Cobb must navigate around in order to accomplish his mission. What's more, Leonard's wife appears only in his memories (or fantasies), and Mal appears only as a projection in Cobb's mind. We never see Mal herself, and the film depicts her suicide not when it actually happens but only as Cobb recounts it to Ariadne. But this absence from the diegetic reality of the films does not preclude a central presence in their fundamental concerns.[13]

Memento uses the contrast between Leonard's wife repeatedly reading the same book and Leonard's inability to understand this kind of repetitive enjoyment to illustrate the antagonism between them. *Inception* distinguishes between Mal's determination to remain with Cobb in the dream and his insistence on returning to reality. If Mal is dead when the film begins—and our certainty about her death depends on Cobb not himself being within a dream throughout most or all of the film—then she dies as a result of Cobb. Though she tells him that she has framed him for her murder so that he must kill himself along with her, Cobb is responsible for her death in a way that she doesn't suspect until he relates his guilt to her at the end of the film. His first successful inception, as he tells Ariadne, involved implanting the idea in Mal that her reality wasn't real. He says, "The reason I knew inception was possible is because I did it to her first. I did it to my wife." In order to bring Mal out of the dream world that they had created together, Cobb planted the idea of unreality in her psyche. As Cobb recounts, even when she finally woke up, she couldn't escape the idea that she remained within a dream, and she killed herself in the real world to wake up.

The guilt that plagues Cobb stems from the role he plays in Mal's suicide. If he hadn't planted the idea of the unreality of reality in her mind, she wouldn't have leapt to her death from the ledge of a building. Cobb furtively gives Mal this idea because of his own investment in the idea of reality. Mal refuses to leave the dream world and return

152

to reality, so Cobb feels as if he has no choice but to perform an act of inception so that she'll doubt the dream world's reality and thus desire to leave it. Before this inception, Mal does not focus on the distinction between the dream world and the real world.

In his brief 1925 essay "Negation," Freud addresses the way that the judgment concerning the reality of things develops. As Freud sees it, this type of judgment is not the most primary one but develops out of attributive judgments. In other words, first we judge whether an object pleases us, and based on this earlier type of judgment, we learn to judge the object's reality. Freud claims that "the real existence of something of which there is a presentation (reality-testing) . . . is a concern of the definitive reality-ego, which develops out of the initial pleasure-ego."[14] Our capacity for judging the reality of an object or of our world depends on the libidinal relation that we take up relative to this object or to our world. Our concern for reality is always secondary or derivative of our concern for enjoyment. Thus, Cobb's obsession with returning to his children in the real world can only form through the abandonment of his enjoyment and an attempt to retreat from its primacy.

Unlike Cobb, Mal's concern is for the relationship that she has to her love object, not the question of whether she is living in reality. At one point, we see her make this distinction clear in a simple riddle that she tells Ariadne. She says, "I'll tell you a riddle. You're waiting for a train, a train that will take you far away. You know where you hope the train will take you, but you don't know for sure. But it doesn't matter. How can it not matter to you where that train will take you?" The answer to the riddle, as Cobb himself divines in the film, is that you will be with the person whom you love.

The idea of an ultimate destination, of going somewhere, serves only as an excuse for sustaining a relation with her object, but Cobb believes in the possibility of obtaining his object, of escaping the dream world and gaining his children back in the real world. In an almost direct response before the fact to Mal's riddle about the train, Cobb says, "I hate trains," as he departs a bullet train after a failed extraction from Saito. And furthermore, it is a train running down the middle of the road that smashes into Cobb and his friends when they first enter into Robert Fischer's dream to perform an inception. Mal sends this train in order to block Cobb's attempted heist and force him to remain with her. For Cobb, the train requires that one wait to arrive at one's destination—or it is an obstacle to arriving at where one desires to go—while for Mal,

ABANDONMENT OF REALITY IN *INCEPTION*

the wait is the destination. There is no destination outside the train ride itself, which is why it doesn't matter to her where the train goes or whether she is dreaming.[15]

The contrast between Mal and Cobb, which manifests itself in their disparate attitude toward trains, parallels Hegel's contrast between the bad infinity and the infinity of the Notion, a contrast that *Inception* develops through the relationship to the laws of physics that it establishes. The dream world that Mal prefers to reality allows one to leave behind the bad infinity that governs the physics of reality and access the infinity of the Notion that Hegel associates with speculative thought rather than with physics. The good infinity or the infinity of the Notion is one that returns to itself while moving forward. It is like the infinite structure of a constant circling motion that moves forward while always returning to the same place. From Hegel's perspective, we can think the infinity of the Notion but we can't picture it. Doing so would require an impossible image in which reality circled back on itself.

While the real world appears to go on infinitely (or at least we never experience its limits), its infinity is what Hegel calls a "bad infinity." The bad infinity is what we deal with when we try to imagine the extension of time, space, or numbers. There is an infinite progress toward an end point that one can never, by definition, reach. One cannot count to infinity, but one can continually be in the process of counting to infinity. When Hegel labels this a bad infinity, he doesn't mean to say that it doesn't count as infinity. Its badness consists in the fact that it signals what one tries to attain without ever attaining it. Hegel believes that we can actually attain infinity, and the bad or mathematical infinity misleads us insofar as it suggests an infinity forever out of reach or transcendent. The bad infinity is always beyond, just like the usual idea of truth that Nolan's films combat.

Hegel contrasts this infinite progress to an unattainable beyond with the proper infinity of the Notion. The infinity of the Notion is not an infinity that we can never reach, but rather one that we already have. As Hegel puts it in the *Science of Logic*, "The universality of the Notion is the *reached beyond*; the bad infinity remains inflicted with the beyond as an unattainable goal, for it remains the mere *progress* to infinity."[16] For Hegel, Christianity provides the great example of the infinity of the Notion: through Christ, humanity attains divine transcendence, and the infinity of God no longer remains separate from the finite human realm. Hegel's investment in Christianity stems entirely from its philosophical conception of the infinite as already attained within the figure

154

of Christ. Rather than progressing toward infinity, Christianity depicts infinity present in finitude.

The problem is that once we create an image of the beyond that we have reached—even the image of Christ—it ceases to be a beyond. This is why Hegel inveighs against "picture thinking" as an obstacle to speculative philosophizing.[17] Picture thinking—forcing thought into an image—misses the infinite of the Notion, an infinity in which the beyond has already been attained but nevertheless continues to exist as a beyond. *Inception* provides, despite Hegel's apprehension concerning picture thinking, an image of the infinite of the Notion.

The contrast between the bad infinity and the infinity of the Notion is perfectly captured in the difference between an unending staircase heading upward (or downward) and the Penrose stairs, which appear in *Inception*. These stairs are impossible in reality but can be depicted by creating the illusion of three dimensions in a two-dimensional drawing. The Penrose stairs reconnect with each other in order to form a square and yet continue to ascend or descend. The drawing can create the illusion of continuous ascension that, brought together with the illusion of depth, creates the sense of an unending square staircase. But no one can actually build a Penrose staircase. Because one can alter the laws of physics in the dream world, the impossible Penrose stairs become a possibility that dream architects, like Ariadne, can realize in the film. As he is introducing Ariadne to the dream world, Arthur takes her for a walk on a Penrose staircase: they continue to walk upward and yet at the same time continue in a circle.

This motion upward while remaining on the same path provides a visual image of Hegel's infinite of the Notion. The staircase itself indicates a movement toward the beyond, but the perpetual circle makes clear that the beyond has already been attained. The existence of the Penrose stairs within the dream world suggests that this realm, in contrast to reality, more accurately represents the structure of desire and the desiring psyche. The existence of these stairs reveals that the dream world is suffused by Mal's logic of the infinite and not by Cobb's. In the dream, one doesn't see Cobb's infinite progress toward an ultimate goal (Hegel's bad infinity) but rather Mal's repetition that moves forward (Hegel's infinity of the Notion).

Nolan reveals the dream world's capacity for visualizing the infinity of the Notion further when Cobb explains dream architecture to Ariadne. While they walk through the streets of Paris, she folds the city over on itself, so that the tops of the buildings rest on each other and the roads

155

all circle around to meet up with themselves. The Paris that Ariadne creates becomes a Paris within a closed loop that includes the beyond within it. Nolan includes this fantasmatic effect of the city folding over on itself not just to wow the spectator with an unforeseen visual spectacle but also to show the infinite structure of the dream world. Here, we see how the film employs astounding special effects to emphasize a precise point about the type of infinity that the dream produces. Even though Ariadne creates this infinity, it reveals that Mal's preference for the dream world is not a desire to escape the truth but to find it. It is only in the dream that one discovers the fiction of the dream world, which enables us to visualize a truth that otherwise remains accessible only through the mediation of speculative thought.

THE FATHER AND THE OBJECT

When Cobb opts for reality instead of Mal, he takes the side of the father against his love object. Freud makes clear the connection between the role of the father and the abandonment of the love object as he first ventures into the social ramifications of psychoanalysis with *Totem and Taboo* in 1913. The primal father of Freud's mythical horde demands that all the sons sacrifice their pursuit of women, with whom he retains a sexual monopoly. The father is the barrier to the enjoyment of the object, and the totem (which plays a central role in *Inception*) is the extension of the barrier. This prohibition does not lessen with the murder of the primal father but rather increases, and the opposition between the father and the love object loses none of its force.[18]

As Freud tells it, the collective of sons conspires to murder the father in order to access the enjoyment that he forbids, but the social order that results from their collective action also deprives them of this enjoyment. This order remains tied to the primal father and his prohibition. Once the social order begins, Freud notes, "what had up to then been prevented by [the father's] actual existence was thenceforward prohibited by the sons themselves, in accordance with the psychological procedure to familiar to us in psycho-analysis under the name of 'deferred obedience.' They revoked their deed by forbidding the killing of the totem, the substitute for the father; and they renounced its fruits by resigning their claim to the women who had now been set free."[19] Even though the collective murder of the primal father succeeds, its aim fails. As long as they remain within their newly constituted society, the sons remain within the same prohibition of enjoyment that ruled over the primal horde. Even after his death, the sons trade their commitment to the father for their enjoyment. The father remains the chief adversary: his enjoyment and his prohibition continue to rule. Freud paints the investment in the father as simultaneously an abandonment of the object. This connection becomes especially evident in *Inception*, though not through any direct conflict between Cobb's father and Cobb's love object.

When Cobb first visits his father, Miles (Michael Caine), in Paris, Miles appears as the voice of reason. He upbraids Cobb for his failure to be a proper father for his children and for turning to thievery. In the midst of doing so, he begs Cobb, "Come back to reality, Dom, please." Here, Miles enjoins his son to give up Mal—who exists for Cobb only in the dream world—for the sake of his role as a father. Cobb must identify with the paternal position, which necessarily involves placing oneself in the social reality rather than in the fantasmatic world of the dream. Paternal identification is simultaneously a psychic investment in the real world and a rejection of the dream. To help bring his son back to reality, Miles sends him to Ariadne.

More than in any of his other films, Nolan uses character names to signal symbolic undertones in *Inception*. The most obvious case of this is Ariadne, whose thread would allow Theseus to escape the Minotaur's labyrinth after slaying him. As the figure who would connect Cobb to reality, she appears to be someone the spectator can trust. But it is Miles, Cobb's father, who points Cobb in her direction. Miles tells Cobb that she is his top student and will serve as an excellent architect, but Miles is not interested in the success of the latest heist. He wants Cobb to return to his position as a father in reality. This is why he proposes Ariadne to Cobb. She will lead Cobb back to reality and thus back to paternity. She acts in the film as the stand-in for Miles and paternal authority.

The complete lack of sexual or romantic tension between Ariadne and Cobb results from her role as the emissary of the father and her connection to the real world. Though Mal immediately views Ariadne as a threat—Mal walks up to her and stabs her—when she encounters her in Cobb's dream world, Ariadne is not a sexual rival. Ariadne never evinces any romantic interest in Cobb. She represents a threat to Mal only through her devotion to the social reality. Nolan chooses an obvious mythological reference not to direct heavy-handedly but rather to mislead the spectator into trusting this character. Ariadne provides a connection to reality just like her mythological namesake, but it is the privileging of reality itself that the film demands we call into question.

157

The importance of the name is not confined to Ariadne. It is also true of Cobb, whose name alludes to the villain of Nolan's first film. In *Following*, Cobb (Alex Haw) creates an elaborate deceit to frame Bill (Jeremy Theobald) for a murder that he didn't commit. Cobb is the name of perhaps the most unequivocally evil character in Nolan's previous films. Ironically, in *Inception* he gives the name "Mal" to the character who evinces the most understanding of where truth is located. Mal, which means evil in French, is played by a French actor, which provides additional resonance for this signification.

Mal is evil because she constantly disrupts Cobb's heists and even his attempts to explain dream architecture to Ariadne. Her disruptions begin in the second sequence of the film and continue until Cobb finally decides to abandon his attachment to her. Certainly from Cobb's perspective, Mal is evil, but she remains so only as long as we remain within his perspective. Her evil depends on an investment in the heists that Cobb wants to perform, which he does for money or self-interest, not for any ethical concern. Mal's status as evil, suggested by her name and by her actions, is a function of Cobb himself, a character on whom the film constantly casts doubt.

Mal is in fact the object-cause of Cobb's desire—in other words, the obstacle that bars the realization of his desire. Desire isn't aroused by the object that it seeks but by the obstacle that renders this object inaccessible. In this sense, Cobb's true object is not the successful heist or the reunion with his children but Mal herself, who obstructs both of these possibilities. The obstacle is the object because desire finds its satisfaction not through the success of attaining its aim but through the repetition of failing to do so. Those who have gotten what they want can readily attest to the disappointment of desire that follows from achieving the goal. But Cobb, in contrast to Mal, cannot recognize the nature of desire.

Cobb's predominant emotion is guilt. Near the end of the film, Mal asks him what he feels, and he confesses, "I feel guilt, Mal, and no matter what I do, no matter how hopeless I am, no matter how confused, that guilt is always there." He feels guilt for causing Mal's death and guilt for abandoning his children. His willingness to take on Saito's job offer stems from its promise of some expiation: if he succeeds in convincing Robert Fischer to break up his father's empire, then Saito will make it possible for him to return to the United States and see his children. But his guilt manifests itself in a quotidian way in the film as well. Mal's constant intrusions in the dream world result from his unconscious and his inability to contain the guilt he feels about her death. He views himself as responsible for her suicide because he gave her the idea of the unreality of her world.

Guilt is, as Freud conceives it in *Totem and Taboo*, a way of sustaining the bond with the father even after his death. After the sons murder their father, a sense of guilt arises, and this guilt cements the obedience of the subject to the father and to the paternal law. It functions as the original inspiration for religion. Freud claims, "Totemic religion arose from the filial sense of guilt, in an attempt to allay that feeling and to appease the father by deferring obedience to him."[20] Jacques Lacan adds an important nuance to this theory while sustaining the association of guilt with the father.

For Lacan, guilt does not result from disobeying and killing the father but from abandoning one's desire and one's object for the sake of the father and his law. As he puts it in his seminar on ethics, "The only thing one can be guilty of is giving ground relative to one's desire."[21] This statement appears to contradict every notion of ethics that we have: ethics involves the restraint of desire, and we feel guilty when we cede control to our desire, not when we give ground relative to it. But Lacan's point here is that the development of guilt has nothing to do with transgressive actions. Instead, it develops when one opts psychically for the father's law and betrays one's object or one's obstacle. Feelings of guilt arise as a result of the father's prominence within the psyche, without which one could act guilt-free. In *Inception*, Cobb chooses paternity over the object, and this explains the massive amount of guilt that haunts him throughout the film.

Nolan undermines Cobb's guilt not only by visually depicting its destructiveness by also through the film's soundtrack. Though Cobb performs the inception on Robert Fischer in order to assuage his guilt and return to his children, the song that the group uses to signal a return to the waking state is Edith Piaf's recording of "Non, je ne regrette rien." Not only does this song dominate the film's diegetic soundtrack, but a subtle version of it plays non-diegetically as well. The film's composer Hans Zimmer relates that part of his score for the film "is constructed from a single manipulated beat from the version [of the song] recorded by Piaf in 1960."[22] The ubiquity of "Non, je ne regrette rien" both within the diegesis and outside it provides a forceful contrast with the guilt that determines Cobb's every step.[23] *Inception* shows us guilt and its manifestations as we hear an imperative to disallow this guilt to seduce us as spectators. Guilt always places one on the side of the father, even if it isn't, as Freud believes, always guilt concerning the desire for the father's death.

When Cobb arrives in Los Angeles after having accomplished his mission and after Saito clears his record with the American authorities through a single phone call, Cobb's father, Miles, greets Cobb and takes him to see his children. The appearance of Miles at the Los Angeles airport is not impossible: though we know he teaches in Paris, he could have easily flown to Los Angeles after learning about Cobb's plan. But it is nonetheless odd, considering that Miles has not been watching Cobb's children and considering that he seems firmly entrenched in Paris.

At no point during this return do we see the grandmother who has been taking care of the children during Cobb's prolonged absence. Nolan leaves this character out of the film at the end—precisely when we would expect to see her—in order to emphasize the role of the father in Cobb's abandonment of Mal and his decision to opt for reality. Miles must be the one who greets Cobb in Los Angeles and takes him to his children since Miles represents paternal law. Social reality, as *Inception* makes evident, is not simply real: it is the terrain of the father, and when we acquiesce to the exigencies of reality and give up the torment of desire, we cede ourselves to paternal authority, which is what occurs at the end of the film.[24]

THE PRIMORDIALLY REPRESSED

Though *Inception* stresses Cobb's decision to cede his desire for the sake of paternity, the film also makes it clear that our desire is never simply our own. Everyone accepts that people borrow ideas from others, but we tend to believe that we know which ideas we have borrowed and which we have discovered for ourselves. But rather than allowing us to distinguish which ideas come from the outside and which are our own, consciousness actually minimizes our capacity for recognizing the Other's influence on our ideas. That is to say, our conscious ideas seem to be are our own, no matter where they actually come from. Nowhere is this more the case than with repressed ideas when they become conscious. Though repressed ideas are by definition unconscious, the act of making them conscious changes how we relate to them, which is why psychoanalysis can never be fully successful. To make an unconscious idea conscious creates the sense that it is ours and inevitably disguises its external origin.

The very concept of inception suggests that the subject is not the author or origin of its own thoughts, even those to which it is most attached. What matters is not the origin of our repressed idea but the relationship that we take up to it. The subject must sustain the trauma of the repressed idea rather than trying to escape this trauma through a return to consciousness. As Nolan sees it, repression is much less a danger than consciousness.

At two major points in the film, we see subjects encounter a repressed idea. When Cobb cannot convince Mal to return to reality, he breaks into a safe hidden within a dollhouse and instills the idea that Mal's reality is unreal, the idea that ultimately leads to her suicide. Toward the end of the film, Cobb narrates this act to Ariadne as Mal looks on, horrified. He says, "I knew we needed to escape, but she wouldn't accept it. She had locked something away, something, something deep inside, a truth that she had once known but chose to forget. But she couldn't break free, so I decided to search for it. I went deep into the recess of her mind and found that secret place. I broke in, and I planted an idea, a simple idea that would change everything, that her world wasn't real." As Cobb tells this story, the film's visuals first show Mal opening the dollhouse and the safe, and subsequently they show Cobb breaking in. We hear the idea that replaces the originally repressed idea, and we see the top—Mal's totem—in the safe. Mal represses her ability to distinguish between the dream world and reality because this very capacity functions as a trauma for her. The same process occurs with Robert Fischer: the film depicts his reconciliation with the father replacing the trauma of his father's dissatisfaction.

Nolan shows that the repressed idea that constitutes the subject— the truth that it has once known but chose to forget—is important for its repression and the position that it has within the psyche. But Cobb works to do away with the traumatic repressed idea. He fills the space of this idea with another idea that is more palatable for the subject, an idea that the subject will no longer choose to forget. He is a psychologist who believes that he can cure repression, but his cure demands an incredible amount of psychic violence, something no psychoanalyst would permit her- or himself.[25] Even Ariadne has a horrified look when Cobb reveals that he performed inception on Mal and gave her the idea that led to her suicide.

Cobb performs inception not just to benefit himself but also to install a comforting idea in the Other. When he and his gang plan to give Robert Fischer the idea of breaking up his father's company, Cobb tells

ABANDONMENT OF REALITY IN *INCEPTION*

the group that "Fischer's relationship with his father is stressed, to say the least." Eames responds, "Well, can we run with that? Suggest splitting up the empire as a 'screw you' to the old man?" Cobb rejects the apparently reasonable suggestion as untenable: it violates what he considers the basic desire of the psyche. He explains to Eames, "No, because I think positive emotion trumps negative emotion every time. We all crave reconciliation, catharsis." Cobb's claim certainly holds for himself: rather than confronting the trauma of Mal's desire for him, he wants reconciliation with his children. But Cobb presents this idea as a general truth rather than a personal one. In this sense, it informs us further about his unreliability as a character and about the fantasmatic nature of any reconciliation that the film presents.[26]

Cobb's plan for Fischer's reconciliation with his father also facilitates Cobb's reconciliation with his own father through a return to his children. For Robert Fischer, the fundamental trauma is linked to a signifier, the last word that his father said to him—"disappointed." The word "disappointed" marks Robert Fischer's failure to live up to the standard that his father had set for him. As *Inception* makes clear, one can change such fundamental traumas, but only when one accedes to another's control. To give up one's fundamental trauma is to give up one's freedom. Robert Fischer wakes up from his dream on the flight to Los Angeles reconciled with his father rather than traumatized by him, but this reconciliation requires a complete betrayal of himself to the thieves who have invaded his mind.

The inception works with Robert Fischer because Cobb manages to alter the signification of the traumatic signifier. When Robert finally reaches his father's deathbed deep within a series of dreams, he hears the traumatic signifier again and tells his father, "I know, you were disappointed that I couldn't be you." Rather than confirm this obvious reading of his last word, the father demurs, "No, no, I was disappointed that you tried." At this moment, Robert's relationship to his father changes completely and the inception succeeds. Breaking up his father's company—the goal of the heist—becomes Robert's method for cementing his reconciliation with his father and becoming his own person, just as he believes his father desired.

This scene of reconciliation between father and son is one of the most moving in the film, and yet it is completely false. The pliability of the signifier makes such reconciliation possible, but it also allows Robert to betray himself. By reconciling with his father, Robert cooperates with those who are robbing him and even trying to destroy him. His reconciliation is simultaneously a betrayal, and in this sense, it fore-shadows Cobb's reconciliation with his children at the end of the film. Of course, genuine reconciliation is possible, but not when it requires that one abandon one's desire, which is what occurs both with Robert Fischer and with Cobb.

The difference between Mal and Cobb resides in their respective re-lationships to their unconscious desire. Whereas Cobb distances himself from his desire by sustaining a link to reality, Mal identifies herself completely with her desire. This is why she initially refuses to leave the world that she and Cobb create in the limbo state and why she insists on killing herself once Cobb implants the idea about the world's unre-ality in her psyche. For Mal, her desire outweighs any sense of reality, even when her desire is the desire to return to reality. Though the film illustrates the destructiveness of this insistence on desire, it does so from the perspective of Cobb, and it is Cobb's inability to confront his desire—his insistence on taking refuge in reality and in paternity—that makes desire itself (or Mal) so evil. To confront one's desire and to sustain one's repressed idea require accepting the failure of desire's realization. One who sustains one's desire doesn't obtain its object and thus fails at every heist.

A HEIST FILM IS NOT A HEIST FILM

Perhaps the most substantive critique of *Inception* concerns its lack of substance. There is no idea about the nature of the unconscious (or "subconscious," as the characters in the film term it), no insight into the nature of dreaming, no development of relations among characters, and not even any advancement of the heist film. *New Yorker* film critic David Denby, for instance, claims that the film "is an astonishment, an engineering feat, and, finally, a folly. Nolan has devoted his extraordi-nary talents not to some weighty, epic theme or terrific comic idea but to a science-fiction thriller that exploits dreams for doubling and redou-bling actions sequences."[27] For Denby, the film disappoints him because it promises much more than it delivers and because Nolan himself has made much more thoughtful films. One should take this critique very seriously. Much of the popular appeal of *Inception* resembles that of the crossword puzzle: it is a puzzle for the sake of being of a puzzle, not for the sake of what it might reveal.

Though Denby calls the film "a science-fiction thriller," the genre that *Inception* most resembles is the heist film.[28] After the opening scene, the film begins with Cobb's elaborate heist attempt to steal trade secrets from Saito for Cobol Engineering. But then the film continues with the characteristics of the heist film while becoming almost an anti-heist film: Rather than trying to steal an idea from Robert Fischer, Cobb and his team try to plant an idea. This reversal of the usual procedure in the heist film is not, however, the only way that *Inception* differs from the genre. It also uses Cobb's relationship with Mal and her intrusions into the heist to call into question the fundamental presuppositions of the heist film as such.

The heist film—even those that play with the conventions of the genre—establishes the object of the heist as the ultimate object of desire that will provide complete satisfaction. The typical heist film promulgates the fantasy of this desire's realization. Instances of this include *Gone in Sixty Seconds* (Dominic Sena, 2000), *Ocean's Eleven* (Steven Soderbergh, 2001), *The Italian Job* (F. Gary Gray, 2003), and *Inside Man* (Spike Lee, 2006). In each case, the film depicts the successful heist coinciding with the fantasmatic realization of desire. The heroes obtain their object and find it satisfying at the conclusion of the film. When the heroes of Steven Soderbergh's remake of *Ocean's Eleven* stand outside the Bellagio in Las Vegas and watch the fountains spray water into the night sky, Soderbergh offers the film's spectators the fantasy of a perfectly realized desire. The spectators and the perpetrators enjoy the immediate aftermath of the successful heist, where the seemingly impossible object of desire has been attained.[29]

There is another set of heist films, however, that thwart this realization of desire. These films attempt to show the impossibility of any such realization and to explode the fantasy that subtends the genre itself. Films such as *Du rififi chez les hommes* (*Rififi*) (Jules Dassin, 1955), *The Killing* (Stanley Kubrick, 1956), and *Heat* (Michael Mann, 1995) all show how some impediment blocks the fantasy of obtaining the fully satisfying object. In some cases, the impediment is external and incidental (as is the case in *The Killing*), but it is often associated with the psychic compulsions of the hero (as in *Heat*). These films make clear that the fantasy that subtends the heist genre is untenable and that one must enjoy the heist itself rather than its successful completion. But *Inception* explodes the genre even more than any of these great heist films. The inclusion of Mal (and Cobb's relationship with her) in the heists makes clear that desire does not involve the seeming object of its focus but the obstacle that stands in the way of obtaining this object.

164

From the beginning of *Inception*, Mal obstructs the heists that Cobb pursues. During the initial heist from Saito, she first appears barely visible in a long shot, and Arthur identifies her in a reverse shot that shows him complaining about her presence to Cobb. After their initial conversation, Cobb has Mal sit in a chair to which he ties a rope to rappel down to Saito's safe. As he arrives at the level of the safe, Nolan cuts to a shot of Mal, who turns her head in apparent frustration with Cobb. After a shot of Cobb looking into the room, the film returns to a now-empty chair, which slides across the room and causes Cobb to fall farther down the outer wall. Mal's act of leaving the chair after Cobb told her to stay disrupts his ability to carry out the heist, but she goes even further and fully undermines it moments later.

Cobb breaks into Saito's safe, removes a manila envelope, and replaces it with another. As we see a close-up of him looking into the safe, the lights in the room illuminate, and Nolan cuts to a shot of Mal standing with Saito and holding a gun aimed at Cobb. Saito's henchmen bring Arthur into the room, and Mal turns her gun on him. She then shoots Arthur in order to inflict pain on him, which forces Cobb to kill him and wake him up. When Cobb flees, we see her say to Saito, "He was close, very close," and moments later Cobb opens an envelope containing blank pages. Here, Mal appears as a figure of evil because she thwarts Cobb's heist, but she does so to show him where the object lies. Cobb—and the thief qua thief—views the object as what one steals, but Mal wants Cobb to recognize that the object is not the goal of the heist but the barrier to its completion. In this case, the object is not the secret that Saito possesses but Mal herself, the obstacle to obtaining this secret.

Later, her obstruction of Cobb's attempt at inception with Robert Fischer again highlights her assertion of herself as obstacle and her insistence on the privileged status of this obstacle. When the group finally brings Robert to the point where he will confront his father and reconcile with him, Mal intervenes. We see Robert looking at the safe behind which lies his dying father, and a blurry figure drops down behind him. A close-up of Cobb looking from afar through a telescopic rifle lens depicts him identifying Mal. Ariadne exclaims that she is not real, but Cobb doubts it and doesn't shoot her. This gives Mal the opportunity to walk toward Robert, who turns around just as she shoots him. Though Cobb quickly shoots Mal, her disruption forces Cobb and Ariadne down to the lowest dream level, limbo, in order to revive Robert and enable his reconciliation with his father that Mal prevented.

Nolan's depiction of the limbo level in juxtaposition with the other dream levels serves as a commentary on the heist film as a genre. He cuts from Arthur preparing to create a jolt for all the dreamers in zero gravity on one level, Eames and Saito fending off attackers on another level, and Cobb and Ariadne exploring the world that Cobb created with Mal on another. The cuts between these different levels reveal the connection between the heist and Cobb's relationship to Mal. At one point, Nolan cuts from Cobb preparing to explain his role in Mal's death to Ariadne as they are descending in an elevator to Eames in a fistfight with someone trying to get into the mountain fortress where Robert Fischer will meet his dying father. Cobb's betrayal of his own desire, which first occurred when he performed inception on Mal, recurs with the heist, which is what the cuts in this section of the film show. The heist—the effort to obtain the ultimate object of desire—is, as the editing of *Inception* indicates, a betrayal of desire through an investment in its realization.

When Cobb first sees Mal at the limbo level, he tells her, "I know what's real, Mal." But then she offers an explanation of the events of the film that casts great doubt on their reality, especially when one considers the dreamlike incidents that have occurred, like Cobb's almost-impossible escape through a narrow passage between buildings or Saito's miraculous arrival while Cobb was being chased by assassins. Mal says to him, "No creeping doubts? Not feeling persecuted, Dom? Chased around the globe by anonymous corporations and police forces? Projections persecute the dreamer. Admit it, you don't believe in one reality anymore, so choose, choose to be here. Choose me." Given the extraordinary happenings that take place in the reality of the film, Mal's explanation makes sense. Nolan cuts from Mal's final plea to Eames still fighting with the attackers, and this cut emphasizes again the contrast between Mal and the pursuit of the object in the heist.[30]

At the limbo level, Cobb finally rejects Mal in favor of Ariadne and the latter's claim to reality, despite Mal's attempt to convince him to choose her as his object. Cobb says, "I can't stay with her anymore because she doesn't exist." After this rejection, Mal stabs Cobb, and then Ariadne shoots her. Even though Cobb does reject her, it is Ariadne who completes this break by shooting Mal. She assures Cobb's return to reality and flight from the dream world. Cobb's abandonment of Mal is not simply the choice for reality over the dream but also the choice for a certain type of object. Throughout the film, Mal functions as an object for Cobb: she is never herself but always what the film labels a "projection" of Cobb's own psyche. Nonetheless, she serves as an obstacle to attaining what he desires. As the film presents it, Cobb—and the subject—can choose between the obstacle and the object of desire that one can attain.

Here, the film displays a sophisticated understanding between the object that causes desire and the object that one desires, between what Lacan calls the objet petit a and the object of desire. The goal of the heist—both in the typical heist film and in *Inception*—is the object of desire, while the objet petit a (or object-cause of desire) is the barrier to this object. Throughout the film, Mal plays the part of obstacle that prevents any realization of Cobb's desire, but the film reveals that the obstacle is the real object. Cobb's guilt stems not from his failure to attain the object of desire but from his betrayal of the obstacle. The obstacle is the subject's real object, the object that demands the subject's fidelity. Despite Mal's apparent evil, she is the de facto hero of the film, much more than Cobb.

THE TABOO OF THE TOTEM

The chief debate surrounding *Inception*—it is almost all consuming for fans and critics of the film—concerns the film's ending. In the film's final shot, Nolan depicts a reconciliation of Cobb with his two children and then pans to a shot of Cobb's top spinning on a table. The top is Cobb's totem, his method for discovering whether he is in a dream or in reality. In a dream, Cobb says earlier, the top can continue to spin without falling, while in reality, all tops eventually fall. The film seems to conclude with a classic open ending: in this final shot, the top appears to wobble somewhat, but it remains spinning during the concluding cut to black. As one would expect, this ending has occasioned multiple theories among viewers concerning Cobb's status at the end of the film.[31]

For some, the wobble of the top suggests that it will soon fall and that Cobb has reentered the real world with his heretofore lost family. For others, the fact that the top doesn't fall offers evidence to the contrary, evidence that Cobb remains in a dream state even when he thinks he has finally come back to reality. The latter have on their side the perfect wish fulfillment that occurs in the ending. Throughout the film, Cobb has fantasized about returning to his children, and the final scene realizes that fantasy. Such realizations, as everyone knows, rarely occur in reality, though they are staples of the dream world.

The great controversy over the ending of *Inception* is yet another one of Nolan's deceptions. The deception does not consist in making us think that Cobb has returned to the real world when in fact he hasn't, but in making the question of the reality of the final scene appear as if it is a—or the—central point of the film. Unlike films such as *The Matrix* (Andy and Larry Wachowski, 1999) or *The Thirteenth Floor* (Josef Rusnak, 1999), *Inception* does not present an illusory reality that characters must escape to access the real world hiding beneath it. In these films, the apparent reality itself is the deception, and overcoming the deception involves ceasing to believe in the reality of the world that one has always taken for granted.[32] This is not the case with *Inception*. Whether the world at the end of the film is real or a dream seems to be the central problem that Nolan presents, but it is entirely false and functions only to misdirect us as spectators. Whereas *The Matrix* deceives spectators about the reality of the world that they initially see, *Inception* deceives spectators with the very question of the reality of the world.

One clue about this form of deception comes early in the film. At first, Nolan suggests that the totem does provide a fail-safe method for determining whether one is in a dream or reality. While explaining the invasion of the dream world to Ariadne, Arthur explains to her the vital role that the totem plays. He says, "When you look at your totem, you know beyond a doubt that you're not in someone else's dream." Just as Arthur provides this explanation, the film cuts to Cobb spinning his top until it stops spinning and falls, which suggests the accuracy of Arthur's statement—that the reality currently being depicted is not that of a dream. It is important, however, that Arthur's explanation is much more limited than we might initially believe: he doesn't say that the totem assured that one is in the real world, just that one is "not in someone else's dream." It provides no guarantee that one is not in one's own dream, as the film explains it.

But immediately before Arthur's explanation, Ariadne asks to examine Arthur's totem, a loaded die. Arthur refuses and cites the absolute singularity of the totem. He tells her that the totem must be "a small object, preferably heavy. Something you can have on you at all times." When Ariadne suggests a coin, Arthur insists on the necessity for the totem being unique and utterly personal for the one who uses it. According to Arthur, the totem is the object that represents the subject's singularity, but it does not serve, despite Arthur's claim, as the object for the subject. Instead, it marks the abandonment of one's object because it connects one to reality rather than to desire, though neither Arthur nor Cobb are able to see this. Both associate the totem with the subject's singularity, despite the evidence against this claim. Arthur is invested in this idea to such an extent that he even refuses to allow Ariadne to handle his loaded die. He says to her, "I can't let you touch it, that would defeat the purpose. See, only I know the balance and weight of this particular loaded die." His refusal to give Ariadne access to his totem suggests that not only will she fail to feel it correctly but that even allowing someone else to touch it might disrupt the totem's value as a guarantor of reality.

Nonetheless, Cobb's totem, the one that seems ready to assure us about the world's reality at the end of the film, is not his own. Mal invented the idea of the totem, and the top was originally her totem that Cobb took over after her death. Hence, even if the totem can distinguish between the dream world and the real world, Cobb's top cannot do so because it lacks any singular attachment to him, which Arthur explains is necessary for the totem to function successfully.

The role that the totem plays in *Inception* underlines the association between reality and paternity. In Freud's account of the development of the totemic religions, he identifies the totem as "the substitute for [the] father."[33] The term "totem," therefore, works on two levels: in the narrative context of the film, it is the object that indicates that things are real, and in the film's psychoanalytic context it is an object that represents the figure of paternal authority. Though Freud never mentions the totem's role as a guarantor of reality, he does, as we have seen, insist that judgments of reality depend on the initial sacrifice of the object, which is also what totemism demands. To bring together the two significations, then, the totem suggests freedom from the dream but capture by the father. The freedom to exist in the real world, which appears to come about at the end of *Inception*, thus has a steep price.

In the film's final sequence, the spectator finally sees the faces of Cobb's children for the first time. When Cobb enters the house where they are staying, he spins the top on a table, and the film cuts from him looking outside to a shot of his children from behind as they play in the grass. This shot corresponds to earlier shots of his last memory of them. But after another shot of Cobb looking out, Nolan cuts to the children turning and looking back at Cobb for the first time. The faces of the children seem to serve as an index of their reality, but the face is no more an assurance of reality than the totem.

Earlier in the film, while conversing with Mal in the dream world, she calls to the children, and Nolan shows them turning to look. He quickly cuts from this shot before their faces become visible to a close-up of Cobb, who turns away and hides his eyes. He says to Mal, "Please, those aren't my children." What is shocking about this scene is Cobb's refusal to look at the faces of the children, as if this would constitute a betrayal of his real children or of his commitment to reality. The faces of his children, for Cobb, become the indication of their reality.[34] But by emphasizing his refusal to look, Nolan makes evident Cobb's psychic investment in sustaining a certain image of them. If he saw their faces, it seems as if it would disturb his fantasy of reconciliation with them, which is why he turns away so vehemently.[35] This sequence, which presages the final moments of the film, suggests that Cobb has a libidinal investment in a certain image of his children and of himself as a father rather than an actual investment in reality for its own sake. He wants the image and certainty of paternity more than he wants reality, though he believes that the latter will provide a vehicle for the former.

The fantasy that Cobb realizes at the end of the film is one of reconciliation with his children, even though this fantasy appears in the guise of reality. When Cobb finally opts for reality, he tells Mal, "I miss you more than I can bear, but I have to let you go." This abandonment of his object frees Cobb for reentry into the real world and the resumption of his duties as a father. But the film subtly makes clear that remaining with Mal is not a retreat from the truth but the only path to it. Reality is the real retreat. One must instead follow the dream or the deception wherever it leads, even when it leads to self-destruction. When spectators invest themselves in the fate of the top in the film's final shot, they share in Cobb's betrayal. Fidelity demands sustaining the dream even when it leads to certain destruction.

Sustaining the dream does not imply a commitment to reality-denying psychosis. *Inception* is not a plea for parents to abandon their children en masse in order to spend all their time dreaming. It suggests rather a marginalization of the question of reality for the sake of one's object or obstacle, an object that comes to the fore in the dream or in the fiction. Instead of seeking new answers in the real world, we must change the question in a way that obviates our obsession with reality. The point is not whether one inhabits the real world but whether one has betrayed or remained faithful to one's object.

THE FICTIONAL CHRISTOPHER NOLAN

When Christopher Nolan began making films and matured as a feature filmmaker, the problem of the lie was central in the activities of two American presidents. Because of his lie to federal prosecutors about his sexual life, Bill Clinton suffered the humiliation of impeachment. George W. Bush, on the other hand, was part of a much more dramatic deception: he and his administration perpetuated the false idea that Iraq, armed with weapons of mass destruction, presented a mortal threat to the United States.[1] Through misleading innuendo, he also led people to believe that Iraq shared some responsibility for the September 11 attack on the World Trade Center and Pentagon. His administration manipulated intelligence data to support these claims and repeated them incessantly. This was not an isolated deception.

Whatever one may think of their character, both Clinton and Bush lied, at least in part, for ethical reasons. Clinton's lie attempted to shield his family (and the country) from the pain and embarrassment of the public revelation of an infidelity. Bush's lie allowed him to destroy an enemy that he believed might one day pose a threat to his country, even if it didn't at the time of the war. Both lies—one on a personal level and the other on a geopolitical level—were the means to what both presidents conceived as good ends.

The lie that serves as the means to a good end is the most acceptable form of the lie. It manifests itself in the white lies that we tell in order to preserve someone's feelings, in the fictions that parents create for their children in order to make holidays more pleasurable for them, in the distortions used to describe society's heroes, and so on. This is the kind of lie that Christopher Nolan embraces at the end of *Dark Knight* (2008) when Batman (Christian Bale) and Commissioner Gordon (Gary Oldman) conspire to deceive the public about the criminality of District Attorney Harvey Dent (Aaron Eckhart). Lying for the greater good indicates a consequentialist morality in which ends count more than means, and this is a morality that the ethics of the lie, as Christopher Nolan develops it in his films, opposes, even if Nolan falls into it at one point

CONCLUSION
LYING WITHOUT CONSEQUENCE

in *Dark Knight*. Nolan privileges the lie for its own sake—in contrast to the lie for the good end—because this lie misrepresents the way things actually stand and thus tears the subject from the dominance of the given situation. Every real lie has the potential to transform both the subject's own existence and even larger social relations.

The problem with a consequentialist morality focused on good ends is that it remains within the ruling order of things and lacks any transformative capacity. The good served by the consequentialist lie remains a predetermined and calculable good that has been structurally accounted for.[2] Clinton's lie about sexual relations with Monica Lewinsky and Bush's lie about the status of Iraq were not only designed to accomplish a good end, but the good end itself, the consequence, was in each case fundamentally tied to the given situation. For both, lying was not the means for a break from the actual situation but a way of sustaining it. This profound conservatism undermines consequentialist morality in whatever form it manifests itself.[3]

But when it comes to lying, it is difficult to imagine a reason for it apart from the good it will bring about, which is perhaps why the great anti-consequentialist Immanuel Kant sees the lie as the worst of all moral failings. Seemingly, one always lies in order to achieve some end, and one treats the audience of the lie as a mere means toward accomplishing this end. It appears as if only the pathological liar escapes the consequentialist lie, which makes it difficult to imagine an ethical lie since no one would consider the pathological liar a moral exemplar. But Nolan envisions a way out of this difficulty by focusing on the creative power of deceit. What is important for Nolan is not what the lie creates—its consequence—but the act of creation that occurs within the lie itself. This is why he can value lying for its own sake or the ethical lie.

The ethical lie has the status of what Alain Badiou calls the event. Though Badiou properly theorizes the event as a shift in terrain or an interruption within the fabric of evolutionary history, he misses, as I have noted earlier, this association of the event with the lie. For Badiou, the event interrupts the lie of the historical situation through the insertion of truth. He identifies the event with truth because he views truth as what is indiscernible and thus irreducible to signification within the ruling symbolic structure. In *Being and Event*, he notes, "The discernible is the veridical. But the indiscernible alone is true. There is no truth apart from the generic, because only a faithful generic procedure aims at the one of situational being. A faithful procedure has as its infinite horizon being-in-truth."[4] Being faithful to the event becomes a way of remaining within truth and avoiding the fictions of the ruling situation. By doing so, one becomes attuned to the indiscernible nature of truth.

Badiou assumes the ontological priority of truth that stems from his investment in mathematics as ontology. Mathematics—specifically Georg Cantor's theory of the infinite set—provides the ontological ground for the event's emergence. Mathematics tells us that being is multiple and indiscernible, and the event returns us to this (true) insight. But if mathematics is not ontology and being is not inherently multiple, then Badiou's association of the event with truth becomes untenable. This association requires that one accept Badiou's ontological presupposition, but Nolan's identification of the event with the ethical lie allows one to avoid such assumptions. The idea of the ontological priority of the lie—an idea that appears throughout Nolan's work—is not an ontological presupposition along the lines of Badiou's. It means simply that our only access to ontology comes through the fiction that we create about being. Whatever truth we come to concerning being must appear through the primacy of this fiction. The ethical lie is this act of creation that unlocks being for us. In this sense, it is an event, though it eschews the truth that Badiou insists on aligning with the event.

The ethical lie is related to the subject's foundational lie, the lie through which the subject organizes its existence. The subject's foundational lie may lead to a series of consequences, but the lie itself marks the moment at which the subject asserts the truth of its desire. This occurs most explicitly at the end of *Memento* (2000), where Leonard (Guy Pearce) decides to lie to himself in order to implicate Teddy (Joe Pantoliano) in the murder of his wife and thereby to continue the search that provides meaning for his life. Leonard's lie to himself is the truth of his desire: he does not want to find his wife's killer but to pursue him or his avatar in the guise of seeking revenge. Without this pursuit, Leonard's life would lose all structural coherence, which is why he cannot accede to the truth about this pursuit even when it confronts him in the most straightforward manner.

Though Leonard reveals the ontological priority of the lie for the subject, he is not an ethical liar. The problem is that his lie does not go far enough; it remains within the realm of his situation. His lie to himself has some creative power—it does result in the death of Teddy and it organizes his own existence—but it is not strong enough to inaugurate a decisive break from his situation. His investment in revenge indicates that he continues to operate within the givens of his world. The quest

173

for revenge is always a way of embracing one's situation in the guise of reacting against it.

The ethics of the lie that Nolan's films champion resides in the act of creating the fiction. By creating an authentic fiction, we evince a refusal to go along with our situation, which indicates again the affinity between the ethical lie and Badiou's event. Nolan's career as a filmmaker is a celebration of the creative power of the artist, and he associates this creative power with the artist's investment in the lie. Through the creation of the lie, the work of art produces a world of meaning that challenges the given world, one that accesses the truth of desire rather than the truth of correlation. The problem with most works of art, however, is that they fail to lie enough. Rather than lying in a way that changes the givens, their lies remain within the prevailing assumptions of the situation itself. Most artists' lies remain too tied to the situational truth. Nolan, in contrast, stands out for the inventiveness of his lies, which enable spectators to experience the truth of their desire at the expense of the truth of the given world.

The failure of the Clinton and Bush lies is not just their investment in a good consequence that they would bring about but, more important, their inability to break from the situation in which they were uttered. That is, there is too much truth in Clinton's denial of sexual relations with Monica Lewinsky and in Bush's proclamation that Iraq had weapons of mass destruction that posed an imminent danger to the United States. These lies had too much truth because they accepted too much of the given situation rather than breaking from it. Real ethical lies would not keep a president's family intact or sustain a country's global hegemony. They would enact a transformative change in social or geopolitical relations. They would accomplish the equivalent of what the magician does in *The Prestige* (2006): they would make a bird appear out of thin air or mysteriously transport a man across a stage. That is, a real ethical lie would perform the impossible. As Nolan's films show, the impossible becomes possible through the lie.

LIE FIRST

By privileging the lie in the way that he does, Nolan as a filmmaker opposes himself to most of the history of Western thought. From Plato onward, Western philosophy has presupposed the primacy of truth. Truth is original, and the lie (or fiction) is a false copy. In his theory of the

174

forms, Plato aligns the ideal forms with truth, and these forms act as the origin for the empirical instances of things that we encounter in the world. The philosopher's task in this arrangement involves thinking beyond the deception of appearances and discovering the truth of their ideal genesis. Philosophy takes us back to the true origin. Plato banishes the poets from his ideal society in Book X of the *Republic* because they treat the representation of an appearance as if it were true, thereby further estranging us from the primal truth that our everyday experience already places at a distance. This alignment of truth with origin becomes the sine qua non of the Western philosophical project for the next two thousand years.

In the late nineteenth and early twentieth centuries, this idea of the primacy of truth begins to come into question. Friedrich Nietzsche identifies the prevalence of deceit and sees that it has the upper hand on truth everywhere in society, but he still maintains an idea of truth as ontologically prior to falsehood. The philosopher, such as Nietzsche himself, has the courage to embrace the truth that the mass of humanity must reject.[5] Martin Heidegger pushes Nietzsche's turn toward the avowal of deceit another degree when he reconceives truth in terms of its original emergence.

For Heidegger, truth is not located in correctness or correspondence; it discloses beings to us and allows us to relate to them. But as it discloses beings, it also conceals them. As Heidegger puts it, "The disclosure of beings as such is simultaneously and intrinsically the concealing of being as a whole. In the simultaneity of disclosure and concealing, errancy holds sway. Errancy and the concealing of what is concealed belong to the primordial essence of truth."[6] Here, Heidegger links the emergence of truth with a simultaneous errancy that holds sway over the disclosing power of truth. The task of the philosophy involves struggling against this errancy and recovering the original unveiling of truth. Thus, despite locating errancy alongside truth as it emerges, Heidegger, like Nietzsche before him, continues to grant an ontological priority to truth.

The real break from the ontological priority of truth occurs almost unnoticed in the thought of Hegel. Despite this break, philosophers after Hegel, like Nietzsche and Heidegger, stealthily return truth to its former position, not recognizing the radicality of Hegel's intervention. His conception of absolute knowledge as the end point of philosophical speculation leads interpreters to see Hegel as the ultimate champion of truth, but in fact his thought carefully grounds every truth in a prior fiction that establishes the possibility for it. Absolute knowledge is not the standpoint of ultimate truth but the recognition that truth can never escape its origin in fiction. No matter how far we travel along the path of truth, we will never arrive at a pure truth independent of falsity and error.

In the *Phenomenology of Spirit*, Hegel rejects all attempts to arrive at the origin of thought or being because he realizes that truth has no ontological priority. Hence, the starting point of a philosophy becomes irrelevant and necessarily erroneous. For Hegel, one must work through deception in order to arrive at truth. As he puts it, "To know something falsely means that there is a disparity between knowledge and its Substance. But this very disparity is the process of distinguishing in general, which is an essential moment [in knowing]. Out of this distinguishing, of course, comes their identity, and this resultant identity is the truth. But it is not truth as if the disparity had been thrown away, like dross from pure metal, not even like the tool which remains separate from the finished vessel; disparity, rather, as the negative, the self, is itself still directly present in the True as such."[7] For Hegel, truth is the disparity with the fiction that leads to it, and any conception of truth that excludes its relation to fiction will inevitably become even more deceptive than straightforward deceit.

This is the line of thought that becomes manifest cinematically in the films of Christopher Nolan. As I've tried to show, Nolan's relationship to cinema parallels Hegel's relationship to philosophy. Rather than denounce deception, Hegel and Nolan see it as the fertile territory out of which truth can arise. According to Hegel's line of thought, the various ideological deceptions that proliferate in history provide the form through which truth can reveal itself. This is why he spends time exploring obvious falsehoods like physiognomy and phrenology. Even during Hegel's time, most serious thinkers understood physiognomy and phrenology as crackpot science—as the perpetuation of a fiction—and yet Hegel takes this fiction seriously enough to include a discussion of it in his first major philosophical work.

Phrenology reveals the dependence of spirit—the power of speculative thought—on the inert material of the skull bone. There is truth to phrenology's claim that "the *actuality and existence of man is his skull-bone*," even though this is not the last word on spirit's limitations.[8] Hegel believes that through these illusory and wrongheaded modes of thinking, we can discover truths that would otherwise remain inaccessible to us. Truth comes through the proper interpretation of the various

176

falsehoods that manifest themselves in history. When we work through the prevailing fictions and finally grasp the interrelation of truth and fiction, we arrive at absolute knowledge. Understood as such, absolute knowledge appears not as the height of philosophical arrogance but as the most profound expression of philosophical humility.

Just as Hegel credits the obvious falsity of phrenology with playing a pivotal role in the unfolding of truth, in *The Prestige* Nolan presents the teleportation invented by Nikola Tesla (David Bowie) as actually existing within an otherwise realistic filmic universe. Nolan's wager in this film is that the idea of teleportation, because of its physical impossibility, makes apparent the possibility of the impossibility: it shows that events that we think are impossible can occur, even though they violate the laws that we associate with reality itself. Like phrenology for Hegel, teleportation for Nolan is an illusion that points toward truth, but this only becomes evident when we see the ontological privilege that the illusion or the deception has.[9]

Nolan's realistic treatment of teleportation in *The Prestige* is the pivotal moment in his cinema. While spectators are prepared for departures from realism in his superhero films, *The Prestige* presents itself as a realistic historical drama. But within this history, Nolan includes the invention of a teleportation device that defies the known laws of physics and the technological capacity of the time. Teleportation is Nolan's ultimate fiction. We know that there was no such invention, and yet the film encourages us to believe. If we refuse to allow ourselves to be deceived, we sustain a safe distance from the cinematic lie. But a safe distance from the lie is also distant from truth. We must risk becoming a dupe of the falsehood if we hope to enter into the realm of truth. This is a risk that all of Nolan's films ask their spectators to run.

The liberatory power of film as an art form is inextricable from its unprecedented power to deceive. Confronted with the deceptiveness of the cinema, Nolan doesn't retreat from it—nor does he become a propagandist. Instead, he sees freedom rather than servitude in the cinematic deception. The diversity of Nolan's films all come back to a single point: the lie will set you free.

1. Despite his investment in the depiction of the lie, Nolan largely respects Alfred Hitchcock's prohibition of the lying visual—the image that shows what didn't actually happen. Inveighing against his own use of the lying flashback in *Stage Fright* (1950), Hitchcock argues that this device violates the implicit pact between filmmaker and audience affirming that what the film shows onscreen actually happens. In his interview with François Truffaut concerning *Stage Fright*, he proclaims, "I did one thing in that picture that I never should have done; I put in a flashback that was a lie." Quoted in François Truffaut, *Hitchcock: The Definitive Study of Alfred Hitchcock by François Truffaut*, rev. ed. (New York: Simon and Schuster, 1985), 189.

2. Friedrich Nietzsche, perhaps the greatest philosophical champion of perspectivalism, does not abandon the idea of truth. Truth arrives for Nietzsche through either multiplying perspectives or finding the most tragic perspective. His famous critique of truth is a call for a new way of understanding it, not ceding the priority to fiction.

3. Jacques Lacan, "Le séminaire XXI: Les non-dupes errent, 1973–1974," unpublished manuscript, session of January 15, 1974. Unless otherwise noted, all translations are my own.

4. The same rule applies for athletes as well. Often, it is the disguise embodied by a nickname, more than the athlete's ability, that enables him or her to win a contest. Simply having the name "Magic" Johnson or "Babe" Ruth is an important part of the struggle.

5. According to Münsterberg, "The fundamental condition of art . . . is that we shall be distinctly conscious of the unreality of the artistic production, and that means that it must be absolutely separated from the real things and men, that it must be isolated and kept in its own sphere. As soon as a work of art tempts us to take it as a piece of reality, it has been dragged into the sphere of our practical action, which means our desire to put ourselves into connection with it. Its completeness in itself is lost, and its value for our aesthetic enjoyment has faded away." *Hugo Münsterberg on Film: "The Photoplay: A Psychological Study," and Other Writings*, ed. Allan Langdale (New York: Routledge, 2002), 123.

6. Theodor Adorno, *Minima Moralia: Reflections from Damaged Life*, trans. E. F. N. Jephcott (New York: Verso, 1978), 25.

7. Robert A. Rosenstone, *History on Film/Film on History* (New York: Longman/Pearson, 2006), 47.

8. Though it emerges in the 1930s in response to the fear that cinematic lies will misshape public behavior, the Hays Code itself in its own way insists that films lie. No criminal can succeed in a crime, no relationship can involve sexual activity, no one can be openly gay, no black woman can marry a white man, and so on. The Hays Code attempts to construct a cinema that preserves a wholly fictional version of American life out of the belief that this fiction will shape American reality.

9. The censorship of the Production Code uses public morality as a fetish to disavow the political agenda informing it. Joseph Breen, the longtime head of the Production Code Administration, was not simply a moralizer but, much more significantly, a conservative ideologue. He wielded the authority of the Production Code to limit any signs of leftist activity that manifested itself in Hollywood cinema. Even negative depictions of Hitler, at least prior to the United States' entry into World War II, earned his censure. Antifascism was, for Breen, every bit as offensive as sexuality or foul language.

10. Mark Crispin Miller points out that cinema has the effect of rendering commodities much more desirable than they appear in our everyday lives. He notes, "Sailing through the movies, the multitudinous labels and logos of our daily lives appear (or so the advertisers hope) renewed, their stale solicitations freshened up by the movie's magical, revivifying light—and by careful steps taken to glamorize them." "End of Story," *Seeing Through Movies*, ed. Mark Crispin Miller (New York: Pantheon, 1990), 197.

11. Jonathan Beller, *The Cinematic Mode of Production: Attention Economy and the Society of the Spectacle* (Hanover, NH: Dartmouth College Press, 2006), 260. In his analysis of the relation between cinema and capitalist production, Beller takes Guy Debord as one of his points of departure. For Debord, one of the key developments in the society of the spectacle is the commodity becoming ubiquitous. According to Debord, "The spectacle corresponds to the historical moment at which the commodity completes its colonization of social life. It is not just that the relationship to commodities is now plain to see—commodities are now *all* that there is to see; the world that we see is the world of the commodity." *Society of the Spectacle*, trans. Donald Nicholson-Smith (New York: Zone, 1995), 29.

12. In his cinema books, Gilles Deleuze contends that films deploying the time image show us things not as objects in a commodified form but as virtualities revealing the act of creation. By contrasting the movement image with the time image, Deleuze articulates the difference between a kind of cinema amenable to capitalist subjectivity and one that resists it, though he never puts it this way. See *Cinema 1: The Movement-Image*, trans. Hugh Tomlinson and Barbara Habberjam (Minneapolis: University of Minnesota Press, 1989); and *Cinema 2: The Time-Image*, trans. Hugh Tomlinson and Robert Galeta (Minneapolis: University of Minnesota Press, 1989).

13. Nolan is not an explicitly political filmmaker. The closest that he comes to an overtly political film is *The Dark Knight*, in which Batman, like George W. Bush, declares a state of exception that permits him to survey the private activity of all the citizens of Gotham. But rather than simply denouncing this surveillance, Nolan complicates it, showing at once its criminality and its necessity.

14. Alain Badiou sees Nicolas Sarkozy as the emblem of this world, one without any value other than the unrestrained maximization of profit. See *The Meaning of Sarkozy*, trans. David Fernbach (New York: Verso, 2008).

15. Fyodor Dostoevsky, *The Brothers Karamazov*, trans. Richard Pevear and Larissa Volokhonsky (New York: Knopf, 1990), 254.

16. Jacques Lacan, *The Seminar of Jacques Lacan, Book I: Freud's Papers on Technique, 1953–1954*, trans. John Forrester, ed. Jacques-Alain Miller (New York: Norton, 1988), 194.

17. Even a film that shows corruption winning out, like Alan Pakula's *The Parallax View* (1974), offers us temporary respite from corruption by giving us a transcendent perspective on it, even if only for a couple of hours.

18. Though Capra predominately uses the cinematic fiction for ideological ends, there are moments in his films where the fiction reveals the truth of life under capitalism, such as the Pottersville sequence from *It's a Wonderful Life* (1946). (I am indebted to Hugh Manon of Clark University for pointing out this exception to me.)

19. In his attempt to articulate an ethics of the lie, Jean-Michel Rabaté claims that the lie is instructive in a way that the truth is not. He says, "We only learn from our lies and errors, and from the lies and errors of other people." *The Ethics of the Lie*, trans. Suzanne Verderber (New York: Other Press, 2007).

20. Sergei Eisenstein's films employ the cinematic lie to reveal a hidden truth to spectators. Deception is a tool that Eisenstein uses in the service of truth. For instance, in *Strike* (1925) he constructs a montage sequence that juxtaposes an attack on striking workers with the image of a cow being slaughtered. This is a clear instance of a cinematic lie: not only are both scenes fictional, but in reality, police officers gunning down striking workers have nothing to do with slaughterhouse workers killing cattle. Montage allows Eisenstein to create a fiction that connects empirically disparate phenomena, but this fiction also communicates the underlying truth that authorities value workers for nothing but what they produce, in the same way that slaughterhouse owners value cattle. Eisenstein's turn to deception in *Strike*, like others throughout his films, is strategic rather than ontological. Christopher Nolan pushes cinematic deception in the opposite direction: his films espouse and develop an idea of deception as ontological and thus ethical.

21. The critique of cinematic fetishism appears in the apparatus theory developed by Jean-Louis Baudry and Christian Metz, among others. For these film theorists, the role that fetishistic disavowal plays in the cinema derives inherently from the cinematic situation itself. The positioning of the camera, the darkened theater, and the nature of the filmic image all work together to create a fantasy that spectators take for reality, even though they know that they are in a movie theater.

22. In his *Seminar VII* on the ethics of psychoanalysis, Lacan adopts a Hegelian position concerning truth. Whereas earlier in his thought Lacan had seen every fiction as an implicit appeal to truth, in *Seminar VII* he formulates the opposite position. He says, "Every truth has the structure of a fiction." *The Seminar of Jacques Lacan, Book VII: The Ethics of Psychoanalysis, 1959–1960*, trans. Dennis Porter, ed. Jacques-Alain Miller (New York: Norton, 1992), 12. This conception of the role that the fictional structure plays in the constitution of truth comes to occupy an increasingly prominent position in Lacan's thought. In a sense, this development reflects Lacan's movement toward Hegel, despite his explicit statements to the contrary.

23. At the conclusion of *The God Delusion*, Dawkins makes clear his investment in the possibility of a fully explicable world (which is to say, an elsewhere). He says, "I am thrilled to be alive at a time when humanity is pushing against the limits of understanding. Even better, we may eventually discover that there are no limits." *The God Delusion* (Boston: Houghton Mifflin, 2006), 374. For Plato's idea of the beyond, see *Republic*, trans. G. M. A. Grube, in *Plato: Complete Works*, ed. John M. Cooper (Indianapolis: Hackett, 1997), 971–1223.

1. Beginning a film with an isolated action that has no immediate bearing on what happens next is common enough in the cinema. Typically, the initial action will provide a key to explaining what occurs in the rest of the film. This structure often manifests itself in James Bond films, which almost always begin with set pieces seemingly disconnected from the rest of the narrative. But during the course of the film, the spectator grasps that the initial action provides the key to understanding the subsequent narrative. In the opening sequence of *The Spy Who Loved Me* (Lewis Gilbert, 1977), for instance, James Bond (Roger Moore) kills the lover of the Russian spy, Major Anya Amasova (Barbara Bach), whom he ends up working with, and this produces much of the narrative tension in the film. Here, the initial action functions as a hidden truth waiting to be uncovered, whereas in *Following* it is a hidden truth meant to mislead us as spectators at the very moment we uncover its status as a truth.

2. In the *Critique of Pure Reason*, Kant attacks the idea of a truth existing beyond the realm of appearance among things in themselves. It is the search for this truth, Kant asserts, that tumbles us into skeptical doubt about the reality of the external world. If we could accept the world of appearances (of experience) as the only possible site of truth for us, we would avoid the metaphysical delusions that ultimately lead to a debilitating skepticism. In a sense, Nolan's film repeats Kant's critique, but it insists on the fictional status of the world of appearances, whereas Kant sees appearances as the realm of truth. This distinction informs Kant's abhorrence of the lie in his moral philosophy and Nolan's embrace of it as an ethical position.

3. G. W. F. Hegel, *The Phenomenology of Spirit*, trans. A. V. Miller (New York: Oxford University Press, 1977), 22.

4. The liar's paradox is really a paradox about sets that should include themselves and yet logically cannot because of their formal structure. Perhaps the most philosophically influential version was Russell's paradox, which concerns the set of all sets that don't include themselves. The communication of this paradox to Gottlob Frege caused the latter great consternation, as it unraveled his attempt to derive mathematics from logic.

5. In the *Symposium*, Plato shows that the attractiveness of Socrates stems entirely from the presumed agalma that he contains and not at all from any material qualities. See *Symposium*, trans. Alexander Nehamas and Paul Woodruff, in *Plato: Complete Works*, ed. John M. Cooper (Indianapolis: Hackett, 1997), 457–505.

6. Jacques Lacan calls this box of secrets the "objet petit a" or the object-cause of desire, though he first develops the contours of this concept in his discussion of Plato's *Symposium* and the agalma in his *Seminar VIII* on the transference. See *Le séminaire de Jacques Lacan, Livre VIII: Le transfert, 1960–1961*, ed. Jacques-Alain Miller (Paris: Seuil, 2001). It is because the subject imagines that the Other has a hidden *objet a* that its desire for this Other is aroused. But the object-cause of desire is not the object of desire: at no time can the subject access the objet a, in contrast to the object of desire, which the subject accesses all the time. But the fact that the object of desire that the subject obtains does not contain the objet a results in the object of desire always remaining unsatisfying for the subject who obtains it.

7. Nolan's use of the term "unconscious" in the dialogue of *Following* indicates

a familiarity with and even acceptance of this concept, which makes the reversion to the idea of a "subconscious" in *Inception* (2010) even more conspicuous. This supports an interpretation of the latter film that views the use of the term "subconscious" as suggesting a misunderstanding of the psyche by the characters who employ it.

8. Cinematic spectatorship as such places one in a structural position akin to Bill's, though it is possible to watch in a different way and see oneself included in the images. This is precisely what Nolan's films aim to encourage.

9. In *Seminar XI*, Jacques Lacan describes our constitutive inability to see that the world takes our look into account. He says, *"They have eyes that they might not see. That they might not see what? Precisely, that things are looking at them." The Four Fundamental Concepts of Psychoanalysis*, trans. Alan Sheridan, ed. Jacques-Alain Miller (New York: Norton, 1978), 109.

10. Films include the spectator through the object gaze, a point in the filmic image that sticks out and remains irreducible to what surrounds it. For an analysis of the object gaze, see Todd McGowan, *The Real Gaze: Film Theory After Lacan* (Albany: SUNY Press, 2007).

11. Hegel, *Phenomenology of Spirit*, 10.

12. Undoubtedly the greatest aesthetic depiction of Hegel's point about the role of the subject in what it sees occurs in Franz Kafka's parable "Before the Law," in which a man from the country seeks access to the law and is denied entrance by a guard. Nothing that the man does brings him any closer to admittance, but at the end of the man's life, the guard reveals the secret to him. The man wonders why no one else came seeking to enter, and in the final words of the parable, the guard tells the man that the door was always meant only for him. The man from the country assumes that the law exists as an independent structure apart from his subjectivity, but in fact its very structure takes this subjectivity into account. This man in Kafka's parable thus makes precisely the same mistake that Bill makes in *Following*. See "Before the Law," in *"The Metamorphosis," "In the Penal Colony," and Other Stories*, trans. Joachim Neugroschel (New York: Touchstone, 2000), 148–149.

13. Bill's incredulous statement—"People don't really do that, do they?"—indicates his inability to recognize the nature of deception within language. Because we are speaking beings, we can hide things in plain sight, and this is typically the best hiding place. Language creates the impression of a hidden essence, something real beneath the surface appearance, which transforms the surface appearance or the obvious hiding place into the best hiding place. In this scene, Cobb plays with Bill's lack of awareness of this paradoxical logic and uses it to entrap him further.

14. Bill fails to think about his experience dialectically. When Georg Lukács defines dialectics as a method through which "the whole totality is comprehended," he means that this method grasps the interdependence of subject and object—how the actions of the subject take the object into account and vice versa. See *History and Class Consciousness*, trans. Rodney Livingstone (Cambridge: MIT Press, 1971), 170.

15. Bill induces Cobb to break into his own apartment because he wants a direct experience of how the Other sees him without the distortion of his own look. He wants, in other words, a direct experience of the gaze, which is how the subject distorts what it looks at. But given its status as a distortion, the gaze is available

183

only indirectly, through distortion rather than outside it. The effort to directly experience the gaze would eliminate the very thing that it seeks.

16. One detail of Bill's apartment that stands out when viewing the film after 2005 is the Batman logo that adorns the door. It is as if Nolan anticipated in 1998 his future renewal of the Batman series that had already become tired and worn out when *Following* appeared.

17. The use of the nonlinear chronology calls attention to filmic discourse in a way that films traditionally avoid doing. In contrast to *Following*, the discursive strategy of most films, as Christian Metz points out, "obliterates all traces of the enunciation" in order that the discourse of the film effectively "masquerades as story." *The Imaginary Signifier: Psychoanalysis and Cinema*, trans. Celia Britton, Annwyl Williams, Ben Brewster, and Alfred Guzzetti (Bloomington: Indiana University Press, 1982), 91.

18. Kant's point in the first *Critique* is not, as many readers assume, an insistence on the subjective nature of all experience. It is rather to show how we can make objective claims about the world and how we can distinguish these claims from merely subjective ones. One of the primary early purveyors of the subjectivist misreading of Kant is Arthur Schopenhauer, who believes that Kant condemns us to the experience of a subjective, dreamlike condition. He states that according to Kant (whom he incredibly aligns with George Berkeley), "the world must be recognized, from one aspect at least, as akin to a dream, indeed as capable of being put in the same class with a dream." *The World as Will and Representation*, trans. E. J. Payne (New York: Dover, 1958), 2:4. Commentators on Kant must constantly work to free him from the delusion of Schopenhauer's reading, which sustains its popularity by reducing Kant's thought to a simple series of oppositions.

19. Immanuel Kant, *Critique of Pure Reason*, trans. Paul Guyer and Allen W. Wood (Cambridge: Cambridge University Press, 1998), 309.

20. Through its reformulating of the basis of objectivity in the subjective fiction, *Following* performs a Hegelian critique of Kant. Nolan's philosophical kinship with Hegel reappears so often because they both recognize the priority of the fiction without then abandoning truth altogether in the manner of the relativist.

21. The assertion that one is speaking the truth operates as an almost-perfect indicator of deception. The insistence on the truth of one's assertion marks an unnecessary point of excess in a declarative statement, and this excess is how the distortion of subjectivity—that is, deception—manifests itself. The phrase "to tell the truth" is the originary form of the lie. This is not to say that one can't simply respond truthfully when suspected of some malfeasance but that the insistence on one's truthfulness necessarily bespeaks its opposite.

22. Sigmund Freud, *The Psychopathology of Everyday Life*, trans. James Strachey, in *The Standard Edition of the Complete Psychological Works of Sigmund Freud*, ed. James Strachey (London: Hogarth, 1960), 6:211.

23. Because the attempt to hide our desire almost inevitably gives it away, the most effective means of disguising it involves openly avowing it. Confession is often the best means for averting suspicion, especially when one confesses without any compulsion. My favorite personal example of this involves a friend from my secondary school who used to hide the fact that he compulsively masturbated by broad-

casting to everyone his great love for masturbation. By doing so, he eliminated the shame associated with masturbation and thus (successfully) created the impression that he didn't partake in any shameful activities at all, unlike the other students at the school. The nature of desire leaves plain sight as the only safe hiding place.

24. Freud, *Psychopathology of Everyday Life*, 6:211.

25. Often we see the unconscious gesture expose even the best liar, as the underrated Carl Franklin shows in his *High Crimes* (2002). In the film, Ron Chapman (Jim Caviezel) creates a completely new identity and life in order to escape punishment for a war crime that he had committed. He plays the role so convincingly that he fools his spouse, Claire Kubik (Ashley Judd), a brilliant defense lawyer, even when the army catches up to him and charges him with the crime. His near-perfect ability to lie allows him to appear completely sincere and to subvert a lie detector. After his acquittal, however, Ron gives himself away at home with Claire by repeating a gesture with his keys that the war criminal, according to witnesses, made with his gun (throwing it back and forth rapidly from hand to hand). Even the best liar cannot avoid the truth of the gesture—which is the truth of desire.

26. The naturally deceptive role that our intentional meaning has leads Lacan to assign it to the imaginary realm. Our meaning is a private affair that has nothing to do with the signification of our statement or with the desire that animates it.

27. This is why there is no such thing as self-analysis, despite Freud's insistence on having accomplished this. The subject needs the Other to draw attention to the errors in which the subject exceeds its intentions. In his *Seminar I*, Lacan describes this process, noting that "the Freudian innovation . . . is the revelation, within the phenomena, of these subjective, experienced moments, in which speech which goes beyond the discoursing subject emerges. An innovation that is so striking that it is only with difficulty that we can believe that it was never previously perceived." *The Seminar of Jacques Lacan, Book I: Freud's Papers on Technique, 1953–1954*, trans. John Forrester, ed. Jacques-Alain Miller (New York: Norton, 1988), 267.

28. The great exception to this rule concerning the twist film's investment in an ultimate truth is *Memento*, which the next chapter will explore. On the opposite extreme, the most egregious turn to truth in a twist film occurs in Ron Howard's *A Beautiful Mind* (2001). The film concludes by allowing the spectator to see the delusion of protagonist John Nash (Russell Crowe) from an objective perspective outside the delusion after earlier identifying the spectator's view with the delusion. In this way, deception becomes firmly anchored inside the field of truth, and Howard affirms truth as entirely distinct from the distortion created by the subject's desire.

29. At the conclusion of *The Village*, we see that the characters in the film have opted for deception instead of truth, but for the spectator, the film rigorously separates the two. The form of the film indicates a prioritizing of truth that the form of *Following* explicitly rejects.

30. The references are to *Double Indemnity* and *Out of the Past* (Jacques Tourneur, 1947), respectively. For the definitive account of how deception and truth functions in film noir, see Hugh Manon, "X-Ray Visions: Radiography, Chiaroscuro, and the Fantasy of Unsuspicion in Film Noir," *Film Criticism* 32, no. 2 (2007/2008): 2–27.

31. Kaja Silverman, *The Acoustic Mirror: The Female Voice in Psychoanalysis and Cinema* (Bloomington: Indiana University Press, 1988), 98.

185

1. See David Bordwell, *Narration in the Fiction Film* (Madison: University of Wisconsin Press, 1985).

2. For a more detailed analysis of *Pulp Fiction* and other films with a nonlinear narrative structure, see Todd McGowan, *Out of Time: Desire in Atemporal Cinema* (Minneapolis: University of Minnesota Press, 2011).

3. According to the correspondence theory of truth (which follows directly from the belief that the subject is always only a subject of knowledge rather than a subject of desire), truth consists in the agreement between our representation and the nature of the object in the external world. The great philosophical exponent of this theory of truth is Bertrand Russell. In *Problems of Philosophy*, he writes, "Truth consists in some form of correspondence between belief and fact." *The Problems of Philosophy* (New York: Oxford University Press, 1997), 121.

4. The critique of cinematic separation finds its most trenchant expression in Guy Debord's *Society of the Spectacle*. For Debord, the fundamental aim of the spectacle (of which the cinema constitutes a central pillar) is thwarting any genuine connection among spectators and assuring their isolation from what they see. As he puts it, "Spectators are linked only by a one-way relationship to the very center that maintains their isolation from one another. The spectacle thus unites what is separate, but it unites it only *in its separateness*." *Society of the Spectacle*, trans. Donald Nicholson-Smith (New York: Zone, 1995), 22.

5. Though it does not employ a reverse chronology, Tom DiCillo's *Living in Oblivion* (1995) also alternates between color and black-and-white sequences. DiCillo does this in order to indicate a shift between fantasy and social reality. Of course, the ultimate precursor of this technique is Victor Fleming's *Wizard of Oz* (1939), in which color marks the fantasy world and black and white the dreary social reality.

6. For a complete mapping of the film's chronological structure, see Andy Klein, "Everything You Wanted to Know About *Memento*," Salon.com, June 28, 2001, http://archive.salon.com/ent/movies/feature/2001/06/28/memento_analysis/index.html.

7. In the beginning of his *Metaphysics*, Aristotle provides a direct alignment of the subject with knowledge. Though other philosophers in the history of metaphysics might avoid such clear statements, they implicitly hold to Aristotle's claim that "all men by nature desire to know." *Metaphysics*, trans. W. D. Ross, in *The Complete Works of Aristotle*, ed. Jonathan Barnes (Oxford: Oxford University Press, 1984), 2:1552.

8. Martin Heidegger, "What Is Metaphysics?," trans. David Farrell Krell, in *Basic Writings*, ed. David Farrell Krell (San Francisco: Harper and Row, 1977), 105.

9. Martin Heidegger, *Being and Time*, trans. John Macquarrie and Edward Robinson (San Francisco: HarperCollins, 1962), 378.

10. Heidegger's conception of Dasein as being-in-the-world accepts the world as a presupposition and thereby fails to grasp the subject's investment in the world. The subject is not just a being-in-the-world; it is a being invested in its world, a desiring being.

11. René Descartes, *Meditations on First Philosophy*, trans. John Cottingham (Cambridge: Cambridge University Press, 1986), 15.

12. Other aspects of Nolan's shot choices in the film indicate Leonard's status as a subject of desire. When Nolan shows Leonard sitting shirtless on a bed with his torso covered with tattoos, it becomes apparent that Leonard takes pleasure in the way that he has structured his search for the truth. Here, the aesthetic dimension of Leonard's search moves to the foreground.

13. The enjoyment that Natalie derives from this exchange is evident in the exaggerated nature of the dialogue and the over-the-top performance of Carrie-Anne Moss, who verbally assaults Leonard as she speaks, stressing each insult as if it were a physical blow. This excess shows that Natalie, like Leonard, acts for the sake of enjoyment rather than on behalf of any teleology. The apparent purpose or final cause—arousing Leonard's anger so that he will beat her and allow her to feign a beating from Dodd—provides a premise for an occasion to enjoy.

14. The problem with the project of radical doubt is that it can never be radical enough. No matter how diligently I work to put everything into question, there remains a point from which I put everything into question, and this point acts as an anchor of certainty. The split in the subject—the distinction between the subject of the enunciation and the subject of the statement—marks the limit that radical doubt continually confronts. The statement of doubt relies on the certainty of enunciation.

15. Hugh Manon (Clark University), private communication, December 8, 2010.

16. Viewers of *Memento* often split over the question of Teddy's reliability. Some insist that he must be the source of an ultimate truth, while others claim equally vehemently that he lies to save himself. As long as one remains focused on the question of the truth of what happens, however, one stays on the terrain of the subject of knowledge. It is only by engaging the film in terms of desire that one can escape this irresolvable antinomy. The film thus operates homologously to Georg Lukács in *History and Class Consciousness*, where he exposes the antinomies of Kantian philosophy as the product of a contemplative rather than a practical attitude toward the world. See *History and Class Consciousness*, trans. Rodney Livingstone (Cambridge: MIT Press, 1971).

17. Jacques Lacan, *The Seminar of Jacques Lacan, Book XX: Encore, 1972–1973*, trans. Bruce Fink (New York: Norton, 1998), 104–105.

18. One mode of subverting the subject of knowledge in the detective film is depicting the solution as indifferent or beside the point. Robert Altman employs this strategy in his films of detection, such as *The Long Goodbye* (1973) and *Gosford Park* (2001). In the latter, the indifference of the solution allows spectators to see class relations as structurally more significant than knowledge.

19. Of course, many detective films provide spectators with the opportunity to experience the crime by showing it in flashback as the detective voices the solution. This is common in films based on Agatha Christie novels, such as *Murder on the Orient Express* (Sidney Lumet, 1974), which matches the account of the murder that Hercule Poirot (Albert Finney) announces with images of the actual murder. But despite the apparent directness of the experience of the crime that it offers, this method nonetheless mediates the experience through the voice of the detective, which has the effect of distancing the spectator from the immediacy of the event.

20. Mary Ann Doane, *The Emergence of Cinematic Time: Modernity, Contingency, and the Archive* (Cambridge, MA: Harvard University Press, 2002), 252.

21. Anna Kornbluh, "Romancing the Capital: Choice, Love, and Contradiction in *The Family Man* and *Memento*," in *Lacan and Contemporary Film*, ed. Todd McGowan and Sheila Kunkle (New York: Other Press, 2004), 135. *Memento* does not simply present its narration as unreliable but as originating from a lie. As a result, the spectator is left not in the position of one who can no longer know with certainty but in the position of one whose project no longer involves knowing. This is the problem with Elliot Panek's insistence on the unreliability of the film's narration. He claims, "The initial block against reading the film as a traditional linear narration was the out-of-sequence presentation of diegetic events. The more substantial block against this reading is the revelation of an unreliable narration." "The Poet and the Detective: Defining the Psychological Puzzle Film," *Film Criticism* 31, nos. 1–2 (2006): 83.

22. Melissa Clarke, "The Space-Time Image: The Case of Bergson, Deleuze, and *Memento*," *Journal of Speculative Philosophy* 16, no. 3 (2002): 179. Clarke sees the film as a Deleuzean affirmation of "shifting, multiply variant possible connections between the present and the sheets of the past" (180). But this reading necessarily elides the way the film renders all these connections moot through its revelation of Leonard as a subject of desire. It is as if Clarke accepts Leonard's own insistence on the primacy of epistemology as the controlling idea articulated by the film itself.

23. The better interpretation of the dream, which Freud would not permit himself (or would not permit himself to publish), is that it exculpates not Freud but his friend and interlocutor Wilhelm Fliess for his negligent act of leaving surgical gauze in the nasal cavity of Emma Eckstein (a patient shared by Freud and Fliess) after an operation. Fliess's error requires the dream because it calls into question the faith that Freud places in him as a partner in pathbreaking scientific inquiry. The trauma of Fliess's incompetence overshadows the guilt of Freud's own therapeutic error. The former confronts Freud with an experience of the lacking Other, while the latter merely confronts him with his own lack, which is always preferable. For a detailed account of this interpretation, see Peter Gay, *Freud: A Life for Our Time* (New York: Norton, 1988), 80–87.

24. Sigmund Freud, *The Interpretation of Dreams (I)*, trans. James Strachey, in *The Standard Edition of the Complete Psychological Works of Sigmund Freud*, ed. James Strachey (London: Hogarth, 1953), 4:119. The contradictory nature of these explanations occasions Freud's famous account of kettle logic, a pattern of justification that gives away its falsity through the multiplicity of explanations proffered. He says, "The whole plea—for the dream was nothing else—reminded one vividly of the defence put forward by the man who was charged by one of his neighbours with having given him back a borrowed kettle in a damaged condition. The defendant asserted first, that he had given it back undamaged; secondly, that the kettle had a hole in it when he borrowed it; and thirdly, that he had never borrowed a kettle from his neighbour at all. So much the better: if only a single one of these three lines of defence were to be accepted as valid, the man would have been acquitted" (119–120).

25. The precise role of fantasy in our lives is to fill in the gaps that populate our life narrative. At moments where trauma or plain forgetting leave a blank space, fantasy provides the filler material that allows us to minimize the disruptiveness of the blank space. Without fantasy playing this role, we would lose all sense of a coherent life narrative and identity.

26. This is why Freud, for better or worse, always interprets anxiety in the face of death as a displaced form of castration anxiety.

27. In contrast to the project of knowledge, the structure of desire constantly defers the solution. Knowledge provides solutions, while desire keeps one waiting because the point of desire—the enjoyment that it offers—derives from relating to the object as lost, not from actually finding it. Having an object of desire is akin to losing it as a desirable object.

28. The book is *Claudius the God and His Wife Messalina* by Robert Graves, the sequel to *I, Claudius*. Though *Claudius the God* is a sequel, Leonard's wife proclaims that she enjoys rereading it without referring to having read or rereading the first novel. Her enjoyment does not require a search for the origin, in contrast to Leonard's pleasure, which is entirely oriented around the discovery of the original lost object.

29. An ordinary object becomes desirable through the act of sublimation, which has the effect of wrenching the object from the realm of utility. For Leonard, however, as for the subject of knowledge, no objects exist outside this realm. All objects are simply there to be used on the quest for truth.

30. René Girard, *Violence and the Sacred*, trans. Patrick Gregory (Baltimore: Johns Hopkins University Press, 1977), 26.

31. Friedrich Nietzsche rejects the idea that vengeance is inherent in human relations. It is, for him, a reaction or a secondary phenomenon. This understanding of vengeance informs his critique of philosophy and Christianity, which he sees as modes of reaction against life. But Nietzsche does not see a subject of desire behind the illusory subject of knowledge. Subjectivity is instead a question of power, which means that Nietzsche has no way to thematize the subject's involvement in its world except in terms of domination or retreat.

32. Garry Gillard, "'Close Your Eyes and You Can Start All over Again': *Memento*," *Australian Screen Education* 40 (2005): 116.

33. There are also a large number of revenge films in the film noir tradition, and the centrality of the revenge motif further locates *Memento* in this lineage. The most significant of these are *Fury* (Fritz Lang, 1936), *Tension* (John Berry, 1949), and *The Big Heat* (Fritz Lang, 1953).

34. William G. Little, "Surviving *Memento*," *Narrative* 13, no. 1 (2005): 80.

35. In contrast to most legal theorists, Hegel does not associate punishment with restoring balance to the social order. Instead, he contends that punishment inheres in crime itself. By committing a crime, the criminal expresses an unconscious desire for the punishment. Punishment thus occurs for the sake of the criminal as much as for the sake of the society. It is not revenge but the actualization of crime. An unpunished crime remains, for Hegel, not actual—and in this way a wrong for the criminal.

36. According to Jacques Lacan, the fact that the Other does not exist forms the basis for the ethical dimension of psychoanalysis. Without an Other to be responsible, the subject must take responsibility for its own enjoyment, and this becomes, for Lacan, the ethics of psychoanalysis.

37. The problem with Jacques Derrida's notion of an impossible justice to come is that it is always to come. By investing itself in future possibility, even if it acknowledges that this future will never fully arrive, the deconstructive version of

189

justice accepts the very temporality that augments injustice through its flight from trauma.

CHAPTER THREE

1. Dennis Lim, "Waking Life," *Village Voice*, May 28, 2002, http://www.villagevoice.com/2002-05-28/film/waking-life/2/.

2. Even reviewers who expressed an exaggerated affection for the film—Andrew O'Hehir compared Nolan to Dostoevsky and David Lynch—nonetheless acknowledged its limitations in relation to *Memento*. O'Hehir notes that "*Insomnia* may disappoint hardcore *Memento* devotees." "*Insomnia*," Salon.com, May 24, 2002, http://dir.salon.com/story/ent/movies/review/2002/05/24/insomnia/index.html.

3. The comparison with *City of Angels* and *Vanilla Sky* is patently unfair. In contrast to *Insomnia*, no one would argue that *City of Angels* or *Vanilla Sky* match the original films, *Der Himmel über Berlin* (*Wings of Desire*, Wim Wenders, 1987) or *Abre los ojos* (*Open Your Eyes*, Alejandro Aménabar, 1997). In these instances, as in most others, the remake falls so far from the tree of the original that it becomes almost unwatchable for the original's fans. Even if one prefers the original Norwegian version of *Insomnia*, this is not at all the case with Nolan's film.

4. As with *Memento*, *Insomnia* leaves the spectator in a state of relative uncertainty about its central event. The fans of *Memento* dispute whether Leonard (Guy Pearce) killed his wife, and fans of *Insomnia* argue about Will's shooting of Hap. Like in *Memento*, however, the importance doesn't lie in the truth of what happens—this is the ultimately unsatisfying path of knowledge—but in how the main character reacts to what happens. The reaction reveals the truth of the subject's desire.

5. Just as *Memento* works as a thematic remake of *Citizen Kane* (1941), *Insomnia* effectively functions as a remake not so much of the Norwegian original but of Orson Welles's *Touch of Evil* (1958). Like *Insomnia*, Welles's film depicts a police officer, Hank Quinlan (Orson Welles), who engages in deceit in order to solve crime. Quinlan plants evidence and frames Manelo Sanchez (Victor Millan) for planting a bomb in the car of Rudy Linnekar. Even more than Will Dormer, Quinlan clearly carries the lie too far, and it ends up destroying him. But the film does show that he frames the guilty person, which forces us to see the link between deceit and capable detective work.

6. Jacques Lacan, "Le séminaire XXI: Les non-dupes errent, 1973–1974," unpublished manuscript, session of January 15, 1974.

7. It is only with Freud that the metaphoric association of light and truth changes to some extent. For Freud, it is the darkness of the night and the dream world that holds the truth of the subject. But even Freud viewed himself as a thinker of the Enlightenment, as someone bringing the light of truth into the darkness of the dream world.

8. J. L. A. Garcia, "White Nights of the Soul: Christopher Nolan's *Insomnia* and the Renewal of Moral Reflection in Film," *Logos: A Journal of Catholic Thought and Culture* 9, no. 4 (2006): 96.

9. Of course, Al Pacino has not only played police officers during his career. He is equally well-known for playing the ruthless criminal Michael Corleone in Francis

Ford Coppola's *The Godfather* (1972) and in the two sequels. This history informs the character of Will Dormer as well and comes to the fore at moments when the criminal underside of Will's police work becomes evident.

10. One can see the exploration of police corruption in films like *L.A. Confidential* (Curtis Hanson, 1997), *Training Day* (Antoine Fuqua, 2001), *Dark Blue* (Ron Shelton, 2002), or *The Departed* (Martin Scorsese, 2006).

11. The scene in Kay's bedroom also provides the first instance of Will making a mistake. He wants to go to the school to question Kay's boyfriend, Randy Stetz (Jonathan Jackson), but he does not realize that it is ten o'clock at night or that it does not get dark in Nightmute during this time of year. This error is of course understandable for someone from Los Angeles, but it suggests the role that the unending light will play in exposing Will's deception. He is accustomed to the cover of night and does not anticipate the effects of an absence of darkness. Police investigation requires the lie, but it must be concealed, which is impossible in Nightmute.

12. The failure of the detective in Skjoldbjaerg's original is in part due to him being Swedish while working in Norway. The other characters in the film emphasize to him that he doesn't belong, and this sense of alienation in the small Norwegian town pushes him further toward criminality. The film is an exploration of an isolated, out-of-place individual more than a study of police investigation as such, as is the case with Nolan's film.

13. It seems most correct to say that the film depicts the shooting of the partner as a parapraxis, an accident that realizes Will's unconscious desire. Though Nolan depicts the shooting in a way that suggests it was not intentional, he also includes the lie to cover up the shooting, which indicates that the shooting was an instance where the unconscious spoke. This dimension is especially evident because Nolan shows the shooting occur just after Will rebuffs Hap's attempt to smooth over their differences concerning the latter's decision to cooperate with the internal affairs investigation.

14. Through Will's efforts to keep the investigation open and thus implicate himself, the film reveals the link between ethics and the death drive. The extent to which Will subverts his own good is the extent to which he acts as an ethical subject. For an unequalled exploration of this link, see Alenka Zupančič, *Ethics of the Real: Kant, Lacan* (New York: Verso, 2000).

15. G. W. F. Hegel, *Phenomenology of Spirit*, trans. A. V. Miller (New York: Oxford University Press, 1977), 19.

16. In the noir universe, parallels between the criminal and the detective might shift suspicion onto the detective, as occurs in the neo-noir *Tightrope* (Richard Tuggle, 1984).

17. The association of money with the classical detective's distance reveals the entanglement of this attitude and a capitalist economy. Like classical detection, capitalism depends on a realist view of the world, a rigorous separation between the subject and the world that it confronts. The capitalist subject who grasps the connection between labor and the world of commodities ceases at that instant to be a capitalist subject. An idea of distance from the world is a prerequisite for both capitalist subjectivity and classical detection.

18. Since the classical detective appears as the subject of knowledge and the noir detective as the subject of desire, I'm tempted to claim that there is no such

thing as the classical detective. Even in the case of Auguste Dupin, the prototype, it is clear that his subjectivity plays a large role in his ability to solve the three cases that Poe recounts. And Dupin's neutrality further comes into question when he ostentatiously displays the enjoyment he receives from solving the cases.

19. Near the end of the film, Finch attests to the noir status of the film when he tells Will, "You made your own choices. It's like I wasn't even here."

20. Many critics have made the claim that film noir concerns visual style rather than narrative structure, which is why many deny it the status of a genre. Janey Place is a representative figure for this position. As she points out, "Unlike genres, defined by objects and subjects, but like other film movements, film noir is characterised by the remarkably homogeneous visual style with which it cuts across genres." "Women in Film Noir," in *Women in Film Noir*, ed. E. Ann Kaplan (London: BFI, 1998), 50.

21. Peter Rainer, "Northern Exposure," *New York Magazine*, May 20, 2002, http://nymag.com/nymetro/movies/reviews/6033/.

22. The film whose mise-en-scène most closely resembles that of *Insomnia* is *Fargo* (Joel and Ethan Coen, 1996). Like *Insomnia*, one could classify *Fargo* as a film blanc rather than a film noir. It has all the characteristics of film noir except the most important one—the darkness.

23. The actual parallel to Copernicus in this analogy is not a particular film director but Dashiell Hammett, the writer who played the largest role in inventing the hard-boiled detective that film noir would bring to prominence.

24. One might say that while film noir accomplishes a Copernican revolution in the history of detection stories, *Insomnia* goes one step further and parallels Kepler's revolution of the Copernican system. Kepler's understanding of elliptical orbits upsets the regularity that Copernicus preserves even as he displaces the Earth from the center of the universe. The ellipsis is homologous to the subject's lie in *Insomnia*. Truth lies in the distortion of the perfect circle, not in its perfection.

25. The deception of the opening credit sequence is enhanced for the spectator who has seen Skjoldbjaerg's original version. The opening scenes of the original do depict scenes from the crime that the detectives are flying to investigate. By inserting Dormer's frame-up in this structure, Nolan attempts to deceive not just the innocent spectator but also the viewer prepared for what is about to happen.

26. Joanne Laurier, "Once Again, Independent of What?," *World Socialist Web Site*, June 7, 2002, http://www.wsws.org/articles/2002/jun2002/inso-j07.shtml.

27. The same logic works with critiques of capitalism. Critiques that single out specific abuses by specific companies or individuals have the effect of immunizing the capitalist system as a whole. The fault appears to lie in those who abuse the system, not in its basic structure. This is why such critiques proliferate today, even as everyone defends capitalism as the sole reasonable economic alternative.

28. The foundational lie that informs every police investigation is that of the detective's neutrality. In order to desire a solution to the crime and pursue the investigation, the detective must take the side of the victim and view every suspect as guilty. This attitude toward suspects results in the arrest and conviction of the innocent, but it is also absolutely essential for the apprehension of a single criminal. Without the universal assumption of guilt, no case would be solved, and every criminal would go free.

29. Given his role in furthering Ellie's investigation of Hap's shooting, it is difficult to see how one might conceive of Will as the villain of the film, as Garrett Stewart does. According to Stewart, "In *Insomnia*, the twist discovers our sleepless detective-hero as himself a nightmare killer. Investigative hero as villain." *Framed Time: Toward a Postfilmic Cinema* (Chicago: University of Chicago Press, 2007), 65.

CHAPTER FOUR

1. The pattern of the independent director being targeted to direct a superhero film begins with Sam Raimi's *Spider-Man* (2002) and Ang Lee's *Hulk* (2003). The success of both Raimi and Nolan led to their involvement in sequels, while the failure of Lee's film necessitated a quasi-remake (*The Incredible Hulk*, 2008) that retold the emergence of the superhero without any attempt to build on Lee's original film.

2. From the launching of the Batman series in 1989, director Tim Burton emphasized the cartoonish aspects of the story. Though we see the inner turmoil of the various manifestations of Batman, villains such as the Penguin, Mr. Freeze, and Poison Ivy tend to create a comic book effect and destroy any hints of verisimilitude. In his first Batman film, Nolan refuses to include any of the comic villains, and when he does include one for the sequel, he creates him as a figure of horror rather than comedy.

3. The Batman comic book series includes an act of reinvention that precipitates Nolan's—and that Nolan would later make explicit reference to in the title of his sequel to *Batman Begins*. In 1986, Frank Miller released *The Dark Knight Returns* series, and the new version of Batman that Miller created and the tone of the comic as a whole became much darker and took on the qualities of film noir. (I owe this point and many others about the Batman series in this chapter to Hugh Manon of Clark University.)

4. When Batman first emerges as a comic book character, he is a classical detective who investigates crimes from a distance. As he becomes a superhero, however, the effect of investigation on his subjectivity reveals itself, and he acquires the status of the hard-boiled detective. In fact, every superhero is a version of the hard-boiled detective because the mere existence of superpowers indicates the distortion of subjectivity that plays a role in the investigation of crime.

5. Jacques Lacan, *The Seminar of Jacques Lacan, Book VII: The Ethics of Psychoanalysis, 1959–1960*, trans. Dennis Porter (New York: Norton, 1992), 319.

6. Spinoza's philosophical elimination of the final cause—he contends that there are no final causes toward which the world moves, no ultimate goals, just an immanent and effective causality—paves the way for the prioritizing of the fiction over truth that occurs first in the Western philosophical tradition with Hegel. Even though Spinoza insists on the ontological priority of truth and on knowledge unpolluted by desire as our true aim, he does contend that truth cannot reside in a transcendent position. We arrive at truth by working through the fictions, but for Spinoza, in contrast to Hegel, this truth exists prior to the fictions, which come about through our failure to conceive the truth properly. The step from Spinoza to Hegel is at once minuscule and gigantic.

7. The critique of the hero who wants to save society by constituting him- or herself as an exception to the corrupt social order becomes manifest in Nolan's sequel

to *Batman Begins*. In *The Dark Knight* (2008), Nolan depicts Batman rejecting the position of heroic exceptionality and accepting the association of that exception with the criminal. See chapter 6 for the elaboration of this point.

8. Fantasy enables the subject to identify with the object because it functions through the erasure of the subject. In the act of fantasizing, the subject imagines a scene that it can see without disturbing through its subjective presence. In this sense, the fantasy scene is impossible: it can occur, but there would be no one to see it. The point of identification in the fantasy thus becomes that of the object. As Juan-David Nasio notes, "The principal organizing mechanism of the fantasmatic structure is the identification of the subject become object." *Le fantasme: Le plaisir de lire Lacan* (Paris: Petite Bibliothèque Payot, 2005), 40.

9. Joan Copjec, *Read My Desire: Lacan Against the Historicists* (Cambridge: MIT Press, 1994), 37.

10. Bruce cannot take the path that his father takes because he experiences the trauma of seeing his father die, which reveals to him the inherent gap within the law that Thomas Wayne's liberal philosophy attempts to deny. Even though Bruce suffers an empirical trauma (the death of his father), his response to it indicates that he interprets this trauma as an ontological one, as concomitant with the gap or fault in the law.

11. Even though enlightened authority figures can avoid recourse to disguise and fantasy, they themselves operate as a fantasy for the subjects who believe in them. The belief that a benevolent dictator could save us from the failures of democracy is simply the fantasy of a social order without a gap, of a law without fault. The point is not that enlightened authority is impossible but that it cannot provide the healing that we imagine it will.

12. In his explanation of the attack by the bats, Thomas Wayne denies the existence of diabolical evil or evil for evil's sake. If one believes this, then the superhero is not necessary, because education should be sufficient to eradicate evil. By taking up the identity of Batman, Bruce acknowledges that there can be evil not tied to a failure of knowledge but instead done for its own sake, even though this form of evil doesn't become fully evident until *The Dark Knight*.

13. Though the film shows the failure of Thomas Wayne's vision to account for the rise in criminality in the city, it nonetheless equivocates concerning his authority. By staging his death early on, Nolan allows us to believe that if Thomas Wayne were alive, Gotham would not succumb to rampant criminality. His death, in other words, cements his status as a non-lacking authority figure. Though the film provides an implicit critique of his position, Thomas Wayne's authority gains additional fantasmatic support through his death, which thus represents a moment where the film compromises with this authority.

14. See G. W. F. Hegel, *Phenomenology of Spirit*, trans. A. V. Miller (New York: Oxford University Press, 1977), 329–349.

15. In his discussion of Lenin's revolutionary politics, Slavoj Žižek notices a similar logic at work. According to Žižek, Lenin's revolutionary gesture doesn't attempt to realize a future utopia but actually allows that utopia to become present in the revolutionary struggle itself. As he puts it, "In a genuine revolutionary breakthrough, the utopian future is neither simply fully realized, present, nor simply evoked as a distant promise which justifies present violence—it is rather as if, in

a unique suspension of temporality, in the short circuit between the present and the future, we are—as if by Grace—briefly allowed to act *as if* the utopian future is (not yet fully here, but) already at hand, there to be seized." "Lenin's Choice," in *Revolution at the Gates: Selected Writings of Lenin from 1917*, ed. Slavoj Žižek (New York: Verso, 2002), 259.

16. Bruce's opposition to his father's position of enlightened authority becomes evident visually at the end of the film through his method of preventing Ra's from destroying the city. In order to stop Ra's, he must destroy the train that his father built to unite Gotham. In a sense, the destruction of Ra's is also the refusal of his father's political position as well.

17. Nolan's attempt to create realistic gadgets for Batman operates in direct contrast to earlier incarnations of the Batman story, including, most infamously, the *Batman* television series from the late 1960s. Here, the appropriate gadget is always ready at hand for the particular crisis, even though Batman would have no way of anticipating the crisis or the gadget required. Furthermore, the gadgets themselves are often completely outrageous, and the series employs these unrealistic gadgets as an integral part of its campy humor. Nolan dispenses with this not in the name of realism for its own sake but to eliminate the distance between the spectator and the superhero as fantasy object.

18. Foucault notes, "Having become a public, disinterested, supervised activity, medicine could improve indefinitely: in the alleviation of physical misery, it would be close to the old spiritual vocation of the Church, of which it would be a sort of lay carbon copy. To the army of priests watching over the salvation of souls would correspond that of the doctors who concern themselves with the health of bodies." *The Birth of the Clinic: An Archaeology of Medical Perception*, trans. A. M. Sheridan Smith (New York: Vintage, 1973), 32–33.

19. According to Žižek, describing the hero's proximity to humanity or humanizing the superhero has a necessarily ideological effect. Like the humanization of the political leader, it serves to obscure the difference that exists between the superhero and the ordinary subject, with the result that the superhero becomes even more mystified for the spectator. He notes, "It is interesting to note how a . . . 'humanization' process is increasingly present in the recent wave of blockbusters about superheroes (*Spiderman*, *Batman*, *Hancock* . . .). Critics rave about how these films move beyond the original flat comic-book characters and dwell in detail over the uncertainties, weaknesses, doubts, fears and anxieties of the supernatural hero, his struggle with inner demons, his confrontation with his own dark side, and so forth, as if all this makes the commercial super-production somehow more 'artistic.'" *First as Tragedy, Then as Farce* (New York: Verso, 2009), 43. While I accept Žižek's argument about the superhero film in general, it does not hold specifically for *Batman Begins* because Nolan's film employs realism not in order to humanize Batman but in order to Batmanize the spectator.

20. One could say the same thing for the medical doctor. All our knowledge about the historical construction of the doctor as an authority figure has the effect of rendering that authority even more mysterious when we experience it. We know it is fictional, and yet we experience it nonetheless.

21. Jean-Paul Sartre, *Being and Nothingness*, trans. Hazel E. Barnes (New York: Washington Square Press, 1956), 4.

22. Jean-Paul Sartre, *Search for a Method*, trans. Hazel E. Barnes (New York: Vintage, 1968), 150.

23. Ludwig Wittgenstein, *The Blue and Brown Books* (New York: Harper and Row, 1958), 65.

24. There is an intimate link between the lie and what Alain Badiou calls the event that goes unremarked in Badiou's own thought. As Badiou sees it, the transformative event that revolutionizes a procedure (science, art, politics, or love) does so by making it possible to see the truth of the procedure, which is why he will sometimes (as in *Number and Numbers*) label the event a "truth event." See Alain Badiou, *Number and Numbers,* trans. Robin Mackay (Malden, MA: Polity, 2008). Badiou himself is not interested in what brings an event about, only in the possibility of fidelity to the event after it occurs. This emphasis allows him to avoid focusing on the role that the lie has in the formation of the event. One inaugurates an event by articulating a truth that is not yet truth—that is, by lying. One proclaims that one is speaking for the people while only having the support of 10 percent of them, or one creates a work of art that claims to capture the horror of the bombing of Guernica with deceptive abstractions. Even the love event is impossible without the lie that expresses love with certainty before feeling that certainty.

CHAPTER FIVE

1. The belief that one might expose and undermine cinematic wholeness through truth rather than fiction is the ruling premise of apparatus theory, which attempts to destroy the fantasmatic power of the cinema by showing how the sense of wholeness embodied by cinematic spectacle is created. Jean-Louis Baudry makes this belief explicit at the conclusion of his essay on the ideological effects of the cinematic apparatus, where he argues that truth can break the power of the fiction. He says, "Both specular tranquility and the assurance of one's own identity collapse simultaneously with the revealing of the mechanism, that is, of the inscription of the film-work." "Basic Effects of the Cinematic Apparatus," in *Movies and Methods: Vol. 2,* ed. Bill Nichols (Berkeley: University of California Press, 1985), 540.

2. Most rivalry occurs on the level of the ego. I view the other as a rival because I see in this other a mirror image of myself—an alter ego. The rival is too similar, and there is only enough space for one of us. The rivalry between Borden and Angier occurs on the level of the real and concerns how each locates his enjoyment. Whereas the ego rivals locate their enjoyment in the same place (which generates the rivalry), Borden and Angier locate it at different points in the artistic process.

3. In contrast to Angier, Borden finds enjoyment in the means of artistic creation rather than the end it produces, which is why his attitude toward his art is perverse. The problem with this perversion—and the problem with perversion as such—is that it blinds the subject to its dependence on the Other. Borden believes that he performs magic for its own sake and that he sacrifices for the sake of the sacrifice itself, and he disdains publicly displaying the results of this sacrifice. But what he fails to see is that the sacrifice would be meaningless without the public performance. His sacrifice could not exist without the goal of the eventual magic trick for the public. He is correct to believe that one's enjoyment is located in the

means, but he doesn't recognize that the means exists only because of the end. Without the performance for the Other, the sacrifice would be nonsensical. This furtive link to the Other is what perversion always misses as it rejects any affirmation of dependence.

4. In the first volume of the *Aesthetics*, Hegel locates the initial development of thought in the experience of wonder. He says, "The man who does *not yet* wonder at anything lives in obtuseness and stupidity. Nothing interests him and nothing confronts him because he has not yet separated himself on his own account, and cut himself free, from objects and their immediate individual existence." *Aesthetics: Lectures on Fine Art: Vol. 1*, trans. T. M. Knox (Oxford: Clarendon Press, 1975), 315.

5. Alain Badiou, *Logic of Worlds: Being and Event 2*, trans. Alberto Toscano (New York: Continuum, 2009), 384.

6. Badiou is actually quite proximate to this position, though in the end he remains on the side of truth rather than deception. His notion that one cannot discover the event through a neutral inquiry but must instead make a decision on its behalf approaches—but doesn't quite arrive at—Nolan's position that the fiction creates the event.

7. Heidegger gives art—and especially poetry—a privileged place in shaping the world in which humanity dwells, but he emphasizes the finite nature of the world that it opens up. Far from enabling access to transcendence, art for Heidegger renders visible the limitations that make it possible to dwell in the world. As he puts it in "The Origin of the Work of Art," "Art is by nature an origin: a distinctive way in which truth comes into being, that is, becomes historical." In *Poetry, Language, Thought*, trans. Albert Hofstadter (New York: Harper and Row, 1975), 78.

8. Hegel, *Aesthetics*, 49.

9. To borrow Herbert Marcuse's terminology from *Eros and Civilization* for other ends, one might say that Angier's inability to recognize necessary sacrifice leads him into surplus sacrifice. Just as Marcuse sees that a certain amount of repression is necessary for human society, *The Prestige* contends that a certain amount of sacrifice is necessary for art. The attempt to eliminate the necessary inevitably produces the surplus in addition to the necessary.

10. The willingness to sacrifice a version of oneself due to the existence of a clone is also prevalent among the pursuers of Adam Gibson (Arnold Schwarzenegger) in Roger Spottiswoode's *The 6th Day* (2000). According to the logic of this film, what separates the ethical hero Gibson from his ruthless pursuers is the willingness to sacrifice one's clone. The villains trying to kill Gibson find the sacrifice of a version of themselves a painful inconvenience, but they accept it as part of their work as henchmen for the cloning mastermind Michael Drucker (Tony Goldwyn), the film's villain. In contrast, when he is confronted with the existence of a clone who has taken his place, Gibson ends up conspiring with the clone to battle Drucker rather than killing his double.

11. Angier is also effectively the murderer of one of the Borden twins. He frames Borden for his own murder by arranging for Borden to be discovered outside the water tank containing his drowned double and by not reappearing himself during the show when Borden goes below the stage to examine the illusion.

12. Bertolt Brecht praises bad acting in the bourgeois theater because he believes that it draws attention to the otherwise-disguised labor that produces the play. But

197

bad acting in the cinema doesn't have the same salutary effect. Unlike the theater, the illusionism in the cinema is so powerful that even bad acting can't break it in any substantive way.

13. Walter Benjamin, "On the Concept of History," trans. Harry Zohn, in *Selected Writings, Volume 4: 1938–1940*, ed. Howard Eiland and Michael W. Jennings (Cambridge, MA: Harvard University Press, 2003), 391–392.

14. Ibid., 392.

15. Max Weber, *The Protestant Ethic and the Spirit of Capitalism*, trans. Talcott Parsons (New York: Routledge, 1992), 159.

16. Slavoj Žižek, "An Ethical Plea for Lies and Masochism," in *Lacan and Contemporary Film*, ed. Todd McGowan and Sheila Kunkle (New York: Other Press, 2004), 183–184. In the *Fragile Absolute*, Žižek offers another formulation of this same dynamic: "In a situation of forced choice, the subject makes the 'crazy' impossible choice of, in a way, *striking at himself*, at what is most precious to himself. This act, far from amounting to a case of impotent aggressivity turned against oneself, rather changes the co-ordinates of the situation in which the subject finds himself: by cutting himself loose from the precious object through whose possession the enemy kept him in check, the subject gains the space of free action. Is not such a radical gesture of 'striking at oneself' constitutive of subjectivity as such?" *The Fragile Absolute; or, Why Is the Christian Legacy Worth Fighting For?* (New York: Verso, 2000), 150.

17. Eric L. Santner, "Miracles Happen: Benjamin, Rosenzweig, Freud, and the Matter of the Neighbor," in Slavoj Žižek, Eric L. Santner, and Kenneth Reinhard, *The Neighbor: Three Inquiries in Political Theology* (Chicago: University of Chicago Press, 2005), 88.

18. Ibid., 103.

19. Karl Marx and Frederick Engels, *The Communist Manifesto: A Modern Edition*, trans. Samuel Moore (New York: Verso, 1998), 38–39.

20. Karl Marx, *Capital: A Critique of Political Economy: Volume 3*, trans. David Fernbach (New York: Penguin, 1981), 127–128.

21. Ibid., 130.

22. Even a writer like Kierkegaard, who is constantly playing with truth and fictionality in his writing through layers of pseudonyms, uses the diary form in *Either/Or* to suggest access to the truth of a specific form of consciousness—that of the seducer. "Diary of a Seducer" reveals the truth about deception rather than immersing the reader in deception in order to reveal it.

23. The film's presentation of the diary form renders evident what the form intrinsically masks: that the diary lies just as much or more than any other art form. The seeming truthfulness of the diary form stems from the absence of an explicit audience, but without an audience, no one would write anything. The actual audience for the diary is the ego ideal that the diarist imagines looking on and measuring the words. Because it is hidden, the ego ideal, as the implicit audience, has the effect of making the diary form *more* deceptive than other arts, not less so.

24. The film shows in a precise way why, as Lacan suggests, truth must have the structure of a fiction. What this means undergoes a dramatic reversal during the course of Lacan's career. In his first seminar, he claims that every lie includes a covert appeal to truth, that lies have their support in reference to an underlying

truth that they implicitly acknowledge. Here, truth has a structural priority over deception, even if deception appears first chronologically. But later, Lacan comes to see deception as the foundation for truth, which is why he titles his late "Séminaire XXI" the way he does—"Les non-dupes errent."

25. Jacques Lacan, "Le séminaire XIV: La logique du fantasme, 1966–1967," unpublished manuscript, session of November 23, 1966.

26. In fact, there are enough hints about Borden's secret that many spectators who pride themselves on figuring out the riddle to puzzle films such as *The Prestige* were disappointed with the obviousness of the solution. One of the chief complaints of the film's spectators was that they saw the end coming from very early on. But trying to figure out a film like *The Prestige* indicates precisely the kind of investment in the idea of truth that the film works to overturn. Those who solve the film's riddle simultaneously miss the film's point.

27. In response to a recognition of the secret behind the magical illusion, spectators experience either horror or disappointment. The film shows both responses. A young boy who figures out that a magician has killed the bird that he causes to disappear breaks out in tears, and even the reappearance of the bird cannot comfort him because he knows the truth. In contrast, when Borden reveals the secret of the bullet catch to Sarah, she loses some of her appreciation for the art. She says to him, "Once you know, it's actually very obvious."

28. Hugh Manon adroitly labels films such as *Unbreakable* and *The Village* "spoilerfilms" because one needs only to speak a single sentence to a prospective viewer of the film to ruin the initial experience. By saying, "The village is an isolated community in the contemporary world," one would completely alter the first viewing that the film attempts to produce for the spectator. This is, as Manon sees it, a profound limitation of such films, and perhaps it explains the dramatic evanescence of Shyamalan's popularity after his initial success. For this point, I am indebted to Hugh Manon (Clark University), private communication.

29. The puzzle film actually works to disguise the deception that inheres in the cinematic form. By focusing spectator attention on the puzzle occurring in what is shown, the film's sleight of hand draws attention away from the act of showing itself, which is where the real cinematic deception lies. Through its use of deception to hide deception, the puzzle film thus represents the highest form of cinematic fetishism.

30. G. W. F. Hegel, *Science of Logic*, trans. A. V. Miller (Atlantic Highlands, NJ: Humanities Press International, 1969), 771–772.

31. Marx, *Capital*, 959.

CHAPTER SIX

1. The necessarily public dimension of the police officer's identity follows from the public nature of the law itself. A law that was not publicized would cease to be a law, and a state that operated with hidden laws would cease to be a state in the proper sense of the term.

2. Film noir represents the aesthetic rendering of what occurs when private interest overruns public law. While public law provides a bond between subjects, the

noir universe shows how the triumph of private interest shatters this bond. As a result, one cannot extend trust to anyone in this universe. As Hugh Manon notes, "The viewer of *noir* is invited to contemplate the objects, people, and events of ordinary daily life in a sinister light." "X-Ray Visions: Radiography, Chiaroscuro, and the Fantasy of Unsuspicion in Film Noir," *Film Criticism* 32, no. 2 (2007/2008): 8.

3. Zack Snyder, director of *300* (2006), turned down the opportunity to direct a Superman film because of the character's lack of moral complexity. Snyder explains, "He's the king daddy of all comic-book heroes, but I'm just not sure how you sell that kind of earnestness to a sophisticated audience anymore." Quoted in Scott Bowles, "Are Superheroes Done For?," *USA Today*, July 28, 2008, 2D.

4. G. W. F. Hegel, *Aesthetics: Lectures on Fine Art: Vol. 1*, trans. T. M. Knox (Oxford: Clarendon Press, 1975), 185.

5. Hegel understands the insufficiency of the legal order and the need for an exception, but he locates the exception not in the hero but in the sovereign. He insists on preserving the monarch even in modernity because he grasps the necessity of sustaining the exceptional position outside the law. See G. W. F. Hegel, *Philosophy of Right*, trans. T. M. Knox (Oxford: Oxford University Press, 1952).

6. Andrew Klavan, "What Bush and Batman Have in Common," *Wall Street Journal*, July 25, 2008, http://online.wsj.com/article/SB121694247343482821.html. After this article appeared, leftist bloggers (such as Christopher Orr) almost immediately pointed out the central problems with Klavan's thesis—namely, that Batman follows an ethic that does not allow him to kill anyone no matter how evil the person may be, that Bush has not reestablished the boundaries of civil rights as Batman does, and that Klavan wants Bush's heroism to be recognized whereas the film insists that true heroism can't be. Nonetheless, there is some aspect of the film that invites Klavan's analysis. With its defense of the need for the figure of exception, *The Dark Knight* grants a fundamental premise of conservative (and even fascist) politics.

7. Ibid.

8. According to Benjamin, the presence of lawmaking violence in a social order does not disappear with the cessation of the violent act itself and the founding of the law. The social order relies on the idea of this violence in order to sustain its functioning. Benjamin notes, "When the consciousness of the latent presence of violence in a legal institution disappears, the institution falls into decay." "Critique of Violence," trans. Edmund Jephcott, in *Walter Benjamin: Selected Writings, Volume 1, 1913–1926*, ed. Marcus Bullock and Michael W. Jennings (Cambridge, MA: Harvard University Press, 1996), 244.

9. The question, for the superhero film, is the precise status of the superhero's violence in Benjamin's terms. Is it merely law-preserving violence, a supplement to the violence of the police? Or is it divine violence, the kind outside the law that renders an infinite justice that goes beyond the balancing of accounts? It is according to this opposition that we must judge each act of exceptional violence.

10. Giorgio Agamben, *State of Exception*, trans. Kevin Attell (Chicago: University of Chicago Press, 2005), 22.

11. The phenomenon of the copycat emerges in response to exceptionality or the perception of it. The copycat serial killer, for instance, views the serial killer as an exception not only to the law but also to ordinary criminality, and thus copies the killings. Exceptionality inspires copycats because of its location outside the

law, which is where we locate enjoyment. From the perspective of those inside the law, the exceptions appear to teem with enjoyment; copycats aim at accessing this enjoyment, though they always come up short because they attempt to do so with hockey pads instead of Kevlar (which is to say, they remain, through the action of copying, within the symbolic law and its world of representation).

12. Agamben, *State of Exception*, 2.

13. Immanuel Kant, *Religion Within the Boundaries of Mere Reason*, in *"Religion Within the Boundaries of Mere Reason," and Other Writings*, trans. and ed. Allen Wood and George di Giovanni (New York: Cambridge University Press, 1998), 59.

14. As Kant puts it, "Whatever his state in the acquisition of a good disposition, and, indeed, however steadfastly a human being may have persevered in such a disposition in a life conduct conformable to it, *he nevertheless started from evil*, and this is a debt which is impossible for him to wipe out." Ibid., 88.

15. The Joker's aesthetic critique of the morality that rules the other characters echoes Nietzsche's condemnation of what he calls a slave morality. Nolan makes the link between the Joker and Nietzsche explicit during the bank robbery that opens the film. As he places a grenade in the mouth of the bank manager, the Joker paraphrases Nietzsche, proclaiming, "I believe whatever doesn't kill you simply makes you . . . stranger."

16. The autonomy of the Joker renders him difficult to understand, even for Batman. At first, he interprets the Joker as just another criminal seeking to enrich himself, but Alfred (Michael Caine) points out the possibility that this interpretation fails to capture what motivates someone like the Joker. Through a story from his own past, Alfred suggests that the Joker acts for the sake of acting rather than for a goal like money. He tells Bruce Wayne, "When I was in Burma, a long time ago, my friends and I were working for the local government. They were trying to buy the loyalty of tribal leaders, bribing them with precious stones. But their caravans were being raided in a forest north of Rangoon by a bandit. We were asked to take care of the problem, so we started looking for the stones. But after six months, we couldn't find anyone who had traded with him. One day I found a child playing with a ruby as big as a tangerine. The bandit had been throwing them away." Wayne asks in response, "Then why steal them?" Alfred says, "Because he thought it was good sport. Because some men aren't looking for anything logical, like money. They can't be bought, bullied, reasoned or negotiated with. Some men just want to watch the world burn." Here, Alfred tries to teach Bruce that the calculation of interest cannot serve as an explanation for evil, that there is the possibility of a diabolical evil that simply delights in the act of performing evil.

17. Immanuel Kant, *Groundwork of the Metaphysic of Morals*, in *Practical Philosophy*, trans. and ed. Mary J. Gregor (New York: Cambridge University Press, 1996), 89.

18. As Alenka Zupančič notes, tracing out Kant's own logic leads to the conclusion that diabolical evil has the exact same structure as adherence to the moral law. Kant's rejection of the possibility of diabolical evil—evil for its own sake—stems, according to Zupančič, from his unconscious recognition of this underlying sameness. She says, *"Diabolical evil, the highest evil, is indistinguishable from the highest good, and that they are nothing other than the definitions of an accomplished (ethical) act.* In other words, at the level of the structure of the ethical act, the difference between good and evil does not exist. At this level, evil is formally in-

distinguishable from good." *Ethics of the Real: Kant, Lacan* (New York: Verso, 2000), 92. This conclusion doesn't lead Zupančič to reject the Kantian moral law but instead to extend it to the figure of diabolical evil. For Zupančič, diabolical evil acquires a moral status because it results from the elimination of all pathological desires or calculations. We can see diabolical evil functioning as a form of morality in a character like Anton Chigurh (Javier Bardem) in Joel and Ethan Coen's *No Country for Old Men* (2007). Though Chigurh acts ruthlessly and kills many people, he also acts against his self-interest out of devotion to his drive.

19. The bond between Batman and the Joker becomes evident on several occasions. When Batman interrogates the Joker in his jail cell, the Joker tells him, quoting literally the famous expression of romantic love from Cameron Crowe's *Jerry Maguire* (1996), "You complete me."

20. The Joker's scars and his conflicting accounts of them have no precedent in the story of the Joker in previous Batman comics or films. Formerly, chemicals disfigured the Joker, and this disfigurement did not take the form of the scars extending from his mouth.

21. The most relentless advocate of utilitarian ethics in contemporary culture is the television program *24*, where the federal agent Jack Bauer (Kiefer Sutherland) confronts a series of ethical dilemmas and consistently reduces them to quantitative problems in order to arrive at the proper ethical decision.

22. Slavoj Žižek, *Violence: Six Sideways Reflections* (New York: Picador, 2008), 66.

23. For Slavoj Žižek, the film's acquiescence to the social lie at this point marks its capitulation to ideology. Without any equivocation, he claims, "*The Dark Knight* is a sign of a global ideological regression." *Living in the End Times* (New York: Verso, 2010), 61.

CHAPTER SEVEN

1. See Nolan's interview with Dave Itzkoff, "A Man and His Dream: Christopher Nolan and *Inception*," *New York Times*, June 30, 2010, http://artsbeat.blogs.nytimes.com/2010/06/30/a-man-and-his-dream-christopher-nolan-and-inception/.

2. Quoted in ibid.

3. Christopher Orr, "*Inception*: Summer's Best, Most Disappointing Blockbuster," *The Atlantic*, July 15, 2010, http://www.theatlantic.com/culture/archive/2010/07/inception-summers-best-most-disappointing-blockbuster/59855/.

4. Robert Samuels, "*Inception* as Deception: A Future Look at Our Everyday Reality," *Huffington Post*, July 26, 2010, http://www.huffingtonpost.com/bob-samuels/eminceptionem-as-deceptio_b_659619.html.

5. The one temporal distortion that occurs in *Inception* occurs with the opening scene. The film begins with Cobb lying on a beach in the limbo state in search of Saito. In the chronology of the film, this scene actually occurs near the end, and when it does occur, we see it repeated almost shot for shot.

6. One might also say that the lie in the big-budget superhero films occurs on the level of content, while in Nolan's other films it also takes place on the level of form. This distinction isn't absolute, but it does largely hold true and testifies to one weakness of *Batman Begins* and *The Dark Knight* in comparison with films like

202

Following and *Memento*. In the case of *Inception*, the deception is clearly formal, which distances it from the Batman films, despite its budgetary similarities.

7. Despite resistance from Cobb and his team against being accompanied by "tourists," Saito insists on entering the dream along with them. Through the character of Saito, Nolan depicts a spectator in the dream who functions as the ideal spectator of Nolan's films. During a gunfight in the dream, Saito is shot and thus becomes both actively engaged in the heist plot and a hindrance to it. Like Saito, as Nolan sees it, the spectator must become invested in the film's fiction and also identify with the obstacle to the fiction's success. This obstacle is the truth within the fiction. (I am indebted to Daniel Cho of Otterbein University for this point.)

8. This is directly stated at one point in the film. When the group comes to recruit Yusef for the mission, he takes them into the basement of his shop, where we see many people sleeping. Eames asks Yusef, "They come here every day to sleep?" An old man responds to him, "No, they come to be woken up. The dream has become their reality. Who are you to say otherwise?" This critique of the realism displayed in Eames's question is sustained throughout the film.

9. Jacques Lacan, *The Seminar of Jacques Lacan, Book XVII: The Other Side of Psychoanalysis*, trans. Russell Grigg, ed. Jacques-Alain Miller (New York: Norton, 2007), 57.

10. For Lacan's discussion of the father dreaming of his son burning, see Jacques Lacan, *The Four Fundamental Concepts of Psychoanalysis*, trans. Alan Sheridan, ed. Jacques-Alain Miller (New York: Norton, 1978).

11. While I was giving a truncated version of this chapter as a talk at Pomona College, Jennifer Friedlander of Pomona College made the point that I recount in this paragraph. I am indebted to her for bringing it to my attention.

12. Cobb's constant use of the term "subconscious" rings false for anyone with even the slightest acquaintance with psychoanalysis. Though Pierre Janet first employs the term in French, it gained popularity in the Anglophone world as a modification of Freud's concept of the unconscious. Unlike the term "unconscious," the word "subconscious" suggests some degree of control, a terrain between consciousness and the unconscious. Such a terrain cannot exist for Freud, which is why he condemns the use of the term in unequivocal language, beginning as early as 1900 in *The Interpretation of Dreams*. The most famous critique occurs in his metapsychological essay on the unconscious, where he argues for "rejecting the term 'subconsciousness' as incorrect and misleading." "The Unconscious," trans. James Strachey, in *The Standard Edition of the Complete Psychological Works of Sigmund Freud*, ed. James Strachey (London: Hogarth Press, 1957), 14:170. Cobb's insistence on "subconscious" rather than "unconscious" reveals his investment in reality at the expense of the truth of his desire, and it is this investment that *Inception* challenges throughout.

13. In fact, Mal's absence in reality—her death by suicide—gives her an increased psychic power within Cobb's unconscious. Presence in reality enables a psychic avoidance that becomes impossible once an object has disappeared. This is why very few people fantasize about the sexual partner who is directly in front of them but rather focus their—often unconscious—fantasies on those who are absent. Cobb can't escape Mal in the dream world because he can't find her in the real world. (I owe this idea to Chris Freyer of the University of Vermont.)

14. Sigmund Freud, "Negation," trans. James Strachey, in *The Standard Edition of the Complete Psychological Works of Sigmund Freud*, ed. James Strachey (London: Hogarth, 1961), 19:237.

15. When Cobb first plants the idea of the unreality of her world in Mal's mind, the method that she and Cobb choose to escape limbo (which they have inhabited for many years) is to put their heads on a railroad track just before an oncoming train arrives. This unusual method of suicide highlights the significance of the train for their relationship and ultimately for distinguishing between their two disparate positions.

16. G. W. F. Hegel, *Science of Logic*, trans. A. V. Miller (Atlantic Highlands, NJ: Humanities Press International, 1969), 647 (translation modified). Miller's translation of "spurious infinity" wrongly suggests that the "bad infinity" is not really infinite, which is not at all Hegel's point. The German term is "schlechte Unendlichkeit," which straightforwardly means "bad infinity."

17. In *Phenomenology of Spirit*, Hegel notes, for instance, that "picture-thinking interprets and expresses as a *happening* what has just been expressed as the *necessity* of the Notion." G. W. F. Hegel, *Phenomenology of Spirit*, trans. A. V. Miller (New York: Oxford University Press, 1977), 465.

18. Even though Freud theorizes women as the love objects in his myth of the origin of society, this is a structural rather than a gender-specific arrangement. Paternal authority—even if a woman embodies it—bars access to the love object, even if this love object finds its representation in the figure of a male.

19. Sigmund Freud, *Totem and Taboo*, trans. James Strachey, in *The Standard Edition of the Complete Psychological Works of Sigmund Freud*, ed. James Strachey (London: Hogarth, 1955), 13:143.

20. Ibid., 145.

21. Jacques Lacan, *The Seminar of Jacques Lacan, Book VII: The Ethics of Psychoanalysis, 1959–1960*, trans. Dennis Porter, ed. Jacques-Alain Miller (New York: Norton, 1992), 321.

22. Davie Itzkoff, "A Film's Mysteries Include a Tease to Édith Piaf," *New York Times*, August 1, 2010, http://www.nytimes.com/2010/08/02/movies/02zimmer.html. Amy Herzog provides an insightful commentary on this aspect of the film's score. See "Subversion Doesn't Come Easily: How the Musical Score in *Inception* Is a Lesson in Collective Dreaming," *University of Minnesota Press Blog*, August 4, 2010, http://www.uminnpressblog.com/2010/08/submersion-doesnt-come-easy-how-musical.html.

23. By choosing to use Piaf's recording of "Non, je ne regrette rien" rather than another version of the song, Nolan subtly connects the absence of guilt that the song denotes with the character of Mal. The woman who plays Mal, Marion Cotillard, starred as Piaf a biographical film of the singer titled *La vie en rose* (Olivier Dahan, 2007).

24. Nolan makes it clear that both the dream world and social reality require a "leap of faith," an act through which we invest ourselves in them and grant them significance. Both Mal and Saito repeat this phrase, telling him that he must make such a leap. Mal wants him to follow her in suicide, and Saito wants him to perform inception on Robert Fischer and thereby return to his position as father.

25. Cobb functions exactly like a benevolent psychotherapist who wants to sub-

204

stitute his healthy and realistic idea for the patient's repressed (and thus diseased) idea. In this sense, his incessant use of the term "subconscious" is consistent with the role that he plays, because this is the term of choice for therapists who take this approach. The problem with this therapeutic strategy is that it wantonly destroys the singularity of the patient and presumes that the normality of the therapist really is advantageous relative to the psychic reality of the patient. *Inception* questions the received wisdom of much psychotherapy in its entirety.

26. The idea of breaking up the would-be monopoly established by Maurice Fischer also seems like an unqualified good—replacing the trauma of monopoly with the normal reality of competition. But rather than endorsing this dogma, the film forces us to question it by associating the dissolution of the monopoly with Cobb's own belief in reconciliation. In this formula, competition becomes a self-reconciled world.

27. David Denby, "Dream Factory," *New Yorker*, July 26, 2010, http://www.newyork er.com/arts/critics/cinema/2010/07/26/100726crci_cinema_denby?currentPage=1.

28. *Inception* is listed as both a heist film and a science fiction film on Wikipedia's list of films within the respective genres.

29. To the credit of Soderbergh, I should note that *Ocean's Eleven* emphasizes the significance of the obstacle by including it within the planning for the heist. The call to the police and the (faked) police response to the robbery are essential to the robbery's success. But the conclusion of the film not only wins millions for the thieves, it also reconciles Danny with his estranged wife, Tess Ocean (Julia Roberts).

30. The central role that editing plays in emphasizing the choice that confronts Cobb leads Hilary Neroni to claim, "While *Memento* is a film about narrative, *Inception* is first and foremost a film about editing." Hilary Neroni of the University of Vermont, private conversation with the author.

31. When I first saw the film on its opening night, the openness of the ending occasioned a collective groan from the audience. This groan seemed to me the culmination of a satisfying response to the film combined with a desire to find a final answer to what seemed to be the central problem that the film posed.

32. Despite the lesser acclaim that accompanies it, *The Thirteenth Floor* actually presents a more complex version of reality as an ideological structure than does *The Matrix*. In the former film, the real resides in the limits and contradictions of the apparent reality, while in *The Matrix*, the real is simply a separate layer of existence out of which the apparent reality is constructed as an illusion.

33. Freud, *Totem and Taboo*, 143.

34. Cobb's investment in the face suggests his commitment to Levinas at the expense of psychoanalysis. The face of the Other for Levinas indicates the Other's absolute alterity, the fact that the Other is not simply the product of my dream. But if he were in fact true to Levinas's thought, Cobb should have no concern about seeing the faces of his children in the dream because it would be clear that these weren't faces as such, insofar as they offered no experience of alterity for him. His fear, in contrast, is that they will, that there will be no difference between the faces of his children in the dream and the faces of his real children.

35. Cobb's visceral act of turning away so as not to see the faces of the children—and Nolan's cut to Cobb's turn, which prevents the spectator from seeing their faces—evinces the fragility of his belief in reality. If he knew with certainty

what their faces looked like in reality as opposed to their appearance in the dream world, he would feel no compunction about seeing them here. In this sense, Cobb prohibits the impossible, which should make us even more suspicious of him, since this is a fundamental gesture of ideology.

CONCLUSION

1. As Slavoj Žižek notes, one indication that Bush was lying rather than simply being unsure about weapons of mass destruction in Iraq is the ground offensive launched against Iraq. He claims, "I am tempted to entertain the hypothesis that the Americans were not simply unsure whether Saddam had WMDs or not, but that they positively knew he did *not* have them—which is why they risked the ground offensive on Iraq." *Iraq: The Borrowed Kettle* (New York: Verso, 2004), 13.

2. According to Immanuel Kant, a consequentialist morality leaves the subject within the realm of heteronomy and constitutively unable to assert its autonomy. One is only autonomous when one does one's duty for its own sake, because this avoids allowing other considerations foreign to the subject itself to enter into duty.

3. Clinton and Bush both nicely illustrate a further problem of the consequentialist lie: one never knows what the consequences of the lie will be. Clinton's attempt to protect his family resulted in their public humiliation, and Bush's attempt to safeguard the country ended up multiplying the terrorist threats against it rather than minimizing them (though one might argue in both cases that these were the intended consequences, at least unconsciously).

4. Alain Badiou, *Being and Event*, trans. Oliver Feltham (New York: Continuum, 2005), 339.

5. Nietzsche's idea of truth as absolute loss that precedes its fictionalization secretly serves as a foundation for his philosophical eschewing of truth. This is why, for example, he says, "'How much truth can a spirit *endure*, how much truth does a spirit *dare?*'—this became for me the real standard of value." *The Will to Power*, trans. Walter Kaufmann (New York: Vintage, 1968), 536.

6. Martin Heidegger, "On the Essence of Truth," trans. John Sallis, in *Basic Writings*, ed. David Farrell Krell (San Francisco: Harper and Row, 1977), 137.

7. G. W. F. Hegel, *Phenomenology of Spirit*, trans. A. V. Miller (New York: Oxford University Press, 1977), 22–23.

8. Ibid., 200. To prove to the phrenologist that spirit is not wholly reducible to the skull bone, Hegel suggests that one might simply smash the phrenologist's skull. This act would make evident that there is more to spirit than just the material bone, and the phrenologist would grasp this truth while dying. Hegel counsels this extreme method of argumentation with tongue in cheek, but given the actual harm that phrenology has helped to inflict throughout human history, it doesn't seem completely disproportionate.

9. Though he presents his thought in large part as a deconstruction of Hegel's, Jacques Derrida actually continues Hegel's insistence on the priority of falsehood relative to truth and the priority of literature relative to philosophy. Though philosophy has tried to assert the purity of truth at the origin, Derrida recognizes the textuality of every origin. The beginning is itself fabricated—and thus fictional. Or

206

to put it in other terms, the first word does not signify directly and then descend into a metaphor. Instead, the metaphor marks the beginning of sense, even as it distances us from sense. There is a distancing or indirectness—a lie—at the origin. We begin with the fictionality of literature, and the truth seeking of philosophy can never catch up. As Derrida contends in *Dissemination*, "There is nothing before the text; there is no pretext that is not already a text. So that, at the moment the surface of attendance is broached and the opening opens and the presentation is presented, a theatrical scene was." *Dissemination*, trans. Barbara Johnson (Chicago: University of Chicago Press, 1981), 328.

Adorno, Theodor. *Minima Moralia: Reflections from Damaged Life*. Translated by E. F. N. Jephcott. New York: Verso, 1978.

Agamben, Giorgio. *State of Exception*. Translated by Kevin Attell. Chicago: University of Chicago Press, 2005.

Aristotle. *Metaphysics*. Translated by W. D. Ross. In *The Complete Works of Aristotle*, edited by Jonathan Barnes, 2:1552–1728. Oxford: Oxford University Press, 1984.

Badiou, Alain. *Being and Event*. Translated by Oliver Feltham. New York: Continuum, 2005.

———. *Logic of Worlds: Being and Event 2*. Translated by Alberto Toscano. New York: Continuum, 2009.

———. *The Meaning of Sarkozy*. Translated by David Fernbach. New York: Verso, 2008.

———. *Number and Numbers*. Translated by Robin Mackay. Malden, MA: Polity, 2008.

Baudry, Jean-Louis. "Basic Effects of the Cinematic Apparatus." In *Movies and Methods: Vol. 2*, edited by Bill Nichols, 531–542. Berkeley: University of California Press, 1985.

Beller, Jonathan. *The Cinematic Mode of Production: Attention Economy and the Society of the Spectacle*. Hanover, NH: Dartmouth College Press, 2006.

Benjamin, Walter. "Critique of Violence." Translated by Edmund Jephcott. In *Walter Benjamin: Selected Writings, Volume 1, 1913–1926*, edited by Marcus Bullock and Michael W. Jennings, 236–252. Cambridge, MA: Harvard University Press, 1996.

———. "On the Concept of History." Translated by Harry Zohn. In *Selected Writings, Volume 4: 1938–1940*, edited by Howard Eiland and Michael W. Jennings, 389–400. Cambridge, MA: Harvard University Press, 2003.

Bordwell, David. *Narration in the Fiction Film*. Madison: University of Wisconsin Press, 1985.

Bowles, Scott. "Are Superheroes Done For?" *USA Today*, July 28, 2008, 2D.

Clarke, Melissa. "The Space-Time Image: The Case of Bergson, Deleuze, and *Memento*." *Journal of Speculative Philosophy* 16, no. 3 (2002): 167–181.

Copjec, Joan. *Read My Desire: Lacan Against the Historicists*. Cambridge: MIT Press, 1994.

Dawkins, Richard. *The God Delusion*. Boston: Houghton Mifflin, 2006.

Debord, Guy. *Society of the Spectacle*. Translated by Donald Nicholson-Smith. New York: Zone, 1995.

Deleuze, Gilles. *Cinema 1: The Movement-Image*. Translated by Hugh Tomlinson and Barbara Habberjam. Minneapolis: University of Minnesota Press, 1989.

———. *Cinema 2: The Time-Image*. Translated by Hugh Tomlinson and Robert Galeta. Minneapolis: University of Minnesota Press, 1989.

Denby, David. "Dream Factory." *New Yorker*, July 26, 2010. http://www.newyorker.com/arts/critics/cinema/2010/07/26/100726crci_cinema_denby?currentPage=1.

Derrida, Jacques. *Dissemination*. Translated by Barbara Johnson. Chicago: University of Chicago Press, 1981.

BIBLIOGRAPHY

Descartes, René. *Meditations on First Philosophy*. Translated by John Cottingham. Cambridge: Cambridge University Press, 1986.

Doane, Mary Ann. *The Emergence of Cinematic Time: Modernity, Contingency, and the Archive*. Cambridge, MA: Harvard University Press, 2002.

Dostoevsky, Fyodor. *The Brothers Karamazov*. Translated by Richard Pevear and Larissa Volokhonsky. New York: Knopf, 1990.

Foucault, Michel. *The Birth of the Clinic: An Archaeology of Medical Perception*. Translated by A. M. Sheridan Smith. New York: Vintage, 1973.

Freud, Sigmund. *The Interpretation of Dreams (I)*. Translated by James Strachey. In *The Standard Edition of the Complete Psychological Works of Sigmund Freud*, edited by James Strachey, vol. 4. London: Hogarth, 1953.

———. "Negation." Translated James Strachey. In *The Standard Edition of the Complete Psychological Works of Sigmund Freud*, edited by James Strachey, 19:234–239. London: Hogarth, 1961.

———. *The Psychopathology of Everyday Life*. Translated by James Strachey. In *The Standard Edition of the Complete Psychological Works of Sigmund Freud*, edited by James Strachey, vol. 6. London: Hogarth, 1960.

———. *Totem and Taboo*. Translated by James Strachey. In *The Standard Edition of the Complete Psychological Works of Sigmund Freud*, edited by James Strachey, 13:1–162. London: Hogarth, 1955.

———. "The Unconscious." Translated by James Strachey. In *The Standard Edition of the Complete Psychological Works of Sigmund Freud*, edited by James Strachey, 14:161–215. London: Hogarth, 1957.

Garcia, J. L. A. "White Nights of the Soul: Christopher Nolan's *Insomnia* and the Renewal of Moral Reflection in Film." *Logos: A Journal of Catholic Thought and Culture* 9, no. 4 (2006): 82–117.

Gay, Peter. *Freud: A Life for Our Time*. New York: Norton, 1988.

Gillard, Garry. "'Close Your Eyes and You Can Start All over Again': *Memento*." *Australian Screen Education* 40 (2005): 115–117.

Girard, René. *Violence and the Sacred*. Translated by Patrick Gregory. Baltimore: Johns Hopkins University Press, 1977.

Hegel, G. W. F. *Aesthetics: Lectures on Fine Art: Vol. 1*. Translated by T. M. Knox. Oxford: Clarendon Press, 1975.

———. *Phenomenology of Spirit*. Translated by A. V. Miller. New York: Oxford University Press, 1977.

———. *Philosophy of Right*. Translated by T. M. Knox. Oxford: Oxford University Press, 1952.

———. *Science of Logic*. Translated by A. V. Miller. Atlantic Highlands, NJ: Humanities Press International, 1969.

Heidegger, Martin. *Being and Time*. Translated by John Macquarrie and Edward Robinson. San Francisco: HarperCollins, 1962.

———. "On the Essence of Truth." Translated by John Sallis. In *Basic Writings*, edited by David Farrell Krell, 117–141. San Francisco: Harper and Row, 1977.

———. "The Origin of the Work of Art." In *Poetry, Language, Thought*. Translated by Albert Hofstadter, 15–86. New York: Harper and Row, 1975.

———. "What Is Metaphysics?" Translated by David Farrell Krell. In *Basic Writings*, edited by David Farrell Krell, 95–112. San Francisco: Harper and Row, 1977.

Herzog, Amy. "Subversion Doesn't Come Easily: How the Musical Score in *Inception* Is a Lesson in Collective Dreaming." *University of Minnesota Press Blog*, August 4, 2010. http://www.uminnpressblog.com/2010/08/submersion-doesnt-come -easy-how-musical.html.

Itzkoff, Dave. "A Film's Mysteries Include a Tease to Édith Piaf." *New York Times*, August 1, 2010. http://www.nytimes.com/2010/08/02/movies/02zimmer.html.

———. "A Man and His Dream: Christopher Nolan and *Inception*." *New York Times*, June 30, 2010. http://artsbeat.blogs.nytimes.com/2010/06/30/a-man-and-his -dream-christopher-nolan-and-inception/.

Kafka, Franz. "Before the Law." In *"The Metamorphosis," "In the Penal Colony," and Other Stories*, translated by Joachim Neugroschel, 148–149. New York: Touchstone, 2000.

Kant, Immanuel. *Critique of Pure Reason*. Translated and edited by Paul Guyer and Allen W. Wood. Cambridge: Cambridge University Press, 1998.

———. *Groundwork of the Metaphysic of Morals*. In *Practical Philosophy*, translated and edited by Mary J. Gregor, 37–108. New York: Cambridge University Press, 1996.

———. *Religion Within the Boundaries of Mere Reason*. In *"Religion Within the Boundaries of Mere Reason," and Other Writings*, translated and edited by Allen Wood and George di Giovanni, 31–191. New York: Cambridge University Press, 1998.

Klavan, Andrew. "What Bush and Batman Have in Common." *Wall Street Journal*, July 25, 2008. http://online.wsj.com/article/SB121694247343482821.html.

Klein, Andy. "Everything You Wanted to Know About *Memento*." Salon.com, June 28, 2001. http://archive.salon.com/ent/movies/feature/2001/06/28/memento _analysis/index.html.

Kornbluh, Anna. "Romancing the Capital: Choice, Love, and Contradiction in *The Family Man* and *Memento*." In *Lacan and Contemporary Film*, edited by Todd McGowan and Sheila Kunkle, 111–144. New York: Other Press, 2004.

Lacan, Jacques. *The Four Fundamental Concepts of Psychoanalysis*. Translated by Alan Sheridan. Edited by Jacques-Alain Miller. New York: Norton, 1978.

———. *The Seminar of Jacques Lacan, Book I: Freud's Papers on Technique, 1953–1954*. Translated John Forrester. Edited by Jacques-Alain Miller. New York: Norton, 1988.

———. *The Seminar of Jacques Lacan, Book VII: The Ethics of Psychoanalysis, 1959–1960*. Translated by Dennis Porter. Edited by Jacques-Alain Miller. New York: Norton, 1992.

———. *Le séminaire de Jacques Lacan, Livre VIII: Le transfert, 1960–1961*. Edited by Jacques-Alain Miller. Paris: Seuil, 2001.

———. "Le séminaire XIV: La logique du fantasme, 1966–1967." Unpublished manuscript.

———. *The Seminar of Jacques Lacan, Book XVII: The Other Side of Psychoanalysis*. Translated by Russell Grigg. Edited by Jacques-Alain Miller. New York: Norton, 2007.

———. *The Seminar of Jacques Lacan, Book XX: Encore, 1972–1973*. Translated by Bruce Fink. Edited by Jacques-Alain Miller. New York: Norton, 1998.

———. "Le séminaire XXI: Les non-dupes errent, 1973–1974." Unpublished manuscript.

Laurier, Joanne. "Once Again, Independent of What?" *World Socialist Web Site*, June 7, 2002. http://www.wsws.org/articles/2002/jun2002/inso-j07.shtml.

Lim, Dennis. "Waking Life." *Village Voice*, May 28, 2002. http://www.villagevoice.com/2002-05-28/film/waking-life/2/.

Little, William G. "Surviving *Memento*." *Narrative* 13, no. 1 (2005): 67–83.

Lukács, Georg. *History and Class Consciousness*. Translated by Rodney Livingstone. Cambridge: MIT Press, 1971.

Manon, Hugh. "X-Ray Visions: Radiography, Chiaroscuro, and the Fantasy of Unsuspicion in Film Noir." *Film Criticism* 32, no. 2 (2007/2008): 2–27.

Marx, Karl. *Capital: A Critique of Political Economy: Volume 3*. Translated by David Fernbach. New York: Penguin, 1981.

Marx, Karl, and Frederick Engels. *The Communist Manifesto: A Modern Edition*. Translated by Samuel Moore. New York: Verso, 1998.

McGowan, Todd. *Out of Time: Desire in Atemporal Cinema*. Minneapolis: University of Minnesota Press, 2011.

———. *The Real Gaze: Film Theory After Lacan*. Albany: SUNY Press, 2007.

Metz, Christian. *The Imaginary Signifier: Psychoanalysis and Cinema*. Translated by Celia Britton, Annwyl Williams, Ben Brewster, and Alfred Guzzetti. Bloomington: Indiana University Press, 1982.

Miller, Mark Crispin. "End of Story." In *Seeing Through Movies*, edited by Mark Crispin Miller, 186–246. New York: Pantheon, 1990.

Münsterberg, Hugo. *Hugo Münsterberg on Film: "The Photoplay: A Psychological Study," and Other Writings*. Edited by Allan Langdale. New York: Routledge, 2002.

Nasio, Juan-David. *Le fantasme: Le plaisir de lire Lacan*. Paris: Petite Bibliothèque Payot, 2005.

Nietzsche, Friedrich. *The Will to Power*. Translated by Walter Kaufmann. New York: Vintage, 1968.

O'Hehir, Andrew. "*Insomnia*." Salon.com, May 24, 2002. http://dir.salon.com/story/ent/movies/review/2002/05/24/insomnia/index.html.

Orr, Christopher. "*Inception*: Summer's Best, Most Disappointing Blockbuster." *The Atlantic*, July 15, 2010. http://www.theatlantic.com/entertainment/archive/2010/07/inception-summers-best-most-disappointing-blockbuster/59855/.

Panek, Elliot. "The Poet and the Detective: Defining the Psychological Puzzle Film." *Film Criticism* 31, nos. 1–2 (2006): 62–88.

Place, Janey. "Women in Film Noir." In *Women in Film Noir*, edited by E. Ann Kaplan, 47–68. London: BFI, 1998.

Plato. *Republic*. Translated by G. M. A. Grube. In *Plato: Complete Works*, edited by John M. Cooper, 971–1223. Indianapolis: Hackett, 1997.

———. *Symposium*. Translated by Alexander Nehamas and Paul Woodruff. In *Plato: Complete Works*, edited by John M. Cooper, 457–505. Indianapolis: Hackett, 1997.

Rabaté, Jean-Michel. *The Ethics of the Lie*. Translated by Suzanne Verderber. New York: Other Press, 2007.

Rainer, Peter. "Northern Exposure." *New York Magazine*, May 20, 2002. http://nymag.com/nymetro/movies/reviews/6033/.

Rosenstone, Robert A. *History on Film/Film on History*. New York: Longman/Pearson, 2006.

212

Russell, Bertrand. *The Problems of Philosophy*. New York: Oxford University Press, 1997.

Samuels, Robert. "*Inception* as Deception: A Future Look at Our Everyday Reality." *Huffington Post*, July 26, 2010. http://www.huffingtonpost.com/bob-samuels/eminception-as-deceptio_b_659619.html.

Santner, Eric L. "Miracles Happen: Benjamin, Rosenzweig, Freud, and the Matter of the Neighbor." In Slavoj Žižek, Eric L. Santner, and Kenneth Reinhard, *The Neighbor: Three Inquiries in Political Theology*, 76–133. Chicago: University of Chicago Press, 2005.

Sartre, Jean-Paul. *Being and Nothingness*. Translated by Hazel E. Barnes. New York: Washington Square Press, 1956.

———. *Search for a Method*. Translated by Hazel E. Barnes. New York: Vintage, 1968.

Schopenhauer, Arthur. *The World as Will and Representation*. Translated by E. J. Payne. 2 vols. New York: Dover, 1958.

Silverman, Kaja. *The Acoustic Mirror: The Female Voice in Psychoanalysis and Cinema*. Bloomington: Indiana University Press, 1988.

Stewart, Garrett. *Framed Time: Toward a Postfilmic Cinema*. Chicago: University of Chicago Press, 2007.

Truffaut, François. *Hitchcock: The Definitive Study of Alfred Hitchcock by François Truffaut*. Revised edition. New York: Simon and Schuster, 1985.

Weber, Max. *The Protestant Ethic and the Spirit of Capitalism*. Translated by Talcott Parsons. New York: Routledge, 1992.

Wittgenstein, Ludwig. *The Blue and Brown Books*. New York: Harper and Row, 1958.

Žižek, Slavoj. "An Ethical Plea for Lies and Masochism." In *Lacan and Contemporary Film*, edited by Todd McGowan and Sheila Kunkle, 173–186. New York: Other Press, 2004.

———. *First as Tragedy, Then as Farce*. New York: Verso, 2009.

———. *The Fragile Absolute; or, Why Is the Christian Legacy Worth Fighting For?* New York: Verso, 2000.

———. *Iraq: The Borrowed Kettle*. New York: Verso, 2004.

———. "Lenin's Choice." In *Revolution at the Gates: Selected Writings of Lenin from 1917*, edited by Slavoj Žižek, 167–336. New York: Verso, 2002.

———. *Living in the End Times*. New York: Verso, 2010.

———. *Violence: Six Sideways Reflections*. New York: Picador, 2008.

Zupančič, Alenka. *Ethics of the Real: Kant, Lacan*. New York: Verso, 2000.

Hill, Jack: *Coffy*, 62
Der Himmel über Berlin. *See* Wenders,
   Wim
Hitchcock, Alfred, 179n; *Stage Fright*,
   179n
Hitler, Adolf, 180n
Hobbes, Thomas, 129
Holmes, Sherlock, 77
Howard, Ron: *A Beautiful Mind*, 185n;
   Ransom, 112
Hulk. *See* Lee, Ang
Husserl, Edmund, 43
Huston, John: *The Maltese Falcon*, 79

I, Claudius. *See* Graves, Robert
ignorance, 51
imaginary, 185n, 196n
Inception. *See* Nolan, Christopher
The Incredible Hulk. *See* Leterrier, Louis
infinite, 107, 120, 154–156
Inside Man. *See* Lee, Spike
Insomnia (American version). *See* No-
   lan, Christopher
Insomnia (Norwegian version). *See*
   Skjoldbjaerg, Erik
Iraq War, 125, 146, 171, 206n
Iron Man. *See* Favreau, Jon
The Italian Job. *See* Gray, F. Gary
Italian Neorealism, 10
It's a Wonderful Life. *See* Capra, Frank

James Bond films, 182n
Janet, Pierre, 203n
Jerry Maguire. *See* Crowe, Cameron
Johnson, Magic, 179n

Kafka, Franz, 183n
Kant, Immanuel, 28–29, 132–135, 141,
   172, 182n, 184n, 187n, 201–202n,
   206n
Kepler, Johannes, 192n
Kierkegaard, Soren, 198n
Kill Bill, Vol. 2. *See* Tarantino, Quentin
The Killers. *See* Siodmak, Robert
The Killing. *See* Kubrick, Stanley
Klavan, Andrew, 125–126, 130–131,
   200n

Klein, Andy, 186n
Kornbluh, Anna, 52
Kubrick, Stanley: *The Killing*, 164
Kurosawa, Akira: *Rashomon*, 4

Lacan, Jacques, 5, 12, 22, 51, 69, 88,
   117, 119, 150, 159, 167, 181n,
   182n, 183n, 185n, 189n, 198–199n
L.A. Confidential. *See* Hanson, Curtis
Lady in the Lake. *See* Montgomery,
   Robert
Lang, Fritz: *Big Heat*, 189n; *Fury*, 189n;
   Scarlet Street, 47
Laius, 63
Last Year at Marienbad. *See* Resnais,
   Alain
Laura. *See* Preminger, Otto
Laurier, Joanne, 82
Ledger, Heath, 123
Lenin, Vladimir Ilyich, 194–195n
Lethal Weapon 2. *See* Donner, Richard
Lee, Ang: *Hulk*, 193n
Lee, Spike: *Inside Man*, 164; *25th Hour*,
   120
Leterrier, Louis: *The Incredible Hulk*,
   131–132, 193n
Levinas, Emmanuel, 205n
liar's paradox, 22, 182n
Libby, Scooter, 123
liberal humanism, 91–94, 96–98, 194n
Lim, Dennis, 67
Little, William, 62
Living in Oblivion. *See* DiCillo, Tom
The Long Goodbye. *See* Altman, Robert
Lukács, Georg, 183n, 187n
Lumet, Sidney: *Serpico*, 71
Lumière brothers: *L'arrivée d'un train
   à la Ciotat* (*Arrival of a Train at La
   Ciotat*), 9
Lynch, David, 190n

The Maltese Falcon. *See* Huston, John
Mann, Michael: *Heat*, 71, 164
Manon, Hugh, 47, 199–200n
Marcuse, Herbert, 197n
Marxism, 109
Marx, Karl, 113–115, 121

217

INDEX

THE FICTIONAL CHRISTOPHER NOLAN